SENTINEL

SEVEN EVENTS THAT MADE AMERICA AMERICA

Larry Schweikart is the coauthor of the *New York Times* bestseller *A Patriot's History of the United States* and the author of *What Would the Founders Say?* and *48 Liberal Lies About American History*. A professor of history at the University of Dayton, he has appeared as a guest commentator on Fox News and has written many academic books and articles on national defense, business, and financial history. He lives outside Dayton, Ohio.

SEVEN EVENTS THAT MADE AMERICA AMERICA

And Proved That the Founding Fathers Were Right All Along

LARRY SCHWEIKART

Sentinel

SENTINEL
Published by the Penguin Group
Penguin Group (USA) Inc., 375 Hudson Street,
New York, New York 10014, U.S.A.
Penguin Group (Canada), 90 Eglinton Avenue East, Suite 700,
Toronto, Ontario, Canada M4P 2Y3
(a division of Pearson Penguin Canada Inc.)
Penguin Books Ltd, 80 Strand, London WC2R 0RL, England
Penguin Ireland, 25 St. Stephen's Green, Dublin 2, Ireland
(a division of Penguin Books Ltd)
Penguin Books Australia Ltd, 250 Camberwell Road, Camberwell,
Victoria 3124, Australia
(a division of Pearson Australia Group Pty Ltd)
Penguin Books India Pvt Ltd, 11 Community Centre, Panchsheel Park,
New Delhi – 110 017, India
Penguin Group (NZ), 67 Apollo Drive, Rosedale, North Shore 0632,
New Zealand (a division of Pearson New Zealand Ltd)
Penguin Books (South Africa) (Pty) Ltd, 24 Sturdee Avenue,
Rosebank, Johannesburg 2196, South Africa

Penguin Books Ltd, Registered Offices:
80 Strand, London WC2R 0RL, England

First published in the United States of America by Sentinel,
a member of Penguin Group (USA) Inc. 2010
This paperback edition published 2011

1 3 5 7 9 10 8 6 4 2

THE LIBRARY OF CONGRESS HAS CATALOGED THE HARDCOVER EDITION AS FOLLOWS:

Schweikart, Larry.
Seven events that made America America : and proved that the founding fathers were right all along /
Larry Schweikart.
p. cm.
Includes bibliographical references and index.
ISBN 978-1-59523-064-5 (hc.)
ISBN 978-1-59523-079-9 (pbk.)
1. United States—History—Miscellanea. 2. National characteristics, American—Miscellanea. I. Title.
E179.S353 2010
973—dc22
2010003098

Printed in the United States of America
Set in Adobe Garamond
Designed by Spring Hoteling

To rock and rollers, here and abroad, now and then.

CONTENTS

PREFACE

When I first sat down to write this book in the spring of 2009, my goal was to present important, even profound, events in our past that, for reasons unknown, have been forgotten, ignored, or underappreciated.

To my surprise, the chapter that generated the most interest and controversy was the first chapter about Martin Van Buren's creation of the national two-party system. Radio interviewers and community groups were particularly taken with the foundations of the American political system. Fox television host Glenn Beck ran a special interview segment on it. In an era when talk of political third parties was on the rise, many seemed to find the information contained in the chapter both reassuring and challenging in its assertion that third parties were functionally impossible, and that engaging one or the other of the existing parties—and fixing them—was the only solution to some of our problems.

But, as expected, some readers dismissed my approach. "These hardly seem like the most important events in American history," they said. "Where is Pearl Harbor? The Declaration of Independence?" and so on. As the title implies, the particular topics I chose were never the most important events, but those that distinctly shaped America's character over time and which either conformed to the vision of the Founders or departed from it drastically. Fortunately, since publication, there have been no natural disasters such as the Johnstown Flood about which to comment. But we have seen continued developments in the area of food nannyism, in jihadist terrorism, and in media malfeasance, the subjects of chapters four, six, and seven, respectively.

For example, when it comes to policing food, New York City has declared a war on salt, and Baltimore has begun fining restaurants who have repeated "trans fat" violations. These are not outliers; they are harbingers of America's future, where Big Brother dictates what can be eaten, smoked, and driven. Indeed, perhaps one of the most inspiring points of hope that remains is that despite having control of the cultural capital (Hollywood), the financial capital (New York City), and the political capital of the country (Washington, D.C.)—the first two for decades, the last for two years—and despite mountains of environmental propaganda, Americans are still highly skeptical of such nonsense as "global warming" or the dangers posed by meat or salt. Of course, on the flip side, they still seem depressingly unready to dismantle the oppressive bureaucracy that threatens to dominate their daily lives.

Certainly music continues to penetrate "walls" around the world, most notably in radical Islamic states. While the recording industry has suffered severely at the hands of piracy and illegal downloading, the democratization of music has ironically allowed it to seep into those oppressive societies where it is most needed. And astoundingly enough, even as jihadis use rap music to spread hate against America and the West, they have already lost the long-term culture war by adopting American music styles. It is profoundly significant that to defeat us, they think they are forced to become us. While the *lyrics* of such vile and hate-filled music are pure jihad, the *structure* and *style* are pure Jerry Lee Lewis—a stunning inversion of the Marxist idea of selling the rope used to hang the capitalist. Therefore, while the dangers posed by radical Islam (covered in chapter six) have not diminished in the least, the methods of defeating that hateful ideology has transformed inadvertently through American culture in a process hardly different from the one that brought down the Berlin Wall. Certainly there are limits to this cultural "warfare." Insightful writers such as Samuel Huntington argue that cultural imports from the West have little impact on changing civilizations ("the fact that the essence of Western civilization is the Magna Carta, not the Magna Mac") and offer as proof the fact that despite absorbing Japanese cars and electronics, we have not become "Japanized."[1] Yet his two points contradict each other: it is *precisely* because the Magna Carta is the essence of the West that commercial products alone have no impact on long-term civilizational change. But rock music, in fact (and certainly to a much lesser degree) *contains* the very essence of freedom that the Magna Carta protects. By its transmission, by Islamic youths copying it, by audiences hearing it, they are absorbing "Americanness" in a way that no driver ever sees a Toyota as representing or embodying Japanese culture. In the case of most foreign products (including McDonalds abroad), they do not inherently demonstrate or reflect key tenets of the civilization from which they are derived— but in this case rock music does.

Most of all, in the brief time since this book was published, we have seen political changes in which the apparent demise of the two-party system with the triumph of liberalism in 2008 was undone in less than two years.

When I first began to write this book, President Obama's supporters were still heralding his election as a pivotal moment in American history— one that would usher in a new era of politics and an upheaval in the status quo. Boy, were they right. Obama's election was historic in that it brought about the most dramatic shift toward socialism and a radical agenda we have ever seen. But while liberals trumpeted the benefits of all of this "hope and change," most Americans were calling for a return to our core beliefs.

Within just a few short months of the book's publication, even the ever-liberal so-called journalists who dominate the mainstream media were joining in the outrage. As of this writing, rumors are awhirl in Washington that the Democrats are fed up with his narcissism and his self-absorption, and that they are desperately seeking to clip his wings before he destroys the entire party. As one-time supporter Mortimer Zuckerman of *U.S. News & World Report* wrote, Obama has come across "as a young man in a grown-up's game—impressive but not presidential . . . . A man who was once seen as a talented and even charismatic rhetorician is now seen as lacking real experience or even the ability to stop America's decline."[2]

Of course, such lamentations may be nothing more than baloney, smoke and mirrors presented to the public to conceal Democrat chaos. But no one can deny the instantaneous grass-roots appearance of the Tea Party movement in 2009 or its impact on the 2010 elections. Several of its candidates, most notably Rand Paul in Kentucky and Marco Rubio in Florida, won, and many more were nominated and ran strong campaigns against entrenched

Democrat incumbents or country-club-backed GOP "moderates" such as Lisa Murkowski (AK). Despite the reality of Tea Party power, the drive-by media has refused to acknowledge the obvious and has continued to try to portray the movement as "kooks," "fringe," or "whackos." Even after the 2010 congressional drubbing, country-club Republicans ran to the media to insist that Tea Party candidates had cost the GOP senate seats. (Scoreboard: GOP *gained* a net of six senate seats at a time where, just a year prior, the brainiacs in the press were insisting the Republicans would lose even more than they had in the previous election).

This political restructuring is not a new phenomenon though. As I point out in the first chapter of this book, American politics differs from almost every other democratic system in that it forces both parties to the middle and punishes radicals on either end. Thus it was almost inevitable that the Democrats—turned loose to manifest their leftist ideology in actual policy through two consecutive elections that they mistook for mandates—would run themselves out of Washington.

Surprisingly to some, this was the largest off-year gain for either party since the 1930s, and the fact that neither Obama nor the leading Democrats in Congress seem penitent for their willful disregard of the public's wishes does not augur well for them in 2012, either. Martin Van Buren certainly wouldn't have known what to do with the Tea Party: his structure was specifically designed to prevent such developments. And the modern news media clearly has not known how to respond, mocking its participants with sexual innuendos or dismissing them as ignorant hicks. Barack Obama has arrogantly ignored them.

There is no way of knowing if, one hundred years from now, the rise of the Tea Party movement will be considered a momentous event in our history. But then again, at the time, it's doubtful that anyone in America thought the freedom suit of a slave named Dred Scott or the collapse of a Pennsylvania dam or a quartet of floppy-haired British rock stars would have had such significant effects either. And that is the beauty of history.

INTRODUCTION

You don't have to be an American history expert to identify certain critical events in our past that shaped our country. Pearl Harbor, the D-Day invasion, 9/11, the assassinations of Lincoln and Kennedy, the Great Depression, important court decisions such as *Brown v. Board of Education*—these are just a few of the milestones in our nation's history that likely spring to most people's memory. On the other hand, not all important changes in our past have unfolded in a single day, but rather were the results of profound unresolved issues (slavery and the Civil War), a slow change in culture (the status of women in the twentieth century), or the response to long-standing international tensions (the Cold War). No one can point to a particular "where were you?" moment with such transformations, as they reflected slow, but important, incremental changes.

The most difficult—and interesting—parts of history to understand are those that spark deep and significant changes but are not necessarily obvious. That is the purpose of this book—to explore and explain some of these forgotten or unheralded moments in an effort to show the profound way in which they influence our history. Yet there is a second purpose in this book, namely, to examine the seven events I have chosen in light of the Founders' vision for America. How would George Washington, James Madison, Thomas Jefferson, and other Founders have interpreted these events? Did the event confirm the vision of the Founders or constitute a departure from their hopes? In short, would the Founders have approved or disapproved of the actions that followed from the event itself? Most important, what can we learn from these events of our past to help build a better future and a stronger America?

For example, Madison wrote with mixed emotions about "factions," or partisan strife, disdaining it (as did Washington), yet acknowledging it as unavoidable and inherent in human nature. "Ambition should counter ambition," he observed. However, he likely would have been appalled at Martin Van Buren's invention of a new, national party machinery, which evoked loyalty by rewarding supporters with jobs in both the party and the government. The result was something none of the Founders desired—an ever-growing federal government. Nor would Madison, having drafted many of the sections of the Constitution relating to a federal judiciary, have dreamed that the United States Supreme Court would seek to make itself the arbiter of personhood itself. It would not have surprised Madison to see that, by wading into such a morass in the case of the slave Dred Scott, the Supreme Court not only mucked up the central object of the case itself but managed to unintentionally start a financial panic as well.

On the other hand, the events following the Johnstown Flood, wherein ordinary private citizens took it upon themselves to provide aid and disaster relief and did so with heroism and efficiency, would have surprised none of the Founding Fathers. Indeed, they would have expected no less from the people, and would not have been surprised at the ineptitude and folly seen in Hurricane Katrina, during which the ill-prepared and ill-equipped federal government stepped in to "help." Of course, even the Founding Fathers might have supported federal disaster relief in a matter of national security, but no logical rationale could justify the government's policing of Americans' diets. Nonetheless, this is exactly what happened after President Dwight Eisenhower suffered a heart attack, and the government, in a misguided campaign against heart disease, began advising Americans on what to eat. But this was only the beginning, with the "war on meat" soon to evolve into a war on sugar, salt, fats, and virtually any other food the government deemed "unhealthy." To say the Founders would have been appalled is an understatement: their (and our) Revolution began when the British tried to dictate what tea we could drink!

Ironically, when it comes to something as foreign (or so it seems) to the

Founding Fathers as rock and roll, a much different story unfolds. In the early 1960s, American rock was languishing, circling in the water until the Beatles arrived on Ed Sullivan's stage. Suddenly, thousands of American musicians found their dreams anew, taking the music of the "British Invasion" and blasting out new, original, and—as it turned out—world-changing sounds. America's new rock rolled through the Iron Curtain—despite several attempts to stop it—and, in the process, helped defeat communism. It did so without a dime of public support, reaffirming the Founders' commitment to ensuring that individuals, not government, remain the source of artistic expression.

Of course, the man most credited with bringing down the Evil Empire, Ronald Reagan, certainly agreed with that principle. But Reagan's role in the demise of communism—his greatest and enduring achievement—was marred by a significant misjudgment, namely, the deployment of marines as "peacekeepers" in Lebanon. When, months later, a terrorist truck bomb killed more than two hundred of the marines, Reagan withdrew them, but this was not enough to stop a new worldwide threat that was only beginning to be understood: radical Islamic jihad. Though the Founders might not have perceived this threat any quicker than the Gipper, they would have warned Reagan about the futility of "peacekeeping" missions.

Washington, John Adams, and Thomas Jefferson would have been more familiar with another modern phenomenon—bias in the news. But, unlike the media conglomerates of today, the newspapers and broadsides that the Founders read were relatively impotent, and almost always countered by a rival paper that took up the other side of any issue. By 2008, however, the mainstream national media had become almost entirely partisan and Democratic, so much so that if it were acting as a government-run propaganda machine, it would espouse almost the identical viewpoints. The pliant and malleable television and print coverage of candidate-turned-president Barack Obama has made a mockery out of "objective" news coverage. What did the Founders see as the role of a free press? Why were they so insistent about protecting *political* speech in the First Amendment?

These seven events allow us to look at oft-overlooked points in our history not only from the perspective of their significance, but also from the standpoint of their conformity to the Founders' visions, hopes, and dreams for this nation. In each case, I think it is clear that it is not always the declaration of war, inspirational speech, famous piece of legislation, or other well-known event we learned about in history class that has had the most long-lasting impact on our lives.

Larry Schweikart

Centerville, Ohio

1.

MARTIN VAN BUREN HAS A NIGHTMARE
AND BIG GOVERNMENT IS BORN . . . IN THE 1820S!

The natural progress of things is for liberty to yield and government to gain ground.

THOMAS JEFFERSON TO EDWARD CARRINGTON, MAY 27, 1788

When New York state senator Martin Van Buren, a leader of the "Bucktail" group of Jeffersonian Republicans, heard about the impending statehood bill for Missouri in 1819, he had a nightmare. Not a literal interruption of sleep—legend has it that, in fact, it was Thomas Jefferson who said the news of the subsequent Missouri Compromise, which admitted Missouri into the Union, awoke him like a "fire bell in the night, awakened and filled me with terror."[1] Van Buren's nightmare involved matters closer to New York, namely, the battle with the forces of De Witt Clinton over control of that state's political machine. But even at that early point in his career, Van Buren feared that the opponents of slavery in Missouri would "bring the politics of the slave states and . . . their supporters in the free states into disrepute through inflammatory assaults on the institution of slavery."[2] The admission of Missouri, a slave state, would threaten to disrupt the volatile harmony the Union had achieved over the issue of slavery. Though sharply divided on the issue, the nation had, it seemed, learned to live with the "peculiar institution," but tipping the balance of power in favor of one side could potentially rend asunder the young Republic. One way or another, the territorial expansion resulting from the vast land acquired during the Louisiana Purchase would elevate one side or the other—pro-slave or anti-slave—to a dominant position in the government, and the loser in that struggle would not accept the verdict.

Compromise had been part of the American fabric from the beginning, and not only because of the slavery issue. As the result of the Constitutional Convention, two titanic compromises shaped the nation from the outset. First, the famed "Connecticut Compromise," which addressed the issue of state representation in the federal government, balanced the concerns of the "big states" and "small states" by providing for a House of Representatives elected by the people of their districts, and a Senate, whose members were (at the time) elected by the state legislatures. All legislation had to pass both houses to become law. A second great compromise at the Convention involved slavery (and representation, too, in a different manner). Southern states wanted to count slaves for purposes of representation, but not for federal taxation; northern states wanted to count slaves for taxation, but not representation. The Convention agreed to count a slave as "three-fifths of a person" for both representation and taxation, over time providing a surprisingly dramatic advantage for the South. Federal taxation as envisioned never materialized, while the South benefited from about a 4 percent increase in their number of House seats.[3]

Where the "three-fifths compromise" endowed the South with a permanent (though shrinking, due to slower population growth than their neighbors to the North) representative advantage, the Missouri Compromise threatened to do just the opposite. Under the agreement, two territories, Maine (free) and Missouri (slave), would become states. A balance in the Senate was maintained, and while no one could predict the eventual populations of either, the change in the House would likely be negligible. Trouble began when Congress established an imaginary line from the southern tip of Missouri all the way through the Louisiana Purchase, located at the 36 degree–30 minute line of latitude. Under the Compromise, from that point forward, slavery would be prohibited in any Louisiana Purchase territories above the line when they became states, while below the line ("Arkansas Territory," an area that amounted to modern-day Arkansas and most of Oklahoma) slavery would be permitted but was not automatic. Free-soil territory encompassed most of modern-day Kansas, Nebraska, Iowa, the Dakotas, Montana, Idaho, Oregon, Washington, and part of Minnesota. No one at the time knew exactly how many states would eventually be carved out of these lands, but Northerners and Southerners alike could anticipate perhaps a dozen free-soil senators and at least twice as many congressmen coming from states that emerged from that land. That possibility threatened to establish a powerful northern majority that at some future date could attempt to legislate slavery out of existence—a consequence the South could not entertain. Ultimately, it threatened disunion and war.

Van Buren's response to this nightmare was to begin shaping a new political structure, first in New York and eventually throughout the nation. As pro- and anti-Clinton newspapers arrayed over the Missouri issue (with Van Buren's Bucktails, so called because of the deer tails they wore on their hats, accused of supporting slavery), Van Buren was more concerned with the politics of sectionalism than with the morality of this so-called peculiar institution. As early as 1819 Van Buren straddled the slavery issue—during one key meeting on his party's response to the Missouri issue he was conveniently out of town—and as state senator he avoided having to take a position when a resolution against slavery passed without a recorded vote. The notion that such a divisive issue could be skirted, perhaps permanently, germinated within the Dutchman. But it required some mechanism to ensure that slavery did not overtake the politics of the nation. The answer, it seemed, was to apply what Van Buren learned in New York to the country as a whole.

Working with other Bucktails, Van Buren became instrumental in creating what was termed the "Albany Regency," which created a new political machine and introduced a new theory of political parties, thereby revolutionizing American politics. Many of the Founders had warned against partisanship—yet none had a reasonable alternative. George Washington, in particular, clung to an unrealistic view of America in which a spirit of national unity and harmony would prevail, warning about the "baneful effects of the Spirit of Party" in his Farewell Address.[4] Interestingly, however, Washington qualified his admonition "with particular reference to the founding of [parties] *on geographical discriminations.*" What was particularly destructive, he saw, were sectional parties oriented around the issue of slavery.

Madison also expressed concerns about the dangerous effects of faction, which he defined as "a number of citizens, whether amounting to a minority or majority of the whole, who are united and actuated by some common impulse of passion, or of interest, adverse to the rights of other citizens, or to the permanent and aggregate interests of the community." Yet he admitted that the only way to eliminate factions was to either abuse liberty, which he found unacceptable, or give "to every citizen the same opinions, the same passions, and the same interests."[5] That, too, was utterly unacceptable. *Federalist* No. 51, written by either Madison or Alexander Hamilton, concluded that parties were probably necessary: "Ambition must be made to counteract ambition."

The Albany Regency developed a much different political theory, though not entirely out of line with *Federalist* No. 51, and in Van Buren's words, "political parties are inseparable from free governments."[6] As his party's newspaper, the *Argus,* put it, parties checked "the passions, the ambition, and the usurpations of individuals."[7] Neither Hamilton nor Madison would have said it any differently. As early as 1821, Van Buren (by then also known as the "Red Fox of Kinderhook") had begun employing the "rule" of "to the victor belong the spoils," the spoils in this case being political patronage. The practice of giving jobs to the election winner's friends constituted a tool in the politician's arsenal by which he could reward supporters. Given the small size of the federal government and most state governments at the time, patronage was usually limited to a few customs positions, a handful of law enforcement jobs, and, in the case of the U.S. government, a growing number of post office appointments. Beyond that, aspiring political leaders had little to promise those who helped elect them.

Van Buren began with a "*general resuscitation* of the *old democratic party*" (emphasis his) in 1822, by which he meant the Jeffersonian democratic party. To modern readers, this invites confusion because by that time the Jeffersonians were known as the *Republicans* (from "Democratic Republicans") as opposed to the opposition party, the Federalists. He allied with Thomas Ritchie, editor of the *Richmond Enquirer,* and other Virginians who were building the

"Richmond junto" up to the same stature as the Albany Regency. Together, the "Richmond-Albany axis" could run the country, terrifying such leaders as South Carolinian John C. Calhoun: "between [them]," he exclaimed, "there is a vital connection. They give and receive hope from each other, and confidently expect to govern this nation."[8] Van Buren—like De Witt Clinton and other political organizers—built on the Jeffersonian foundation of the caucus. Caucuses were state bodies of largely self-appointed men who had money and influence and acted as regional kingmakers. But the caucus began to lose its power as the property requirement to vote was lifted in state after state, meaning that the vote of the "common man" suddenly counted for almost as much as the support of a few wealthy individuals. Van Buren did not create this, and he certainly did not initiate the end of voting restrictions; nor did he originate party newspapers as propaganda tools. But like Henry Ford with the auto and Bill Gates with operating systems, he immediately grasped the totality of the parts and began reshaping New York politics from the inside, convincing others to develop a party organization that reached down to local levels through a state, district, ward, and precinct arrangement. Under this framework, the party established levels of responsibility for getting out the vote on election day: the state coordinated and funded candidates and directed the districts or counties; district and county organizations made sure that every ward and precinct was staffed with "captains," who, on election day, literally walked the streets and encouraged voters to go to the polls. County and district organizations also helped transmit funds downward to local candidates from the state level. Over time, Van Buren and his allies added newspapers as rallying devices to further ensure turnout.

When Van Buren—by then known as the "Little Magician" for his dexterity at putting together political deals—became a U.S. senator and left for Washington in 1821, he sought to transplant his new party on a national level. Still technically a slave owner (his slave had run away eight years earlier), Van Buren again sought to have it both ways, arguing on the side of Northerners to limit the spread of slavery while comforting Southerners by defending the existence of slavery in the South. His thinking evolved slowly, but steadily, toward a position of strong states' rights, constrained further by a national party that would avoid direct confrontation with slavery, all enforced by the discipline of spoils. This would, he thought, prevent disunion and war.

Within forty years, however, it became shockingly obvious that Van Buren failed in this immediate objective and, ironically, the very system he founded would help bring on the pivotal and decisive conflict over slavery. Yet the carnage and heartbreak of the Civil War reached far beyond the 600,000 dead and the decades of sectional hatred and distrust. Van Buren's legacy to the American people contained one final paradox: seeking to limit the power of the federal government to act on slavery within the states, Van Buren forged a system that ensured and accelerated the relentless, permanent, and inescapable growth of government. When critics of modern-day "special-interest politics" bemoan the fact that presidential campaigns (like all others) have descended into exercises in pandering to interest groups, it's not unfair to lay this at the feet of Martin Van Buren. And when Barack Obama won the presidency in large part by appealing to formerly "oppressed minorities," it's fair to say Martin Van Buren elected him . . . in 1820.

Creating a massive bureaucracy beholden to special interests was absolutely not Van Buren's intention. Indeed, he never even imagined the possibility of such a state of affairs. State and national expenditures were not only small at the time, but tightly confined by both the U.S. and most state constitutions: what little money there was could not be spent willy-nilly or handed out to cronies. For example, in 1800 the entire U.S. government spent only $11 million for a nation of 5.3 million people.[9] By 1820, the budget had nearly doubled, but so had the population, with over half of the spending dedicated to national defense and none to "welfare" or "education." Interest on the debt claimed one-quarter of the government's revenues (as opposed to, depending on the calculation, 8 to 10 percent today), and "other spending," or transfers within government agencies and to the states, made up the final quarter.

That's not to say there was not an inherent bias for growth, however tiny, built into the system. U.S. government employees numbered 5,000 in 1816, but multiplied dramatically after 1830, to over 25,000 by 1850. Of course, the population of the United States also rose, but even adjusted per capita, the number of government employees per person nearly doubled over that same period. Although real per capita government expenditures fell slightly under Jefferson, Monroe, and John Adams, and rapidly under Van Buren, they spiked radically upward under Madison (partly as a result of the War of 1812), Jackson, and John Tyler. But even in Madison's first two nonwar years in office, real expenditures rose; James Monroe promised in his inaugural address to build a network of canals and roads to "shorten distances . . . and bind the Union more closely together"; and under Jackson (supposedly a small-government president) government spending skyrocketed, more than doubling with no foreign conflict and no major land acquisitions.[10] Despite a general trend of increasing expenditures per person, federal government spending prior to 1850 still amounted to less than $3 per person per year.

The remarkable hands-off approach of government to the economy, however, simultaneously resulted in per capita income growth of just about 1 percent per year prior to 1850, while government grew at only a rate of three-quarters of 1 percent per year. Put another way, even though government grew slowly but inexorably in the early 1800s, it *shrank* relative to the personal income growth of most Americans.[11] This was not only because public expenditures remained light, but also because the young nation's gross domestic product (GDP) was an astounding $700 million, or *seven times* the gross public debt of $91 million. In such a wealthy nation, where there was more money to be made outside of government than inside with even the most lavish political favors, elected officials had little to pledge to supporters, and thus even fewer favors to actually perform once in office.

The astonishingly rapid growth of government, particularly (but not only) at the federal level, over the last half-century has led many Americans to think of it as a recent development. In fact, with the exception of a couple of panics and depressions—hardly examples of political restraint—U.S. government spending has grown consistently, in actual and per capita terms, with every single administration. Indeed, the expansion of government started almost immediately with George Washington and John Adams. Washington proposed a national (government-funded) university, and both he and Adams appreciated the need for a larger navy as a means to protect the country's shipping. James Monroe and John Quincy Adams supported the national road, and for more than national security reasons. In his inaugural address, the younger Adams noted:

> nearly twenty years have passed since the construction of the first
> national road was commenced. The authority for its construction
> was then unquestioned. To how many thousands of our country-

men has it proved a benefit? To what single individual has it ever proved an injury?[12]

Virtually all of the Founders agreed that certain functions of government required the expansion of federal power, particularly defense (which often consumed at least half of the national budget), but also the mail system, the customs network, and the bureaucracy that supervised the surveying and distribution of land. By the time of Thomas Jefferson's administration, "internal improvements" covered not only repairs to, but construction of, roads and the clearing of harbors and rivers and was supported by both Federalists and Republicans. Politicians of all stripes endorsed spending public money for transportation networks, often invoking national security as requiring the rapid movement of troops and supplies.[13] Despite the fact that private contractors built and maintained most roads (turnpikes) through a system of tolls and fees, Jefferson tasked his secretary of the treasury, Albert Gallatin, to design a large transportation network that would include federally funded roads and canals. When Gallatin presented the proposal, it had a whopping price tag of $10 million—an amount equal to the *entire* federal budget—and Congress predictably voted it down. But the fact that it came from Jefferson's administration is telling: even small-government Founders like Jefferson expressed a willingness to spend public money, and a lot of it, on what they deemed appropriate, based on often flimsy justification.

When it came to institutionalizing a national debt, few Founders have suffered as many slings and arrows as Gallatin's predecessor and Washington's treasury secretary, Alexander Hamilton, who viewed *limited* debt as a blessing because it enabled the government to borrow money it could use immediately, while tying men of capital to the nation's financial future.[14] He called debt the "price of liberty." Hamilton, certainly a big-government advocate by any standard, nevertheless has earned something of a bum rap by conservatives in that he first and foremost called for limitations on government borrowing that would seem draconian by today's standards. His recommendation in his 140,000-word *Report on Public Credit* (1790) that all national debt be processed through a "sinking fund," in which state debts assumed by the federal government were subordinated to a new lower-yield debt, thus gradually reduced the overall debt burden of the nation. Hamilton also excelled when it came to appreciating the motivations of investors, offering lenders a menu of bond options so as to encourage the wealthy to ally with the young Republic, ranging from original debt at 6 percent to new funded debt options available at 4 percent.[15] But the notion that Hamilton favored unending debt is ludicrous: he advocated extinguishing the debt "in the very *first* communication" which he ever made on the subject, called debt "perhaps the NATURAL DISEASE of all governments," and as biographer Ron Chernow notes, Hamilton's "warnings about oppressive debt *vastly* outnumber his paeans to public debt as a source of liquid capital."[16]

At the time, it wasn't necessary for individual politicians to resist "big government" because the system the Founders had established fought against it in myriad ways on its own. One important restriction came in the requirement that most voters still had to own property, hence they were reluctant to suffer high taxes or accept burdensome regulations. Property requirements also ensured high voter turnout because voters had a stake in the system. However, the single most energizing and galvanizing characteristics of elections prior to 1824 that ensured voter participation were *ideas* as embodied in the presence of competitive parties. Richard McCormick, who produced seminal works on the early party systems, published a classic article in the *American Historical Review* (1960) in which he found that voter participation commonly reached 70 percent of the adult white males in states where there were competitive parties (but under 50 percent where one party dominated). Even he noted "curious exceptions" in the case of Alabama (one 1819 election reported 97 percent turnout) and Tennessee (an 1817 election netted 80 percent turnout).[17] McCormick rejected notions that simply adding more turnout made the process any more "democratic," noting, "I have the impression that the 'new' voters tended to divide between the two parties in much the same proportion as the 'old' voters."[18] His classic study of North Carolina and New York voters in the *Mississippi Valley Historical Review* revealed "whether or not a man owned fifty acres or more of land seemingly had little or no influence on his party affiliation," leading him to conclude, "It does not appear that the liberalization of the franchise had any measurable effect on the relative strength of the contending parties. . . ."[19]

A second feature of the early "first" (pre–Van Buren) party system was that it seemed to provide a means to express the will of the majority and to enable conflicting sides to settle their differences peaceably.[20] No event better captured this spirit than Jefferson's ascension to the White House in

1800—a first-of-its-kind election in which the loser, John Adams, not only relinquished power without a fight, but an entire governing philosophy was removed and another substituted for it without a single bayonet being brandished.[21] Nevertheless, the notion that the contentious issue of slavery could be resolved without a major struggle was an illusion, reinforced by the fact that until 1820 the nation had escaped any serious discussion of the issue. Moreover, until 1820, the mechanisms by which the tensions between individuals and groups were worked out within the American political process relied heavily on deferential politics, in which elites in the state legislatures (and, to a lesser degree, in the U.S. House of Representatives and Senate) spoke for the "common man." To some degree, rabble-rousers, rebels, and ambitious newcomers were routed into the state organizations with low-level appointments and thus somewhat neutralized and co-opted by the system. They could work their way up the ladder, and over a long period of time join the governing elites, or they could seek to overturn the system by appealing to the electorate directly. For the most part, that was a difficult row to hoe: the state electoral structures were extensively decentralized. In short, everything was built to resist rapid change.

Politicians recognized that promoting their constituents' interests automatically gained the support of some and the antagonism of others. Thus, choices had to be made on policy grounds, and since votes were needed to enact those policies, legislators took a keen interest in the outcome of congressional elections. The ability of a New Jersey congressman to deliver favorable policies for his constituents depended in part on the successful election of like-minded men in Delaware and Georgia who would vote with him on bills in Congress. Consequently, within twenty years of the Constitutional Convention, state races were already becoming nationalized, with implications for citizens in every state.

Still another development involved the growing importance of the presidency as a politically symbolic lightning rod for all policy outcomes. After Washington's two elections, however—in which he was the obvious choice—it became easier to associate legislation with an individual president than with dozens of legislators whom no one recognized. By identifying the cause of faction itself as liberty—the desire of people to express their opinions and join with like-minded people in that effort—Madison had to admit that "the latent causes of faction are . . . sown in the nature of man" because different abilities led to different outcomes. The only alternative, however, was an unconstitutional and undesirable restraint of freedom of association. As Justice Clarence Thomas noted in his dissent in *Nixon v. Shrink Missouri Government PAC*, "The Framers preferred a political system that harnessed such faction for good, preserving liberty while also ensuring good government. Rather than adopting the repressive 'cure' for faction that the majority today endorses, the Framers armed individual citizens with a remedy."[22] (The Court as a whole disagreed with Thomas, upholding the *Buckley v. Valeo* limitations on campaign contributions as "property . . . not speech.") The remedy to which Thomas alluded was a regular vote and, as Madison put it, letting "ambition counteract ambition" through competing factions.[23]

Over time, the American Left came to argue that factions were necessary to protect minorities. In 1982, Garry Wills, for example, claimed:

> Minorities can make use of dispersed and staggered governmental machinery to clog, delay, slow down, hamper, and obstruct the majority. But these weapons for delay are given to the minority irrespective of its factious or nonfactious character; and they can be used against the majority irrespective of its factious or nonfactious character. What Madison prevents is not faction, but action. What he protects is not the common good but delay as such.[24]

But as soon as liberal administrations became the dominant political culture in America, and when it was convenient for liberalism to benefit from the absence of competition, liberals abruptly made a U-turn. Justice John Paul Stevens, in his dissent to the *California Democratic Party v. Jones* (2000) case, which set up a blanket primary (as opposed to a closed, "partisan," primary), wrote that "Parties ranked high on the list of evils that the Constitution was designed to check."[25] To sum up, parties and factions were good for liberals when they worked on behalf of liberal interest groups, but as soon as partisanship began to work against liberals, suddenly factions made the evil hit list.

Between 1800 and 1840, the variable most likely to bring out voters, particularly for presidential elections, was a highly contested race that elevated different ideas. Washington's party, the Federalists, had lost their clout in the War of 1812, then completely disappeared by 1816, essentially leaving America a one-party state, and the result was predictable—voters didn't care. McCormick found that in the 1824 election, for example, none of the eighteen states that had electors chosen by popular vote reached the percentage of voter participation that they had witnessed before 1824.[26] The significance of Andrew Jackson's unsuccessful presidential run in 1824, then his election in 1828, came in the fact that for the first time in years, a "sharp cleavage in almost every state" appeared, which is to say that partisan competition resurfaced.[27] As flamboyant a character as Old Hickory was, "Jacksonian democracy" had more to do with a fundamental reordering of the American political structure than it did with any of Jackson's ideas or policies. Nor did Jackson himself cause people to flock to the polls, contrary to the hyperbole of historian Charles Beard, who claimed democracy "foamed perilously near the crest."[28]

Among these factors reshaping the system, the caucus—a device that dominated the first American party system—lost influence rapidly, especially when it came to nominating the presidential candidates, and was replaced by national nominating conventions.

Originally, only New Jersey and Delaware had state nominating conventions, but under the second American party system, states adopted the convention process. Along with this came a sharp devolution of power away from state legislatures.[29] A second structural change involved the relaxing, or elimination, of property requirements for white males to vote, with most states nearing universal (white) male suffrage by 1810, and by 1826, only Rhode Island, Virginia, and Louisiana had any restrictions on white men voting at all. With more people involved and the state legislators losing influence, there were greater opportunities for ambitious newcomers to become activists. These new activists appeared first at the state political level, as reflected in the fact that elections for state offices had higher turnout than presidential elections.

A third, socioeconomic change in politics occurred after Andrew Jackson's election, wherein the old, deferential model of acquiescing to the caucuses' coronation of candidates simply because they were from an older, elite class was abandoned in favor of ideological selections. Lynn Marshall once described the Whig Party as "stillborn" because even as it embraced the new Jacksonian political structure of patronage, it still relied on candidates drawn from the pools of the established political class.[30] Merely adopting the tactics and machinery of the Jacksonian Democrats proved insufficient to win elections on a consistent basis. Ultimately, however, it came down to more than mere machinery. Even the insightful McCormick puzzled over the motivating factors behind political interest, admitting it could "scarcely be comprehended in purely political terms."[31]

Martin Van Buren's solution for quelling dissension over the slavery issue in the 1820s began with the simple reality of the centrality of the South in national politics. Four of the first six presidents were Virginians; of the fifteen presidents before Abraham Lincoln, six were from Virginia, nine were from the South or the West, and all but the two Adamses were what historian Richard Brown would call "northern men of southern principles." That is to say, all but two of the first fifteen chief executives actively or passively supported slavery. What endowed the South with such power and national influence? The overwhelming consensus among southern voters about the issue of slavery dampened all other political divisions in the region.[32] Van Buren quickly recognized this, noting a "remarkable consistency in the political positions" of southern politicians. New York senator and Van Buren's friend Rufus King put it more bluntly, saying all Southerners agreed on the need for the "black strap" of slavery.[33] Indeed, coalescence around the pivotal principle that only Southerners could act on slavery within the South had shaped the drafting of both the Declaration and the Constitution, and had propelled what was a numerically inferior region into a national majority position through a system of alliances outside the South, particularly with New York, but including Kentucky, Tennessee, and Pennsylvania.

Ironically enough, trouble began with the demise of the Federalist party. Left without opposition (or a reason to cater to the whims of the South), the dominant Republicans—that is, the Jeffersonian Republicans—lost touch with their southern support. In the process, Brown claimed, "in victory the Republican party had lost its identity—and its usefulness."[34] Others besides Van Buren recognized the opportunity for political realignment caused by the unresponsiveness of the Republicans during the Missouri controversy. John Quincy Adams noted that "here was a new party ready formed," which he perceived as "terrible to the whole Union, but portentously terrible to the South [by] threatening . . . the emancipation of all their slaves, threatening in its immediate effect that Southern domination which has swayed the

Union for the last twenty years."[35] No less than the aging but mighty Sage of Monticello, in his previously noted "fire bell" letter, referred to the Missouri bill as the "knell of the Union." "It is hushed for the moment," he wrote, "but this is a reprieve only, not a final sentence."[36] He went on to identify the central issue of any compromise over slavery: "A geographical line, co-inciding with a marked principle, moral and political, once conceived and held up to the angry passions of men, will never be obliterated; and every new irritation will mark it deeper and deeper."[37]

Whatever political balance the Missouri Compromise achieved was guaranteed to be short-lived for the reasons already discussed. At the same time, it blunted a growing tendency on the part of most political leaders to-ward nationalism, or joining the sections together in the "market revolution" of commerce, transportation, manufacturing, and finance. Obscuring the stark differences over slavery, observers of the day and some historians have referred to the "Era of Good Feelings," at the very time that the ship of state had entered a slow-brewing maelstrom.[38] In particular, southern politicians increasingly emphasized the close connection between party and slavery, while in the North this had the effect of "handing the keys to national party success . . . to whatever Northern leader could surmount charges of being pro-Southern and command the necessary northern votes to bring the party to power."[39] Again, in Brown's simple but accurate summation, the only plausible national candidate was a northern man of southern principles or a Westerner with no particular ties to slavery, but who took no stand against it (hence the ascendance of Westerners such as Jackson and James K. Polk).

Reaction to the proceedings related to Missouri statehood reflected anything but "good feelings." One reporter noted that the response in Richmond was as "if affected by all the Volcanic Eruptions of Vesuvius."[40] Nathaniel Macon (of Macon's Bill No. 2 fame in 1810, which lifted the embargoes on both Britain and France) warned that the Compromise would acknowledge Congress's right to interfere with, or legislate, slavery. Boxing in slavery, without the prospect of territorial expansion, would leave South-erners "dammed up in a land of slaves" (according to Spencer Roane) and "cooped up on the north" (according to Thomas Ritchie) without a safety valve.[41] Nevertheless, the congressional vote in the South was almost evenly split for and against the bill.

Throughout the process, Van Buren had his eye on higher political office, as well as on a watered-down view of republican liberty based, supposedly, in small government.[42] He similarly fretted about the corrupting power of money in the political process, which he saw as less pervasive in the South. He might have simply kept trying to refurbish the Old Republicans had the election of 1824 not taken such an odd turn, with the election of John Quincy Adams under the murky aspersions of a "Corrupt Bargain" with Henry Clay. That election killed "King Caucus," which had "acquired the stigma of aristocracy," sweeping away the last impediment to a new national political party that would, as he noted, combine the "planters of the South with the plain Republicans of the north."[43]

But the conundrum facing the architect of such a party was how to simultaneously join the slave South and the increasingly anti-slave North, and Van Buren hit upon the only solution. How could he redraw the old party lines? Since any new party could not embrace *either* the northern or southern position, it had to identify a more powerful incentive than the ideology of pro- or anti-slavery, to substitute *"party principles* for *personal preferences."*[44] During a tour of western New York, Van Buren's answer became obvious; he would appeal to economic self-interest to supersede ideology. He would substitute specific rewards bestowed on individuals through jobs in either the party or the government for broader economic interests accrued through support of, or opposition to, slavery. Put bluntly, a dollar today in the hands of a party loyalist would trump potentially higher but uncertain returns in the future. One unnamed opponent marveled at the scheme: "the perfection of Mr. Van Buren's party discipline," he said, was that "the wires [of] political machinery [were] attached to strings in every county."[45] A Van Buren ally, newspaper editor Duff Green, wrote that *"party* is everything."[46] For example, as Van Buren returned to run for governor of New York, the Regency perfected the practice of handing out clerkships and sheriff positions. It was as governor, where he wielded the ability to directly appoint friends, that Van Buren finally made the connection between spoils, party discipline, and a national party agenda.

By 1826, Van Buren had identified Andrew Jackson as a safe Westerner whom he could support for president in two years. "If Gen Jackson & his friends," Van Buren wrote, "will put his election on *old party grounds*, preserve the old systems, avoid if not condemn the practices of the last campaign we can by adding his personal popularity to the yet remaining force of old party feeling, not only succeed in electing him but our success when achieved will be worth something."[47] The new organization soon became known as the "Jacksonian Democrats" or, more commonly, merely "Democrats."

The scheme was both shocking in its simplicity and repellent in its characterization of American selfishness. But in theory, at least, it seemed to overcome sectionalism. More remarkably, a few years later, when the Whigs emerged as a national competitor to the Democrats, they operated under the same assumption that men could be bought. Cloaking their application of patronage in more patriotic terms, the Whigs and their "American System" promised to improve the well-being of all through a system of tariffs, internal improvements, and a national bank. Such a program, they promised, would bind the nation together in a web of commerce. However elevated the rhetoric, at its most basic level, the American System constituted only a broader dispersion of spoils. The key, however, was that *both parties avoided slavery and the central issues of the day and ran for office on the assumption that principles were for sale.* The tariff, in particular, constituted direct federal funds targeted to the vote-rich northern textile regions and, not surprisingly, next to slavery the tariff became one of the most divisive antebellum issues. "Internal improvements" was often a code phrase for specific investments in river towns, coastal cities, or railroad lines that benefited targeted groups of voters.

The structure of the new party, which built on the organization of the old, employed a division of national, state, county, district, ward, and precinct divisions of the electorate, assigning to each level a partisan director charged with getting out the vote. Electoral success was then rewarded with promotions, in which ward captains became district directors, and so on, until all possible job holders in the party organization were appointed to paid government positions. For example, Van Buren, as New York governor, moved his longtime supporter William Marcy to the state supreme court, then slipped Albany mayor Charles Dudley into Van Buren's old Senate seat. But these were only two examples of the across-the-board process of handing out positions to customs collectors, sheriffs, county clerks, and hundreds of other plum political jobs. Since the total number of government jobs remained small, however, the bureaucracy grew slowly—a few thousand new jobs per every state and general election—concealing the corrosive dynamic at work. So to make up the difference, Governor Van Buren quickly got approval for a new Bank Safety Fund bill that would reward his financial supporters and had the New York City health commissioner ship $8,000 a year to the Society for Reformation of Juvenile Delinquents, another well-cloaked political sop.[48]

A prime example of the spoils system at the national level, the Post Office accounted for more jobs than any other government office or agency, including the U.S. Army! By the 1830s, there were over 8,700 postal positions in the United States. This amounted to three-quarters of the entire federal civilian workforce, making postmaster general the most plum appointment in government outside of secretary of state. (It's difficult today to think that individuals once actually aspired to be postmaster general as a life's ambition!) The postmaster general had the political appointment power for *all* postal workers in the era before the civil service exam. Thus, depending on the outcome of an election, one might see a completely new postman (virtually no women worked for the Post Office at the time) every four years. Moreover, with post offices in every state, the postmaster general had unmatched national patronage powers.

The postal system had another function besides its role in delivering spoils. Early in American history, a Faustian pact had been sealed between newspapers and "exchanges," in which postal law permitted printers to exchange their papers without postage through the mail.[49] This policy, first codified in 1758 by Benjamin Franklin and William Hunter, deputy postmaster general for the American colonies, locked together the Post Office and the early newspapers in a relationship that would dramatically reshape the way Americans read. Since the postal system shipped newspapers for only a fraction of the cost of transporting them, a strong incentive arose to print—and mail—more newspapers. Between 1800 and 1840, the number of newspapers shipped through the mail rose from just under two million to almost 40 million. If the newspapers had paid the same postage rate as other publications, their transmission costs would have been *seven hundred times higher*. By the 1830s, the number of news-related items equaled the number of letters that passed through an average post office.[50] The mastheads of these publications—from the *Richmond Whig* to the *Arkansas Democrat*—stated the obvious: these were partisan papers, and by the 1830s, partisan propaganda constituted almost half of all postal deliveries. An even more ominous trend developed in which editor Thomas Ritchie "used postmasters as intelligence agents to check up on subscribers who did not pick up the Richmond *Enquirer* . . . ," turning the postmaster into a highly paid political snitch.[51]

Originally, the news network consisted of a channel of communication that went out from the printers in New York, Boston, Philadelphia, or Baltimore to secondary cities such as Albany, Hartford, or New Haven, before then penetrating the hinterland around Philadelphia and Baltimore. Eventually, cities on postal routes farther inland, such as Cincinnati or Detroit, would receive the news. At each step of the journey, local papers were free to "cut and paste" from the original source, thus standardizing information as it was transmitted inland.[52]

During the colonial and revolutionary periods, "news" consisted of mostly local events, although a few overtly partisan papers existed. The *National Gazette*, edited by Philip Freneau, opposed George Washington and the Federalists, as did the anti-Federalist *Aurora*, while the *National Intelligencer* supported the administration. The *Intelligencer* received a government contract for reprinting the speeches of members of Congress, which constituted a monopoly contract, persuading many of the members to hold up publication of their remarks until they, or the party, could alter them. Once again, Van Buren perceived an opportunity, viewing the newspapers as the perfect propaganda instruments to take the message of his new party to the citizens—by the 1858 Senate race between Abraham Lincoln and Stephen Douglas, Douglas mailed more than 350,000 news clippings containing his speeches back to Illinois. Papers had to be faithful to the party's ideology (which is to say, lack of ideology), meaning they—like other organization loyalists—would be procured with cash.

As historian Robert Remini contended, this constituted "perhaps the single most important accomplishment" of the Jacksonians—the "creation of a vast, nationwide newspaper system" that supported their ideology.[53] The Jacksonians blatantly established their own party organs, such as Duff Green's Washington-based *United States Telegraph* (1826), by lending the editor the money to start the paper. Green obediently repaid his political masters with pro-Jackson editorials and obligingly turned out a special extra paper during the 1828 election with a circulation of forty thousand.[54] He also played Johnny Appleseed to the Jacksonian news nexus, helping to set up other Jacksonian papers around the country. Defenders of Green point to the fact that he was "struggling financially" and thus could not possibly have been "on the take," but in fact he relied on increasing sales to distant subscribers, and like all other papers of the era, his fell victim to the reluctance of subscribers to actually pay for the paper.[55] So the evidence suggests that Green was every bit as partisan as his accusers have claimed and that he was likely just a poor businessman.

Printing profits, for example, averaged 40 percent a year during one ten-year stretch, and an official paper could be charged tremendous lithographing, printing, and engraving fees.[56] The motto of the *United States Telegraph*, "Power Is Always Stealing from the Many to the Few," seems an apt description of what Green and his friends were doing. Not only did he receive official party monies, but Jacksonian loyalists endorsed Green's personal notes and funneled "soft money" to him on a regular basis, but without this steady flow of funds, the paper never could have survived on its subscriptions. Indeed, as more Democratic papers proliferated, and as Whig papers rose in opposition, almost *none* made money aside from the political cash infusions they received.

Surprisingly, Green himself recognized the dangers of a politicized press. In 1826, he wrote that "it is in vain to talk of a free press when the *favor of power* is essential to the support of editors, and the money of the people, by passing through the hands of the Executive, is made to operate as a bribe against liberty. . . . if liberty shall ever expire in our country, it will die of the poisonous draught of corrupt patronage."[57] Nor was Green alone in his concerns. The same *Richmond Enquirer* editor Thomas Ritchie, who used postmasters as political spies, worried about "showering patronage too much on Editors of newspapers and on Members of Congress, and the rights of the people themselves are exposed to imminent danger."[58] Of course, with patronage dollars flowing in, such concerns tended to be fleeting. Francis Preston Blair's paper the *Congressional Globe*, supported initially by the State Department to publish session laws, perhaps even exceeded Green's *Telegraph* in its loyalty to the party. The *Globe* functioned solely as an organ of the Jackson administration, and Blair's attitude on any given current issues was "determined by Jackson's stand on them."[59] Indeed, the *Globe* served as the political handbook for the party, printing marching orders for other editors around the country to follow.

Unwilling to consider the dangers of a politicized press, or unable to contemplate the political results, political parties propelled newspaper circulation upward, with circulation growing more than five times as fast as population by 1840, having been roughly equal to population in 1790. This tsunami of newspapers had little to do with market forces and everything to do with political patronage. Publishers carried delinquent customers for months, their deficits offset through political contributions, "loans," and subsidies from Congress.[60] Historian Gerald Baldasty found that in 1830, the state of Georgia had eleven newspapers, "all of them embroiled in political fights," and the party had at least three patronage papers in each state, with the *Globe* serving as their pilot for editorial policy.[61] By 1850, political bias so dominated the newspaper industry that the U.S. Census estimated nearly 80 percent of American papers were partisan, while other estimates put the number of partisan papers at close to 100 percent![62]

Thus, at the time "newspapers" emerged as a driving force in American political life, they had almost nothing to do with objective news. To the contrary, they deliberately slanted every report and openly advertised their partisan purposes through their names. Partisanship was their primary raison d'être.[63] Editors viewed readers as voters who needed to be guided to appropriate views, then mobilized to vote.[64] Green's *Telegraph* flatly condemned neutrality as an absence of principles, and overall, editors increasingly discarded news in favor of propaganda.[65] A Louisville paper criticized the neutrality of an Indiana paper, noting, "in this State, people have more respect for an open, independent adversary than for dumb partisans . . . who are too imbecile to form an opinion."[66] One Jacksonian editor stated that "we most of all abhor and detest . . . a neutral paper. It pretends to be all things to all men."[67] This attitude has been confirmed in studies of content, in which the percentage of editorial comment in "news" stories increased, then nearly doubled between 1847 and 1860.

Many editors owed their jobs directly and specifically to the Jacksonians, frequently slipping back and forth between editor positions and postmaster jobs. Jackson himself appointed numerous editors to salaried political positions, including many postmasters, while nationally it is estimated that fifty to sixty editors had been given plum political jobs.[68] Rewarding political friends was nothing new—the Federalists had appointed nearly one thousand editors to postmaster positions over a twelve-year period—but the Jacksonians transformed an ad hoc approach to appointments into a strategic political plan.[69] Under such circumstances, few readers of "news" doubted where a paper stood on particular positions, nor did people think they were receiving objective facts upon which to make reasoned decisions.

Ironically—keeping in mind that the entire purpose behind founding the Democratic Party was to exclude slavery from the political debate—newspapers had for more than a century provided a cheap and reliable way of catching runaway slaves and overcoming cost barriers of distance.[70] One historian of slavery noted that eighteenth-century slave owners used "print to counter the mobility of the unfree, to establish or reestablish confidence in slavery and servitude."[71] This aspect of the public discussion of slavery apparently went unnoticed in Van Buren's schemes, but it reflected a truth about slavery and the press, namely, that to not take a stand against slavery was to endorse it.[72] Put another way, at the local level, "printers and post-masters . . . served as agents for masters. They were go-betweens" who supported the slave structure through the dissemination of information needed to reacquire runaways.[73] This fact clashed on the most profound level with the Jacksonian imperative that required that slavery be pushed out of the public sphere, subtly and consistently pushing maintenance of "the peculiar institution" into the public sphere. Over time, as northern states ended slavery, even pro-Jacksonian papers that ran ads about runaways began to vanish, further distinguishing northern and southern papers, and "free" and "slave" papers, all in stark contrast to what Van Buren had hoped would occur.

With the end of "King Caucus," the elimination of restrictions on voter qualifications, and the erection of a massive network of newspapers supported by the federally funded postal system, Van Buren had constructed a political party that conceivably could restrain the trend toward disunion over slavery. It bears repeating: at every turn, Van Buren's system was designed to *suppress* all political discussion of slavery. Of course, this proved impossible to enforce since virtually every debate involved sectional tensions, and sooner or later slavery became the unspoken topic. The stultification of free speech through the very newspapers established to spread the Democratic message was an inevitable by-product. Southern Democrats attempted to manipulate and control the press even more over time, seeking to stem the influx of hostile, abolitionist literature between 1820 and 1860. This affected the nature of news-gathering itself as editors depended less on "clipped news" (which

fell from 54 percent of the stories in 1820 to just 30 percent by 1860) because of the potential for pro- or anti-slave views to surface in the text.[74]
Instead, reporter-generated stories doubled between 1820 and 1860, a trend
that shifted the location of stories to a geographical area within the editor's
reach, allowing him to tell the slavery story as he saw fit.[75]

It was a futile effort. Even as news emanating from Washington, D.C.,
fell by 3 percent from 1820 to 1860 as a share of total news at a time when
the federal government played an increasingly important role in the lives
of ordinary people, over that same period discussion of sectional problems
"increased steadily . . . from 5% of the coverage in the early years to 12%"
by the election of Lincoln.[76] Even that sharp increase in sectional issues did
not adequately reflect the profound impact slavery had on the party system
and the press, due to the understanding of a "gag" on all discussion of slavery
on the part of southern editors. In essence, the increasingly sectional tone
of newspaper discussions occurred even while a gag on debate over slavery
was imposed in the South. It seems reasonable to conclude, therefore, that
despite Van Buren's grand design to push it onto the back burner, slavery
had become the single most important topic in America.

At the same time that free speech was being stifled under the guise
of preserving the Union, Van Buren's scheme frayed at other edges. The
requirement, for example, that to maintain a national party presence, the
presidential candidate had to be a "northern man of southern principles"
or a westerner meant that if a northern man of *northern* principles ever ac-
ceded to the highest office, it would constitute a threat of the most profound
kind. So long as the Whigs remained the loyal opposition—winning only
two presidential elections between 1836 and 1860, and both presidents died
in office—little danger existed that they would raise the issue of slavery.
Indeed, one reason Lynn Marshall labeled the party "stillborn" is that from
its inception, the Whig Party's chief components were irreconcilable. Daniel
Webster of Massachusetts, an ardent opponent of slavery, and John C. Calhoun of South Carolina (the first major politician to term slavery a "positive
good" as opposed to a "necessary evil") had virtually nothing in common,
save their hatred of Jackson.

If, however, the Whigs faltered and another party took their place—a
party whose chief issue was the restriction or elimination of slavery—then
Van Buren's presidential safeguard would likewise collapse. Such was the case

in 1860 when a northern man of northern principles, Abraham Lincoln, explicitly campaigned on the principle that slavery should not be allowed into the western territories. While he promised repeatedly not to touch slavery where it then existed, as we will see keeping such a vow was an impossibility, as Lincoln himself had acknowledged with his "House Divided" speech.

Quickly, all supporting elements of Van Buren's scheme fell apart. In 1836 Congress officially adopted the "gag rule" to prohibit all debate or discussion of slavery, which itself became the source of endless conflict and debate. Anti-slavery forces had begun inundating Congress with thousands of petitions calling for the abolition of slavery in 1831. The pro-slavery forces found support from, of all people, newly elected president Martin Van Buren, who urged them to find a compromise. The result came in the Twenty-fourth Congress, using the Pinckney Resolutions of 1836, which packaged all anti-slavery petitions together and referred them to a select committee.[77] South Carolina representative Henry Laurens Pinckney's committee concluded that Congress had no constitutional authority to interfere with slavery in the states, and therefore proposed to table all petitions so that none were brought up for discussion or debate. Attempts by Whigs to derail it were themselves gagged. Because this was a "resolution," and not a House "rule," every new session had to renew the gag rule. In both 1837 and 1838, new gag resolutions passed, but not without a backlash, which in part contributed to the first Whig majority in the Twenty-seventh Congress. Nevertheless, in 1840, the Twenty-first Rule was passed, which converted the resolution to permanent status and prohibited the Speaker from even receiving an anti-slavery petition. Far from ending debate, the gag rules by their very wording required that new and expanded language be added as new territories joined the Union as states.

Throughout, the star in Congress was former president John Quincy Adams—the only U.S. president to return to the House of Representatives after a term in the White House. Adams's speaking skills enabled him to follow the gag rule while still raising anti-slavery issues.[78] For example, Adams forced the Speaker to rule on whether each individual petition he received fell under the jurisdiction of the latest gag rule, altogether violating the intent of the rule itself. His actions finally resulted in a motion to have Adams censured. Then, when the Whigs had the majority, he got himself appointed to head the Rules Committee, which reported out rules that removed the gag provision. When finally, in 1844, the House rescinded the gag rule by a 28-vote margin, the victory belonged to Adams more than any other man.

Repeal of the gag rule constituted only the first thread to unravel from Van Buren's garment to exclude slavery from national debate, and even there, the Democrats could not maintain party discipline. During the debate over the settlement of the Mexican War, Democratic congressman David Wilmot of Pennsylvania introduced a provision that slavery be prohibited in all territories acquired by the United States in the conflict. Hence, Van Buren's own party abandoned the principle that slave politics should be excluded from the halls of Congress.

Two other key elements of Van Buren's scheme to suppress the slave issue also spun out of his control. Government at the federal level had grown consistently bigger and more powerful. Ironically, the man who gave it the most muscle was Van Buren's champion, Andrew Jackson. Old Hickory's reputation as a small-government president is ill deserved, a myth based largely on his famous "war" on the Bank of the United States in 1832. In fact, the Bank War was a highly partisan power struggle with the influential president of the bank, Nicholas Biddle, who had great support among Jackson's congressional foes. It had nothing to do with either economics or federalism, and certainly was not an example of limited-government libertarianism as so many of Jackson's admirers have attempted to paint it. Jackson had ordered the drafting of his own plan for a national bank in 1829, and when he killed the BUS, he put the government deposits in state banks run by his political pals. Considerable evidence exists that he hoped to completely eliminate state paper money.[79] Jackson issued more vetoes than all previous presidents combined, reversing the long tradition of "Whig" governance (the term in this instance does not refer to the party, but rather the view that the main source of popular will lay in the Congress, not the presidency).

The oft-overlooked aspect of Jackson's many vetoes is that as *negative* demonstrations of presidential authority, they nevertheless *increased* the scope and power of the office itself, regardless of the intention that lay behind them. In other areas, though, Jackson made no mystery of his intention to dominate other branches. When the U.S. Supreme Court ruled against him in the Cherokee removal, he uttered the famous phrase, "Justice Marshall has made his ruling. Now let him enforce it." Jackson (with legitimate cause) threatened to invade South Carolina and enforce the collection of tariff duties there. Nothing Andrew Jackson did actually weakened the federal government, and most of what he did greatly expanded the size and reach of the presidency. It was only a matter of time until someone who did not share Martin Van Buren's goal of suppressing all discussion of slavery reached the White House.

A final failure of Van Buren's plan involved the issue of patronage, for as the Whigs learned to play the game, with every election came more government jobs to be given away. Ensuring electoral success meant that a candidate had to promise more jobs than his opponent. Jefferson may have answered the White House door himself in his bathrobe and slippers, but the trends were such that by 1860 Abraham Lincoln spent every moment not fighting the war dealing with a seemingly endless line of political office holders, whose letters of appointment he had to sign. Even though he still ran the U.S. government essentially with only three personal aides, the burdens of dealing with the spoils at the end of every election had started to become apparent.

Thus, Van Buren's nightmare only increased national debate about slavery (when he had sought to exclude it), increased the presence and intrusion of the federal government (when he had counted on limiting it), and increased the likelihood that if the government ever fell into the hands of a contrary ideology, its power would be such that slavery itself would not be safe. And that was precisely the case when Abraham Lincoln was elected. The Democrats had by then ceased to be a national party at all, fracturing into northern and southern wings that could not even agree on a presidential candidate. An entirely new party—using spoils as its instrument to win elections, but this time fueled and directed by a specific anti-slavery ideology— the Republicans, ditched Van Buren's concept of a party devoid of principle and elevated the principle of anti-slavery to the top of its agenda.

Not only had he failed to keep slavery out of the national debate, Van Buren had devised a system that ensured it would be addressed at the national level, with the machinery of a vastly larger federal government. During the Civil War which followed, both the Union and Confederate governments accelerated the growth of government power. Both imposed income taxes, confiscated private property, enacted draft laws, printed unsecured money, silenced free speech, engaged in arrests that violated habeas corpus, and committed dozens of other violations of the principles of limited government. The excesses of Lincoln's government were substantial, but research has shown that the Confederacy in fact was far more oppressive to the rights of free white citizens than the North.[80] As historian Richard Bensel found, during the war, "two central states . . . were locked in mortal combat," and the Confederacy pursued a "relatively statist war mobilization. In contrast, the northern war effort mobilized materiel and men by relying on voluntary contracts within a comparatively robust capitalist market."[81]

Another unintended consequence of the war was that a giant lobbying organization, the Grand Army of the Republic, was formed to acquire benefits for veterans. Between 1865 and 1888, the GAR emerged as the largest nonbusiness special interest group in America, padding its rolls with thousands of "veterans," many of whom never served in combat; it pleaded for those who had received war wounds to obtain restitution. Yet many never served, more still never fought, and still more were never wounded. Its ranks swelled beyond all imagination—when, given the age and physical health of the war survivors, the numbers should have declined steadily—until after the Compromise of 1877, the GAR floated the notion of paying veterans' benefits to *Confederate* soldiers.

Eventually, the courageous president Grover Cleveland would personally rein in the GAR, by which time other unintended consequences of Van Buren's party structure would be out of control. As long as government remained relatively small, the excesses of the spoils system likewise remained minimal. On a micro level, one could see the inevitable results, however: the Tweed Ring in New York City in the 1850s turned spoilsmanship into a high art, as the political agents of "Boss" William Marcy Tweed doled out largesse to anyone and everyone who helped keep the ring in power. Alexander Callow has detailed the staggering graft that went on under the Tweed Ring, which honed Van Buren's political machine to perfection, stealing millions from the taxpayers of New York City.[82] At one point, Tammany Hall (as Tweed's operation was called, for the building out of which it operated) counted almost twelve thousand people whose livelihood directly depended on the Tweed Ring staying in power. The modus operandi for getting out the vote was accurately captured in Martin Scorsese's film *Gangs of New York,* and was epitomized in the saying, "It's not who votes that counts, but who counts the votes." Tweed's boys used intimidation to prevent opponents from getting to the polls, while at the same time they elevated to a fine art the practice of getting out the vote among their own supporters. Their practices included outright cash bribes, multiple voting by the same person, and scouring every alley and saloon for any breathing citizen who could cast a ballot for Tammany Hall.

It was a far cry from the voters in the age of Jefferson, who turned out at up to 80 percent rates because of a sense of duty, patriotism, and pride. Tweed's voters were herded like livestock, told whom to vote for, and warned to not think for themselves.

Ultimately, though, the ring's power came from the cash it doled out in the form of rewards to friends, particularly the Manufacturing Stationer's Company, which got virtually all of New York City's printing. On top of that, every patronage job involved a salary that the ring vastly inflated. But that was only the tip of the spoils iceberg. Because the ring controlled the Corporation Counsel office under Richard O'Gorman, it allowed cronies to file claims against the city, collect a commission, and then pay the claims at inflated prices. Judgments against the city attained all-time highs (over $400,000), while O'Gorman's office racked up almost $153,000 in expenses. The Manufacturing Stationer's Company proved to be the most fortunate, though, in sucking money out of the system. In 1870 alone, it received from the city $3 million, typical charges to those found on almost any other annual billing to the city.

While outrageous and astonishing on its own, the Tweed Ring demonstrated the direction patronage was sure to take, and spoils became the focus of political reform in the late 1860s and early 1870s—with "reform" itself usually making matters worse. Various groups, mostly within the Republican Party, sought to rein in the spoils system, in the process backing or opposing candidates who either favored spoils or wanted to end it. The most prominent of the patronage supporters were the "Stalwarts," headed by Roscoe Conkling, who battled reformers such as Rutherford B. Hayes. Another prominent Stalwart, Chester A. Arthur of New York, was nominated as James Garfield's vice president. Garfield, a "Half Breed" (the name given to enemies of the spoils system), favored instituting a civil service system based on examinations and a merit system. Garfield had been tainted in the Crédit Mobilier scandal, but not seriously so, and had only been in office a few months when Charles Guiteau, who had failed to get a spoils job, shot him in a railway station. Guiteau shouted, "I am a Stalwart. . . . Arthur is president now."[83]

Garfield's assassination galvanized the forces of reform, resulting in the passage of the Pendleton Civil Service Reform Act in 1883, which created the United States Civil Service Commission, placing most federal employees on a merit system. No longer would competent postmasters and customs collectors be yanked from their jobs merely because of the results of an election.[84] While that appeared both humane and practical, it constituted a massive expansion of the spoils system and patronage, taking it to an entirely different level. Where Boss Tweed and Martin Van Buren only had to promise a few thousand jobs directly to supporters in every election to ensure victory, that option disappeared after 1883. Instead, the Pendleton Act made matters worse because it forced politicians to promise entire programs and legislation in scattershot form that would appeal to larger numbers of voters. Thus, instead of promising a few ward and precinct jobs to cronies, the post-Pendleton politician had to promise masses of jobs cloaked in "support" for such programs as public works, then later, NASA, defense, protectionism for industry, the environment, and hundreds of other areas.

For example, a presidential candidate speaking in Dayton, Ohio, before a large crowd of residents dependent on Wright-Patterson Air Force Base for employment could legitimately say, "I favor a strong national defense" and certainly some in the audience applaud him for supporting the military. But just as many would interpret that as saying, "I favor a strong commitment to Wright-Patterson Air Force Base and all the jobs it brings," and they would be right. The same candidate in Iowa might support ethanol subsidies because he genuinely believes it would improve America's energy problem, but it would just as likely represent that candidate's awareness that he needs the votes of Iowa's farmers. What changed between Van Buren's original structure and the Pendleton "reform" was not the fundamental element of the system—that politicians exchanged jobs for votes—but merely the *number* of those directly affected by such giveaways!

The Founders, both Federalists and anti-Federalists, were suspicious of big government and terrified of the tyranny that an unchecked government might bring. James Madison carefully balanced the executive, legislative, and judicial branches, while the other members of the Constitutional Convention worked diligently to secure the rights of the states within the federal system. To *all* of them, "big government" constituted a serious threat. Even Hamilton, widely considered to be a big-government politician, feared that the masses would gain control of the Treasury and vote themselves taxpayer benefits. While Federalist fathers such as George Washington, John Adams, and James Madison all agreed that a more powerful central government than the Articles of Confederation offered was necessary, none approved of handing out jobs for political support, and all detested the concept of national leaders running for office by, essentially, buying votes. Van Buren not only failed to prevent the war that he intended to avoid, but he bequeathed to the United States a party system that depended on the delivery of jobs as its lifeblood. It's hard to imagine one man, regardless of his good intentions, who has done more damage to the nation, unless it would be our next subject, Chief Justice Roger B. Taney.

2.

THE *DRED SCOTT* DECISION WRECKS AN ECONOMY
AND HASTENS A WAR

To consider . . . judges as the ultimate arbiters of all constitutional questions [is] a very dangerous doctrine indeed, and one which would place us under the despotism of an oligarchy.

THOMAS JEFFERSON TO WILLIAM JARVIS, 1820

Seldom do Supreme Court decisions make an immediate impact on American life. *Roe v. Wade*, probably the most important Court decision of the twentieth century, and *Brown v. Board of Education* are clear exceptions. Others, however, may settle a case, but they hardly settle the issues surrounding it. For example, *Bush v. Gore* may have settled an election, but it hardly settled the debate about how elections should be handled. More commonly, the impact is felt over long periods. When courts confirm damaging legislation or executive branch policies, the result normally reinforces practices that had existed during the long appeals process. If courts overturn legislation or block executive actions, markets often have already factored in a likely response. Such events as the breakup of Standard Oil Company in 1911 under antitrust concerns, or the Microsoft decision in the 1990s, had long been discounted before the final verdict. Even the implementation of *Brown* was delayed for almost a decade, then fought out on still other battle-fields of busing, property taxes, and school vouchers.

But a few Supreme Court decisions have been unexpected in terms of their scope or implications. The 1857 *Dred Scott* decision is one such case. In it, the Court reached far beyond the immediate question of the "person-hood" of slave Dred Scott and weighed in on the critical issue of slavery in America. As a result, it produced a remarkable trifecta of consequences: it triggered a financial panic, greatly sped up the arrival of the Civil War, and disgraced the Court itself. The *Dred Scott* decision represents the law of un-intended consequences in almost every imaginable way. Historians James Huston and David Potter have both argued that the decision accelerated the drift toward war, perhaps past the point of no return.[1] More recently, Judge Andrew Napolitano has re-examined its continued influence on Ameri-can race relations.[2] The case's impact on slavery and on sectional strife has been established, but not only did *Dred Scott* potentially affect all existing southern slaves (more than three million), but it threw open the question of whether the American land that still remained to be settled—the vast western territories—would allow slavery or not. In the process, it injected immediate uncertainty into financial markets and perpetuated a depression that had implications for the impending sectional breakup. Not only was *Dred Scott* bad law in itself, but it also demonstrated the law of unintended consequences, sparking a panic and virtually ensuring a war by taking criti-cal questions out of the hands of the people.

The case began eleven years before the Supreme Court issued its final decision when, in 1846, a slave named Dred Scott filed a suit for manumis-sion in the slave state of Missouri. Scott was born in 1799 as a slave of a Virginian, Peter Blow, who sold Scott in 1833 to a U.S. Army doctor, John Emerson. With Emerson, Scott went to a post in Illinois, then to Minne-sota, where slavery was illegal. He then was taken with the family to other states, finally arriving in St. Louis, Missouri. There, he took advantage of the Missouri legal system, which permitted blacks to purchase their freedom. After Emerson's widow, Irene, rejected his offer of $300 to purchase his own liberty as well as his wife's, he sued in state court in 1846.

While the historiography of slavery remains divided between those who see the propensity in the Constitution toward confirming an unjust system of human bondage and those who see the Founders as institutionalizing a series of remedies in the wording and in subsequent acts (such as the Northwest Ordinance), the purpose here is not to join that argument except to note that in Scott's case, it should strike the reader as rather astounding that in a *slave state*, Missouri law permitted Scott access to the court to sue for his freedom.[3] In *Winny v. Phebe Whitesides*, the Missouri Supreme Court noted for the first time the precedent of freeing slaves who had resided in a free state or territory by citing an 1807 territorial statute that allowed anyone held in slavery to petition the court for freedom as a "poor person."[4] Winny won her freedom. Of course, all suits did not work out so well for the petitioners: a circuit court case in 1818, *Jack v. Barnabas Harris*, featured a slave named Jack who unsuccessfully sued for his freedom. Scott, then, was only one of many—though certainly the most famous—to use the instruments of the law to seek his freedom. In a truly "closed" system, however, with a bias toward the status quo or maintaining elites (including slave owners) in a permanent position of power, no such avenues ever would have been available to Scott or any other slave.

Scott's case rested on proof that he had been free in Illinois or in the Wisconsin Territory (Minnesota). He initially lost the case, then appealed to the Missouri Supreme Court, which held that the case should be retried.[5] At that point, the St. Louis circuit court found that Scott and his family were indeed free in 1850, whereupon Mrs. Emerson—her husband having died several years earlier—appealed to the Missouri Supreme Court in 1852, which reversed the circuit court decision. By that time, John Sandford, Eliza Emerson's brother, was given title to the slaves, and thus inherited the case. Scott, meanwhile, had been freed by the sons of his original owner, Peter Blow, who had paid for his legal fees during the court battle. Denied liberty by Missouri's state courts, Scott then filed a suit in the Missouri federal court, which agreed with the Missouri Supreme Court, leaving Dred Scott with an appeal to the United States Supreme Court and a date with history.

From the outset, the odds were stacked against Scott: seven of the nine justices had been appointed by southern presidents, and five came from slaveholding families, including Chief Justice Roger B. Taney of Maryland, who had personally owned slaves. As a young man, Taney had befriended Francis Scott Key, whose sister he married. Taney was a Jacksonian partisan of the worst kind, personifying the term "political hack." A Catholic and a states'-rights champion, the skeletal, stooped, and ailing Taney, nearly eighty years old at the time of the *Dred Scott* case, read his decision for over two hours in a strained voice as his hands trembled from the stress of holding the paper. He had emancipated his own slaves in the 1820s, but philosophically he still believed in the "peculiar institution." And he had a track record on the matter. In 1850, Taney's Court in *Strader v. Graham* had ruled that slaves from Kentucky who had gone to Ohio and similarly claimed freedom were bound by Kentucky law, not Ohio law.[6] As is well known, all Taney and his fellow justices had to do was agree with the Missouri court system that, as a slave, Scott had no right to bring suit. But as we have also seen, Missouri and Maryland, in particular, were subjected to a constant stream of emancipation cases, and, indeed, the frequency with which they were brought in Missouri (as opposed to neighboring Illinois) suggests that in fact the law was in flux. If an owner's word *alone* was not sufficient to characterize a black person as a slave, then the very essence of personhood was an issue, and if slaves were persons, then they were dangerously close to being the "men" who were "created equal" under the Declaration.

Whatever Taney's motivations, he and the other justices went far beyond a quick resolution of the case by merely upholding the lower court and instead issued a manifesto on property rights and slavery in America. In an unusual development, all nine justices rendered separate opinions in the 7–2 decision against Scott. It was a case of remarkable judicial activism, even more stunning for its lack of logic. (There were seven justices appointed by Democrats, one by the Republicans, and one by the Whigs.) Taney began his opinion by stating that it was "too plain for argument, that [blacks] had never been regarded as part of the people or citizens of the State, nor supposed to possess any political rights which the dominant race might not withhold or grant at their pleasure."[7] Moreover, the Court maintained that the Founders had not intended to endow blacks with citizenship rights (a strange claim, given that blacks could vote in ten of the thirteen original states).[8]

Since Scott was not a citizen of Missouri, the federal courts, including the United States Supreme Court, lacked jurisdiction to hear the suit—but then Taney's Court went on to render a decision anyway. Engaging in judicial activism by addressing the Missouri Compromise, the justices said that the compromise had been unconstitutional, and therefore the prohibition against slavery there had likewise been unconstitutional. The property of a slaveholder had full protection under the Constitution's Fifth Amendment. At the same time, the Court held the concept of "popular sovereignty"—in which the people of a territory could decide the fate of slavery at their state territorial conventions, touted by Senators Stephen Douglas of Illinois and Lewis Cass of Michigan—to be equally null and void. The protections of slavery could not be eliminated except by an existing state, meaning that the bias for all new territories to begin their statehood with slavery would be henceforth universal. Put another way, Taney's Court had essentially said that Congress could not prohibit slavery, nor could the people prohibit slavery in their territorial legislatures. Only the institution of the state, after achieving statehood, could enact laws to prohibit slavery, but even those laws would not extend to any other states.

Both Abraham Lincoln and Stephen Douglas—the opposing U.S. Senate candidates in Illinois in the election of 1858—recognized the destruction caused by the decision. Each addressed it in the famed Lincoln-Douglas debates, but only Lincoln predicted that it would lead to war. Lincoln's June 1858 "House Divided" speech warned that the nation would become either all slave or all free. Douglas had attempted to skirt the issue by supporting popular sovereignty. However, Douglas also supported the *Dred Scott* decision, and Lincoln pounced on his inconsistency by demanding that the "Little Giant" reconcile support for popular sovereignty with the Court's decision that the people of a territory could not exclude slavery. At Freeport, Douglas's answer, known as the Freeport Doctrine, killed his presidential chances. Douglas said he supported the *Dred Scott* ruling but that people could keep slavery out of their state by refusing to pass legislation that would protect slavery and by electing officials who would not enforce it. With the "Freeport Heresy," as Southerners labeled it, Douglas's political hopes crumbled and the Democratic Party split along sectional lines, ensuring the election of an anti-slavery Republican in 1860. When that occurred, war became almost inevitable.[9]

Lincoln knew popular sovereignty was not an answer for any question of moral and constitutional proportions. He considered it the equivalent of allowing a vote on whether, say, all blonds should be imprisoned or all fifty-year-olds executed. More important, Lincoln sensed, as implied in the "House Divided" speech, that the debate over slavery in the territories was a mere proxy for the reintroduction of slavery into free states as well. It eventually came down to a question of constitutional property rights, and sooner or later, the issue of whether slaves were *people* or *property* would eventually require a final resolution.[10]

Needless to say, anti-slavery forces in the North were shocked and outraged by the Court's decision. In addition to Lincoln, who had wondered in January 1857 if the Court would use the occasion to rule on "the constitutional restriction of the power of a territorial Legislature, in regard to slavery in the territory," others expressed concern.[11] Chicago's *Democratic Press* expressed a "feeling of shame and loathing" for the Court; Horace Greeley believed the decision held the same weight as one rendered "in any Washington bar-room."[12] The New York *Independent* charged that the ruling was a "Moral Assassination of a Race and Cannot be Obeyed," while a competitor, the *Tribune*, prophesied that no one who cherished freedom would submit to the results handed down by "five slaveholders and two doughfaces."[13] Washington's *National Era* observed, "The Slaveholding Oligarchy have the Administration, the majority in the Senate and in the House, and the Supreme Court. What is left to the People?"[14] Of course, southern and Democratic papers were ecstatic: the *Philadelphia Pennsylvanian* called the decision the "funeral Sermon of Black Republicanism," and the New Orleans *Picayune* gleefully boasted that now "the whole basis of the Black Republican organization [is] under the ban of the law."[15]

Obvious to most was the implication that if Scott's residence on free soil had not entitled him to emancipation, then any slave could be brought into the North permanently. This was precisely what Lincoln cautioned against in his "House Divided" speech—that one way or another, the issue had to be decided nationwide, and on the grounds of either property or personhood. He had warned, "Either the *opponents* of slavery, will arrest the further spread of it, and place it where the public mind shall rest in the belief that it is in the course of ultimate extinction; or its *advocates* will push it forward, till it shall become alike lawful in all the States, *old* as well as *new*—*North* as well as *South*."[16] Taney's Court had chosen the former. In the Lincoln-Douglas debates, the future president warned about a "nice little niche [that might be] filled with another Supreme Court decision" that would prohibit free states from excluding slavery."[17] Lincoln, however, was well ahead of his contemporaries and fellow Republicans in realizing that "the negative principle that *no* law is free law" meant that the Constitution had a presumption of human liberty over property rights.[18] In this way, Lincoln said what many southerners feared in their hearts: that without "positive" law, slavery would become the subject of a majority vote. They began to fear that Northerners would never permit new slave states, leading the South to demand with increasing intensity a national approval of slave property. Merely admitting the right wasn't enough: Northerners had to approve of the institution, which they would never do. Calhoun had already broached the subject during the debates over the Wilmot Proviso in 1847 by saying:

> I go farther, and hold that if we have a right to hold our slaves, we have the right to hold them in peace and quiet, and that the toleration in the non-slaveholding States of the establishment of societies and presses, and the delivery of lectures, with the express intention of calling into question our right to our slaves [and enticing runaways and abolition, are] not only a violation of international laws, but also the Federal compact.[19]

This was a chilling prophecy of gag laws in modern-day Europe and Canada, where religious criticisms of homosexuals or Muslims even on a purely theoretical basis are muted on the grounds that they abridge the rights of people who engage in homosexual behavior or subscribe to Islam.

Once again, though, Calhoun raised the ugly hand of the whip: if a free man dared criticize slavery, he would be punished for his opinion that it was wrong. To repeat, acceptance of the institution was not enough: approval was the goal. As James Huston put it, "southerners hoped to control the actions of the federal government and never lose."[20] Democratic republics can only endure as long as the losers agree to go along peacefully with the will of the majority and so long as private rights are protected. But Southerners felt that if property rights of slaves were endangered in any way—even by restrictions on movement into the territories—then property rights of slaves in the states themselves would soon be up for grabs. Hence, the battle increasingly involved forcing a national acceptance of the southern definitions of property. Jefferson Davis, in 1850, asked, "What is there in the character of that property [slaves] which excludes it from the general benefit of the principles applied to all other property?"[21]

All of the debate over property, of course, also obscured the fact that *Dred Scott* was bad law. The decision cut the ground out from under the logic used in *Lemmon v. People*, a New York Superior Court case in which a slave owner who stayed in New York with his eight slaves on a steamship was sued under habeas corpus laws and Justice Elijah Paine cited "the law of nature [that] all men are free, and where slavery is not established and upheld by the law of the state there can be no slaves."[22] The ruling was appealed, reached the New York Supreme Court on a writ of certiorari, and the original decision was upheld. It was then appealed to the New York Court of Appeals, where it was upheld yet again. By that time—1860—the New York court was fully aware of the *Dred Scott* decision but ignored it. Judge William Wright took a dig at Taney's Court when he wrote:

> Men are not the subject of property by such law, nor by any law, except that of the State in which the status exists; not even by the Federal Constitution, which is supposed by some to have been made only to guard and protect the rights of a particular race. . . . [23]

War broke out before the case could come to the United States Supreme Court, where it almost certainly would have met the same fate as Scott's. As Don Fehrenbacher wrote, the decision "legitimized and encouraged an expansion of slavery that never took place; it denied freedom to a slave who was then quickly manumitted."[24] Of course, the central reason the "expansion never took place" was because the South seceded rather than risk the results of the democratic process that it knew was sure to come.

But the most obvious unstated fact was that Taney's Court did not acknowledge the evil or basic injustice of slavery, and Lincoln did. Modern angry black writers, such as Lerone Bennett, have claimed Abraham Lincoln was a racist, a notion accepted by a handful of otherwise sensible thinkers on the right.[25] Lincoln's dream, "like Jefferson's dream," Bennett wrote, "was a dream of a lily-white America without Negroes, Native Americans, and Martin Luther Kings."[26] Those are cockamamie comments about a man who said, "I can not but hate [slavery]. I hate it because of the monstrous injustice of slavery itself."[27] More important, for those who cite Lincoln's comments about black inequality, a remarkable exposition exists that proved just the opposite—that in freedom equality was assumed:

> You say A. Is white, and B. Is black. It is *color*, then; the lighter, having the right to enslave the darker? Take care. By this rule, you are to be a slave to the first man you meet, with a fairer skin than your own. You do not mean *color* exactly?—You mean the whites are *intellectually* the superiors of the blacks, and, therefore have the right to enslave them? Take care again. By this rule, you are to be the slave to the first man you meet, and with an intellect superior to your own.[28]

In the short term, Abraham Lincoln used the *Dred Scott* decision as a sledgehammer to pound Senator Stephen Douglas during the famous Lincoln-Douglas debates of 1858. Douglas, running for reelection, already had his eyes on the presidency. As noted in the previous chapter, until 1860 virtually every American president after Monroe had been a "northern man of southern principles" or a Westerner who acquiesced in the existence of slavery, and Douglas, from Illinois, certainly fit that mold. Under the structure of Van Buren's party system, the national parties had to run candidates who had appeal in both Albany and Richmond.

Douglas, however, had already antagonized many Southerners. First, he helped orchestrate the Compromise of 1850, which admitted California as a free state and the New Mexico and Utah territories under the new concept of popular sovereignty. This idea, originally elaborated by Michigan senator Lewis Cass, embodied a solution to slavery wrapped in the guise of democracy, namely, that the people of a territory could choose whether or not to have slavery within their borders. As Harry Jaffa, the most insightful critic of the Lincoln-Douglas debates, has argued, it elevated the concept of moral relativism above that of natural law for the first time in the young Republic's history.[29] Douglas earned the further antipathy of the South when he introduced a bill for Nebraska statehood in 1854 into the Senate, employing popular sovereignty to organize two new states, Nebraska and Kansas.

Already the sectional balance was off, with Minnesota set to come into the Union, and according to one Southerner, the idea that Kansas alone would compensate for Minnesota's admission was "vile hypocrisy" and "flimsy twaddle."[30] Over the short run, slave owners flooded into Kansas, setting up a pro-slave capital at Lecompton and drafting a constitution that protected slavery. But the principle that slavery could be excluded by a mere vote of the population did not sit well with those in the South who could read a map, and who knew that even if they won a new slave state in Kansas, future states carved out of the old Louisiana Purchase territories and the new Mexican Cession territories were more likely to be free soil than slave lands. Thus, in their minds, Douglas had consorted with the enemy, handing the anti-slave forces a means to deny Southerners their constitutional rights. The breakup of the Democrats as a national party had begun.

Lincoln, representing the new Republican Party, ran against Douglas in the Illinois senate election of 1858 with little hope of winning. His party had been founded specifically on the principle of opposing the expansion of slavery into the territories, and now the *Dred Scott* case gave Lincoln his opportunity. He could make Douglas choose between supporting a bad *Dred Scott* decision or the fundamentally unconstitutional position of popular sovereignty—or, even better, Lincoln could weaken him on both issues simultaneously, making him vulnerable for some other Republican candidate in 1860. Douglas walked into the trap at the debate in Freeport, Illinois, by stating:

> [The right to hold a slave] necessarily remains a barren and worthless right, unless sustained, protected and enforced by the appropriate police regulations and local legislation [which] depend entirely upon the will and wishes of the people of the Territory. . . . Hence the great principle of popular sovereignty and self government is sustained and firmly established by the authority of this decision.[31]

While simply restating the maxim that an unpopular law is difficult to enforce, Douglas's statement had the effect of nullifying the *Dred Scott* ruling in virtually every free territory.

Besides the obvious moral problem, in which any issue is subject to a majority vote without any constitutional rights superseding it, popular sovereignty also contained a practical issue. By turning the problem of slavery over to the states, Congress withheld its authority (or, perhaps more accurately, transferred it). However, the same inaction could be read by pro-slave forces to mean Congress lacked such authority to act on slavery. Yet if that was the case, how could Congress then *delegate* such authority that it lacked to a subordinate state power? Douglas and most leading Democrats of both sections had already reached the conclusion that in fact Congress possessed no such authority to restrict slavery, and had arrived at that point almost a full year before the *Dred Scott* decision.

Already the country had divided into pro-slave and free-soil sections. The last southern abolition societies had vanished by 1837, and most southern states had laws that punished the public advocacy of abolition. Itinerant peddlers and northern travelers were viewed with increasing suspicion. Local "vigilance" committees "ferreted out subversives, administering whippings or other chastisements."[32] Northern states, meanwhile, may not have whipped pro-slave advocates, but they had eliminated slavery throughout the North, refused to comply with the federal Fugitive Slave Law derived from the Compromise of 1850, and even engaged in anti-slavery mob violence from time to time.[33] Virtually every major sectional event of the decade seemed to symbolically capture the evils of slavery: Preston Brooks's caning of Senator Charles Sumner on the floor of the Senate was reminiscent of the slave-master whipping his chattel; the gag rule seemed a metaphor for the owner's silencing of dissent by slaves; then finally the *Dred Scott* decision constituted the ultimate expression of the "slave power conspiracy's" grip on the levers of power.

Kansas statehood spelled disaster for northern Democrats, costing them over 70 percent of their seats in free states in subsequent elections. Yet those were not gained by Whigs, who for all intents and purposes were "me-too Democrats," refusing to take a position on slavery. Thus, Democratic losses did not translate into Whig gains—quite the contrary, the Whigs vanished, replaced by the new Republican Party whose platform elevated slavery to the top of the national debate. Nor was the narrower issue of Kansas resolved. Thousands of pro-slave settlers had poured in and established Lecompton as the territorial capital, only to be offset belatedly by an influx of free-soilers who created their own capital at Topeka. There were two legislatures, two territorial governors, and two state constitutions sent to the U.S. Senate for ratification. All attempts at compromise failed: "An angel from heaven could not write a bill to restore peace in Kansas that would be acceptable to the Abolition Republican party," Douglas intoned.[34]

Worse, the bloody factional skirmishes throughout the state started to escalate. One thousand pro-slave men, led by Sheriff Samuel Jones, converged on Lawrence, Kansas, a bastion of the free-soil New England Emigrant Aid Company, in May 1856, burning a printing office and ransacking the local hotel. No one was killed, but the "Sack of Lawrence" immediately made headlines in northern papers as an example of pro-slavery lawlessness. Just a few days later, abolitionist John Brown, who had come to Kansas with his sons to "make it a Free state," marched to Pottawatomie Creek and executed five pro-slavery "ruffians" who had arrived to make Kansas a slave state. Both sides had volunteer armies; weapons flowed in, most memorably the "Beecher's Bibles"—rifles delivered by Henry Ward Beecher in boxes labeled "Bibles." Between 1856 and 1858, some fifty-five people were killed, and, while less in the news, vigilantes in Iowa had taken that many lives as well.

Murders constituted the worst, but not the only slave-related escalating violence in the territories. Mobs in Missouri burned out 50 families and expelled 150 more in 1856. Free-soilers drove out 300 settlers from Linn and Bourbon counties.[35] Arguing that "most settlers came [westward] with the usual frontier motive: the desire for new opportunities and better land," David Grimsted was partially correct.[36] At the same time, the ideology of "free soil" had so embedded itself in northern settlers that separating opportunity from slavery became impossible. To many new immigrants in Kansas, Nebraska, and other territories, there could be no opportunity so long as slavery threatened to undercut wages and large slave-based plantations loomed as a dominant competitor to small, free farms.

Meanwhile, the young Republican Party had profited from the Kansas-Nebraska Act, which created two new territories, Kansas and Nebraska, each of whose status regarding slavery would be decided by a vote of that territory's legislature under Douglas's popular sovereignty concept. Nevertheless, both parties struggled to process the most expedient use of the *Dred Scott* case while remaining within their ideological grid. Lincoln and the Republicans attempted to remain locked in on the issue of slavery in the territories, but after *Dred Scott* they had another troubling political issue to raise, that of judicial activism and the tyranny of the Supreme Court. To disregard the decision would be rebellion, Lincoln argued, and added that he thought it possible to persuade the Court to reverse itself. In any event, the Taney Court was hideously wrong on both its history and the law. Lincoln cited numerous instances of free blacks who had citizenship rights prior to the Constitution, and de facto were included in the phrase "We the people." Moreover, he argued, the Declaration should be correctly interpreted to mean that all men were equal in their inalienable right to life, liberty, and the pursuit of happiness, and while all men did not enjoy such rights, the Founders nevertheless had declared that such rights existed and that when circumstances permitted they should be made real to all.[37]

Events in Kansas only seemed to confirm that the decision was not only legally flawed but practically unenforceable. Bribery, cajoling, and threats from Congress all failed to convince free-soil Kansans to go along with the Lecompton slave constitution and statehood for Kansas that would have come with it. Trickery was tried, too, with a constitutional vote between a "Constitution with slavery" and a "Constitution without slavery," concealing the fact that the latter would only affect the introduction of *new* slaves into the state. When a legitimate vote was held (and with the pro-slave voters abstaining), the votes totaled as follows: 138 for the constitution with slavery, 24 for the constitution without (but with existing slavery), and 10,226 against either. Heedless of the wishes of the citizens, President Buchanan sent the pro-slave Lecompton constitution to Congress with his blessing, while warning of "disasters" if it was rejected.

If *Dred Scott* moved the nation closer to war by unwittingly contributing to the demise of the national Democratic Party, it also greatly accelerated the impetus toward war by sending the nation into a major panic. At the time, observers thought the Panic of 1857 was unrelated to the Supreme Court's ruling, and indeed the view that the two were unconnected remained common until recently, as historians blamed the Panic of 1857 on the failure of the Ohio Life Insurance and Trust Co. or the impact on the wheat market of the Crimean War. In fact, it was the *Dred Scott* decision that triggered the runs that precipitated the failures of the New York banks and even Ohio Life. Economists Charles Calomiris and Gary Gorton have conducted extensive research into why, and under what conditions, depositors engage in panic behavior. In the antebellum period, the most important factor in depositor behavior was the realization that an adverse shock had occurred, even if the depositors didn't fully understand the cause of it.[38] Anything that spread bad news about bank assets, including future stock prices, could send the markets into a spin and cause increased commercial failures.

How, exactly, did the *Dred Scott* decision ignite the Panic? An investigation begins with the bankruptcy of securities brokers who financed dealings in bond markets, mainly railroad bonds. Railroads were *the* hot stock of the 1850s, the equivalent of dot-com stocks in the 1990s, but within railroad securities, three types existed. First, there was a series of older eastern railroads. A second group consisted of roads that ran along shorter, established routes that served local distribution. Finally, a third group was built westward to connect western markets with the East Coast.[39] It was in these new lines, "with their aggressive land-purchasing policies and far-reaching plans for transcontinental expansion," that the "principal speculative opportunities for railroad investors of the 1850s" lay.[40] From 1853 to 1854 especially, investment in western railroads soared.[41] Foreign investment in American roads was heavy, reaching $44 million in railroad bonds and another $8 million in stocks out of a total of $550 million.[42] (It should be noted that slave prices rose rapidly as well, increasing 30 percent from 1850 to 1856.)[43] Income from those roads depended on a steady flow of western settlers, which in turn relied on high levels of confidence in the prospects of the territories. And in early 1857, confidence was high.

The *Cincinnati Enquirer* noted a "railroad fever" related to the completion of the Southern Illinois Railroad through Ohio, particularly the link from Cincinnati to St. Louis.[44] Historian Allan Nevins described "a fever of speculation in Kansas lands was raging, men selling homes, giving up well paid positions, and even borrowing money at ten percent to purchase farms."[45] Newspapers of towns situated on the main travel routes reported "a veritable torrent of humanity," with some speculators expecting Kansas lands to "increase by seventy thousand people" in 1857 alone.[46] By April, a thousand settlers per day were arriving in the Kansas Territory.

Obviously, the railroads were the immediate beneficiaries of such traffic. Railroads lowered rates, indicating expectations of continued increases in the volume of business, as well as sound business strategy in encouraging still more immigration. Rate reductions of up to 25 percent were advertised, while builders and entrepreneurs laid ambitious plans for new construction. The *Leavenworth Herald*, for example, reported on May 8, 1857, plans to connect that town with the Hannibal and St. Joseph Railroad. Major politicians and businessmen leaped into these ventures, occasionally for purely speculative gains. Town lots could pass through "two dozen hands within sixty days" as speculators beamed at the relentless flow of settlers to their lands. By the time Governor Robert Walker arrived in May, he found the best Kansas lands, "especially along projected railroad routes," had already been snapped up by the speculators.[47]

Then something happened. A sharp change in expectations occurred. What was it? By late summer, optimism was shattered, the price of western lands plummeted, and railroad securities took a nosedive. Yet not all railroad securities dropped, and many remained flat—but not the trunkline western roads that served the territories. From July to early September, securities in the trunk lines, Kansas land warrants, and stock in the Ohio Life company dropped sharply (with Ohio Life suspending all gold and silver payments on August 24). During the crash of these particular stocks and bonds, something unusual had become apparent: none of the other railroad stocks were dropping. But by October, a banking crisis had struck the major financial centers, and banks in Philadelphia, Washington, and Baltimore suspended specie payments, followed by the banks in New York. Even when all securities took a tumble in October, though, they soon recovered, but not the trunk lines that ran from the western territories.[48] Several railroads defaulted, including the Illinois Central, the Erie & Pittsburgh, the Reading, and the Fort Wayne & Chicago, and some went bankrupt altogether, such as the Delaware, the Lackawanna & Western, and the Fond du Lac.

The first clue that a dramatic change had occurred could be found in the land prices. Between 1856 and early 1857, lands were purchased for

$1.83 an acre, or approximately $0.83 more than settlers who had military warrants had paid for the land.[49] Then the land market collapsed: between 1858 and 1860, 45 out of 102 mortgages in Osage County met with foreclosure, 81 of 246 in Anderson County, and 54 of 366 in Lyon. Ultimately, observers predicted two-thirds of all mortgages would end in foreclosure in Kansas.[50] At the same time, virtually no land values were falling in the South or East. At the same time that land prices crumbled, immigration westward declined. For six of the major east-west arteries that traversed Ohio, the number of passengers fell from 581,000 in 1857–58 to 367,000 the following year, and the number of westbound passengers arriving in Chicago from the East—a measure of net migration—collapsed, going from 108,000 in 1856 to one-tenth of that in 1860.[51] Records kept by the Western Railroad showed its passengers dropped from 63,246 in 1856 to 41,674 in 1860.[52]

In other words, the asset declines that preceded the panic lay in a particular class of investments in the West, and were not reflective of overall market conditions. Those asset declines occurred rapidly in mid-1857, then accelerated from August through September. Were these declines the result of falling wheat prices due to the declining international demand for grain after the Crimean War?[53] The war ended in 1856 and prices would have reflected that much earlier (as indeed they did: wheat prices tumbled in October 1856, but rebounded by July 1857). And British prices in wheat barely changed at all during this time—but had adjusted to the end of the Crimean War in 1856. Something much deeper was at work in the western American territories.

With the announcement of the *Dred Scott* decision on March 6–7, the prospects for free-soil western lands rapidly deteriorated, and with them, the hopes and dreams of thousands of potential settlers. Reaction to the *Dred Scott* decision, in part, came with the defeat of pro-slavers in the St. Louis mayoral election a month later. This was followed by the continued deterioration of the situation in Kansas, where, by July, the prospects for bloody violence were all too likely.[54] In June, for example, the anti-slavery community at Lawrence began setting up a separate municipal government without newly appointed territorial governor Robert Walker's consent, whereupon he marched dragoons into town and asked President James Buchanan for federal troops.

Free-soilers had sat out the June constitutional convention, and thus a new ballot was scheduled for October 1857, but when the results of the June election appeared, they only provoked more outrage. In one county, which contained only six houses, some 1,600 votes were cast for the pro-slave constitution, all on a single long sheet of paper (and obviously copied directly from the *Cincinnati Directory*).[55] More than 1,200 votes came from McGee County, which only had 20 registered voters on its rolls. By May 1856, when John Brown hacked up his victims at Pottawatomie, various rifle companies, volunteers, local militia, and other armed groups traversed the Kansas Territory routinely, and gunplay was frequent. After *Dred Scott*, it seemed like "Bleeding Kansas" would not only continue, but spread to every other open territory in the West. Against this backdrop, interest rates had risen in New York beginning in June 1857, although New York bank stocks remained firm until September.

Another interpretation of the Panic assigned its cause to the failure of the Ohio Life, an Ohio bank thought to have large mortgage holdings, on August 24. In fact, Ohio Life also had a strong connection to the railroads— its assets consisted mainly of securities and loans to a number of lines, particularly the Cincinnati, Hamilton, and Dayton Railroad, whose dividends were payable at Ohio Life. To facilitate these payments, the company opened an office in New York City and named Edward Ludlow as the director there. Ludlow engaged in massive lending, not on mortgages, but on railroads. He loaned out an amount equal to the company's capital, or $2 million, to various railroads including a single loan to the Cleveland and Pittsburgh Railroad of $500,000.[56] Of its total $4.8 million in assets, the bank invested $3 million in railroads, and the Cleveland & Pittsburgh stock had sunk from $0.39 in July to just half that in August, then dropped to only $0.15 after Ohio Life suspended. If western railroad stocks were troubled, then it could be expected that any banks holding western railroad securities would be the hardest hit, and that's exactly what occurred.

In other words, there is a smoking gun tying the *Dred Scott* Supreme Court decision to the ongoing events in Kansas and a further expectation about that kind of civil war and lawlessness spreading throughout the territories based on the Court's verdict. The next link was economic, whereby investors either put money into projects or pulled it out based on expectations about business climate. Those expectations were made abundantly plain with the collapse of the western trunk-line railroad securities. Three destabilizing elements now combined to turn a region-specific shock (the railroad stocks) into a national financial crisis.[57] First, as railroad invest-ment in western and midwestern roads plummeted, New York note hold-ers rushed to convert their bank debt into gold and silver (specie), putting a drain on New York banks, which addressed it by selling bonds. As one contemporary put it, the "causes which alarm one bank alarm the whole. Upon any shock to confidence, they [will] all call [in their outstanding loans] at once."[58]

This depressed bond prices further. Second, outside of the city, banks used correspondents to send a flood of their notes to New York banks for conversion into specie, further depleting the city banks' reserves. Finally, when bankers started to grow concerned about the value of the securities, they refused to roll over the debt of the brokers, forcing still more bond sales as brokers scrambled to get liquid. Suddenly, the New York City banks that seemed unaffected by events in Kansas or by the declaration of the Supreme Court found themselves facing bankruptcy. The connection between the de-cline of the securities/note prices with bank suspensions in New York seems well supported.[59]

On September 25, the Bank of Pennsylvania failed and other banks in that state suspended, which only placed more pressure on New York City banks, and was followed by the failure of the respected firm of E. W. Clark, Dodge, and Company. Then, on October 13, a massive run struck the banks, which paid out between $4 and $5 million before suspending. New York bank superintendent James Cook lamented, "The banks went down in a storm they could not postpone or resist."[60] Deposits among New York banks had plummeted by $10 million in just under two weeks. But the dam-age done by Taney's Court did not end there, as fear soon rippled through the banking systems of other states. Ohio saw its reserves reduced by half; a mad scramble for specie hit Baltimore and Philadelphia. Outraged citizens and terrified merchants met in major cities—often the business communi-ties demanded their own banks suspend while they still had gold and silver in their vaults, as occurred in citizen meetings in Virginia, Georgia, and Tennessee.[61]

Financial distress soon had its very real effects on manufacturing. Within a month of most of the large suspensions, more than two-thirds of New York's shipbuilders were laid off. In Providence, Rhode Island, of the almost 1,500 employees who made jewelry, only one-fifth of them still had jobs by October.[62] Newspapers begged depositors to fight "FEAR" and "unreasoning panic."[63] Mercantile activity was curtailed, swelling jobless-ness in most major cities and leading the editor of the Louisville *Courier* to prophesy "terrible suffering for the poor."[64] New York's unemployed num-bered between 30,000 and 100,000, and Mayor Fernando Wood promised relief FDR-style through public works, with payment to come in the form of "cornmeal, potatoes, and flour."[65] Mass demonstrations by the unemployed struck Philadelphia, St. Louis, Chicago, Louisville, and Newark. But the Panic's effects were just beginning in some sectors, such as Pennsylvania's iron industry and coal fields, where the furnaces went cold in October and didn't reopen until April 1858. Production fell from 883,000 tons in 1856 to 705,000 tons in 1858.[66]

When the worst of the Panic was over and stocks began to rise, as one Wall Street veteran noted, "Wizened bank cashiers, having recovered from their fright, sallied out from their fortresses to take a turn in the street. Merchants, weary with brooding over piles of protested notes, came down to try to repair their losses. . . ."[67] It took until January 1859 for most banks to reach their pre-crash levels. Contemporaries disagreed on the causes of the Panic of 1857, and virtually none of the observers of the day pinned the blame on the U.S. Supreme Court. Nathan Appleton, a Massachusetts textile magnate and banker writing in *Hunt's Merchant Magazine*, blamed New York City's banks for contracting loans; James S. Gibbons criticized the so-called country banks for their part in a credit contraction.[68] New York's banking superintendent was stumped, finding it "without apparent reason derived from past experience."[69] Wall Street insider William Fowler attrib-uted the panic to overexpansion of credit due to the new gold finds in 1849, then to the failure of the Ohio Life and Trust.[70] Historians subsequently blamed the failure of the Ohio Life Insurance and Trust Co. (Ohio Life) for triggering a bank run, or looked to a long-term decline in railroad invest-ment that began in 1854.[71] Still others claimed that a rapid reversal in the profitability of western grains, related to the decline of foreign demand after the Crimean War, was the culprit.[72]

Most—North, South, merchant, laborer—blamed "the banks." Nathan Appleton complained that the New York banks had brought about the contraction without "the slightest necessity."[73] In fact, the culprit was the Supreme Court, and most observers had missed the immediate causes and thus had poor remedies often grounded in sectional partisanship.

Historian James Huston, in his analysis of the panic, got the causes wrong but the impact right.[74] Immediately, discontent in the North swung large numbers of previously Democratic voters over to the new Republicans. At the same time, political and financial analysts in both sections erroneously concluded that the South had been insulated because of "King Cotton." Southerners misinterpreted that as evidence that they could sustain an independent economy that sold primarily to Europe, and that in any event the preeminence of cotton was such that the North would never "make war" on King Cotton. In reality, the southern branch banking system had protected it from the worst of the runs—but in a war, that system would be quickly "nationalized" by the Confederate States of America and would become impotent.[75]

An appreciation for *Dred Scott*'s true impact on the national economy cannot be understood outside of an analysis of what both sides in the slavery debate saw as the dominant (and, increasingly, *only*) issue, namely, the definition of property. As Huston explained:

> Southern slaveholders searched for a sanctuary founded on the absolute guarantee that all members of the Union would view slaves as property and agree that no law at any level of government anywhere within the Union could directly or indirectly harm the value or ownership of that property—the absolute sanctity of property rights in slaves.[76]

If property rights rested in government, it became vital that government not fall into the "wrong" hands. Assurances of goodwill were no longer enough: "Northerners could not afford to let the South win control over defining property rights in slaves because it meant the possible extension of slavery into the North and the ruination of their society."[77]

This reality was contrary to the conclusion of many historians, including the great Allan Nevins who wrote, "it was plain that *if* the country held together, every step forward would strengthen the free society as against the slave society."[78] Stephen Douglas argued in 1849 that "the cause of freedom has steadily and firmly advanced, while slavery has receded with the same ratio."[79] That was only true if, in fact, the nation could arrive at some definition of a "person" versus property. Even then, however, two factors militated against an inexorable march to freedom: first, slave values themselves—as all economists agree—continued to escalate; and second, the value of slave labor over free labor (certainly in the short term) was obvious. While the slave South may have trailed the North in innovation, patents, and inventions, on the playing field that mattered—direct competition between slaves and free laborers—little question existed in anyone's mind as to which was more cost-efficient.[80] Even Douglas, in 1858, rested his argument about slavery on profitability, in that while Illinois was still a territory, residents "*had no scruples about its being right* [i.e., about slavery being legal], but they said, 'we cannot make any money by it. . . . [emphasis his]."[81] He repeated this position in 1860: "We in Illinois tried slavery while we were a Territory, and found it was not profitable; and *hence* we turned philanthropists and abolished it."[82] Douglas thereby twice affirmed that which Lincoln charged him with, namely, not caring about the morality of slavery, only its profitability. Even the superiority of free labor was a moot point if slave values as property were appreciating faster than the differential of their labor earnings compared to free laborers. Such was not the case.

To appreciate the significance of slavery as *property* in antebellum America, no less than Alabama Fire-Eater William Lowndes Yancey, in 1860, said southern slaves "are worth, according to Virginia prices $2,800,000,000—an amount easy to pronounce, but how difficult to conceive."[83] As early as the 1830s, Thomas R. Dew found that Virginia slaves constituted almost one-third of all asset values in Virginia. By 1859, the pressure on the South to force permanent constitutional definitions of slavery into the halls of government was apparent: in the eleven states of the Confederacy lived 5.4 million whites and 3.5 million slaves, and even when including the border states, one-third of people below the Mason-Dixon line were slaves. As property, these people constituted $3 billion (1860 dollars) in wealth, or approximately 18.75 percent of U.S. wealth. This was more than railroads and manufacturing *combined.*[84] Sliced yet another way, when ranking the wealth of the states based on a per capita (not gross) measurement, an astonishing picture emerges. Traditional measures put New York, Pennsylvania, and Ohio at the top of the list of

wealthiest states in 1860, but when adjusted for population, South Carolina, Mississippi, Louisiana, and Georgia are at the top, followed by Connecticut, then Alabama, Florida, and Texas, interrupted by Rhode Island,
with Virginia, Maryland, and Kentucky rounding out the top twelve. Put
another way, except for Connecticut and Rhode Island, the Union's ten
richest states were all slaveholding states.[85]

It would not be an exaggeration to say that the single most important
asset in the American economy in 1860 was a slave. Protecting rights in those
slaves became paramount, for economically the only possibility of slavery
ending was if or when slaves themselves became worthless. Just the opposite
was happening: slave values were increasing on the eve of the Civil War.[86] At
the same time, the "free soil" movement had swept the North, and it had a
well-grounded fear of direct competition with slavery. What changed by the
1850s, though, was that due to the railroad and steamship networks, slavery
for the first time came into proximity to, and direct competition with, free
labor. *Dred Scott* meant that free labor and slave labor would be in direct
competition with each other not only across borders but even *within states*—
and within *northern* states.

Outside of the South, small farmers dominated the American scene,
with 70 percent of the farms of more than five hundred acres located in the
South. For those who did not own slaves, "wealth meant land, buildings,
carriages, and tangible objects, not people; for southerners . . . ownership
of slaves revealed success at worldly endeavors."[87] More important than the
different views of property was the approach to labor, which in the North
meant a means of advancing economically, while in the South labor was
equated with servility. Until the 1840s, travel between the sections was so
difficult that few Northerners ever had to witness the dangers to free soil that
slavery presented. (In the Civil War, most of the soldiers on either side had
never been far outside their hometowns until they served.) As late as 1830, a
coach ride from Cincinnati to New York could cost several days' wages and
the stagecoach itself could be expected to be overturned at least once—one
rider on a New York–Cincinnati trip had the misfortune of having his coach
overturned nine times![88]

But while the transportation revolution brought the sections together in
a sense, the so-called market revolution—despite the claims (or wishes) of
some economists and historians—was not having any impact on liberating

slaves. Virtually all of the market instruments and practices already existed in the South, including the sanctity of contract, free markets, competition, impartial government "referees," and so on. Indeed, while the South trailed the North in manufacturing, invention, patents, and innovation, the southern banking system was far superior to that of the North because of its preference for branch banking. Simply exposing Southerners to northern free farms generated no incentive whatsoever to emancipate slaves, and every inducement to keep them (and increase their number). Lincoln, Henry Clay, and others had bought into the flawed solution of "compensated emancipation" without realizing that with every slave purchased and freed, the value of all remaining slaves *would rise*. And that was if the slave owners agreed to sell in the first place, which proved illusory. Despite profits in the manufacturing sector some four or five times that of plantation agriculture, southern slave owners clung to slavery out of economic comfort, for reasons of racial superiority, and because of fears of social upheaval in a society where half the population consisted of free blacks.[89]

Lincoln, while ostensibly referring to "Bleeding Kansas" in his speeches, constantly broadened the debate to slavery itself, particularly the morality of slavery. It was "not only the greatest question, but very nearly the sole question of the day," he said.[90] Failure to resolve the issue of slavery, he argued, and not just *slavery in the territories*, would doom the republican experiment, for political liberty could not last alongside human slavery. The natural right to eat the bread of one's own hands—one of Lincoln's most repeated examples—was a universal right stated in the Declaration, and the fact that Lincoln himself cited *political* equality of blacks in some northern states prior to the war is clear evidence that he thought full equality, if not present in 1857, was attainable. Slavery for some, however, meant inevitable slavery for all—precisely what George Fitzhugh, a Virginia socialist and admirer of Karl Marx, had been advocating.[91]

The *Dred Scott* decision only increased sectional tensions, while at the same time providing Abraham Lincoln the noose to slip around the political neck of Stephen Douglas and shattering the Democratic Party as a national entity. It did not spark any immediate political upheaval, but did trigger a national panic that, in turn, affected the politics of secession. It marked the next-to-last event in a long series of seesaw moves in which each section temporarily had the edge. The Missouri Compromise had seemingly skewed the sectional balance in favor of the North, resulting in an inevitable legislative attack on slavery; but that was nullified, it seemed, by the appearance of the national party, the Jacksonian Democrats, whose avowed goal was to eliminate slavery as a political issue. That party discipline immediately broke down because the very dynamics of party success demanded an ever-growing government at every level, but with power increasingly flowing to the federal government. Moreover, in the Webster-Hayne debate, in other land and tariff debates, and in the ongoing fight over the gag rule in Congress, slavery was becoming *more frequently discussed than ever.* With the annexation of Texas, the South seemed to gain a vast new extension of slavery, only to have the Mexican War, the Wilmot Proviso, and the Compromise of 1850 swing the pendulum back in the other direction toward free soil.

The South's great victory within the Compromise of 1850, the Fugitive Slave Law, was undone by the publication of *Uncle Tom's Cabin* and the mass civil disobedience of Northerners unwilling to enforce the law. Yet the South seemed to gain in the initial Kansas-Nebraska Act, only to see the slave state of Kansas yanked away from them in an influx of free-soilers and political intrigue. Then came *Dred Scott*, which seemed to ensure the survival of slavery permanently, only to have the new Republican Party, under Lincoln, force Douglas into the "Freeport Heresy" and negate the decision. Lincoln's election in 1860 constituted the final, inevitable swing of the pendulum against slave property rights. Despite the new president's assurances, it was bountifully evident to all that slavery's clock was ticking, and that the time would soon come when the concept of people as property would no longer be tolerated.

On the road to that political end point, the *Dred Scott* decision produced another, unintended consequence: it generated a brief depression whose "lessons" were badly misinterpreted. That flawed analysis of the causes of the Panic of 1857 was piled on top of the other disastrous fruits of *Dred Scott* to push the nation to war. Thus, *Dred Scott* yielded not one, but two separate paths to the Civil War.

It would not be the last time that American court decisions would result in damaging, unintended, and unforeseen consequences. In the early 1900s, seeking to apply the new antitrust laws and thereby protect small business from predatory trusts, U.S. courts would in fact do great harm to smaller firms. George Bittlingmayer analyzed stock performance of small businesses supposedly protected by antitrust rulings, and found that action against large firms coincided with business downturns and that smaller firms did poorly during such judicial/regulatory activity.[92] A similar study of the antitrust case against Microsoft showed a pattern of the securities of competitor firms, which should have benefited from a Microsoft defeat, falling every time the case against the computer giant advanced, and strengthening every time the case suffered a setback.[93] In far more cases—the *Kelo v. New London* decision, for example—while the economic impact is likely to be long-lasting and significant, it has not been immediate.

Dred Scott combined bad law with bad timing. It was exceptional in its judicial activism, with that activism made possible in part by the inability of the nation to address the festering issue of slavery through legislative and constitutional channels. Discerning the Founders' intentions on slavery is difficult, and there were indeed mixed signals. None expected it to last long, yet none would risk disunion to extinguish it. Many thought the presumption of freedom within the states would relegate it to obsolescence. By the time of the Civil War, there had been no test case on the definition of personhood, and for all its overreach, *Dred Scott* also sidestepped that issue constitutionally. As Alexander Hamilton wrote, "Laws are a dead letter without courts to expound and define their true meaning and operation."[94]

What is clear is that the Founders did not favor a supremely powerful, activist judiciary. Virtually all of the Founders were immersed in, and fully accepted, the concepts of government known as "Whig" principles that derived from John Locke and included such English writers as Henry St. John (Viscount Bolingbroke), Thomas Gordon, and John Trenchard. As proto-Whigs, the Founders had deeply held views about limiting the power of government, particularly the sovereign. Courts were to provide impartial bars of justice, that is to say, they were to fairly interpret the laws of the legislature or parliament—but never "make" law themselves. For the most part, the Whig concerns involved making certain one was tried by a jury of his peers, and that people had the right to file writs of habeas corpus so as to prevent mysterious and permanent disappearances to such places as the Tower of London.[95]

Virginia's 1776 constitution declared that "all power of suspending laws, or the execution of laws, by any authority, without consent of the representatives of the people, is injurious to their rights, and ought not to be exercised."[96] When the Founders drafted the Articles of Confederation, they did not even include a judiciary act, but instead put their faith in state courts.[97] The delegates to the Constitutional Convention had explicitly rejected the notion that the judiciary should be included in the review process for laws, but a much different problem threatened earlier courts, namely insufficient power. [98] The *Federalist Papers* focused on the immediate problem of ensuring the independence of the (then nonexistent) federal judiciary, as both the legislative and executive branches were endowed with considerable power. Alexander Hamilton, James Madison, and other Founders were deeply concerned that the courts not become mere pawns of the legislature, and retain their autonomy, but "instead of being subsumed by Congress or the president, the judiciary [subsequently] has subsumed substantial authority over the other branches."[99] Thomas Jefferson argued in 1820 that "the Constitution has erected no . . . single tribunal "above the other branches of government," adding that "to consider the judges as the ultimate arbiters of all constitutional questions [is] a very dangerous doctrine indeed, and one which would place us under the despotism of an oligarchy."[100]

The *Dred Scott* decision constituted perhaps the final tear in the fabric of the Union in 1857 and illustrated perfectly what the Founders feared could happen if the Court overstepped its authority. Shortly thereafter, in the debate at Freeport, Illinois, Abraham Lincoln maneuvered Stephen Douglas into his fatal political misstep, in which Douglas invalidated the Supreme Court decision by saying that ultimately the people could exercise an 1800s version of "jury nullification" by simply refusing to enforce unpopular laws. Thus political reality, and the grimmest reality of all, the Civil War, overturned de facto what was not overturned de jure. And by that time, the other malignant impact of the *Dred Scott* decision, the Panic of 1857, had also been mitigated by economic growth. Yet the status of the territories was not decided except by the sword, and Kansas and its sister territories stood to remain nineteenth-century versions of Beirut or Belfast a century later until the question of who had authority over those areas was established once and for all. In the decades following the Civil War, the Supreme Court would routinely weigh in on economic matters, almost always with the same unintended and pernicious results, whether in antitrust rulings, eminent domain, or property rights. Roger Taney's decision in 1857, however, represented a unique moment in which the Supreme Court managed to simultaneously abuse the Constitution, rule against human rights, severely damage the economy, and help start a war, all in one fell swoop.

3.

JOHNSTOWN FIGHTS A FLOOD AND
DEMONSTRATES THE POWER OF PRIVATE COMPASSION[*]

I cannot undertake to lay my finger on that article of the Constitution which granted a right to Congress of expending on objects of benevolence with the money of their constituents.

JAMES MADISON, 1794

What does the federal government do right? While a cynic might answer "nothing," the United States government actually handles several tasks—namely, those delegated to it by the Founders—with competence and, occasionally, extreme skill. America's military, for example, has proven exceptionally adept at overcoming setbacks, defeating more numerous foes, and building a culture of victory.[1] The United States Coast Guard, while perhaps unable to stop the flow of drug traffic, has nevertheless proven ex-

---

* Special thanks to Peter Cajka, who provided research for this based on his unpublished paper, "The National Cash Register Company and the Neighborhoods: New Perspectives on Relief in the Dayton Flood of 1913," July 1, 2009, copy in author's possession.

tremely capable in handling rescue operations and preventing major terrorist attacks by sea. America's federal courts have, at least until recently, maintained the sanctity of contract and encouraged the profit motive for the free-enterprise system. In other cases, however, even where the Constitution permits the federal government certain nonexclusive powers—such as the establishment of a postal system or the coinage of money—and where, at one point, those became either temporarily or permanently monopoly powers, the record has not proven as favorable.

A more important question for our discussion might be, "What is the federal government empowered to do?" Is it empowered to respond to natural disasters? If so, under what circumstances and for what reasons? The Constitution is explicit on this: the federal government is empowered to act to maintain order—and only to maintain order—when conditions at the local and state level endanger the nation as a whole. The Constitution does not allow it to engage in charity or "disaster relief" out of goodwill, and, as major disaster relief efforts such as those used in Hurricane Katrina have proven, when the government does so, it circumvents normal community and local responses and generally mucks things up.

The Founders knew that, intrinsically, the government lacked the proper incentives to do many things and that private individuals and smaller communities would put resources to far better use. Despite the fact that the young Republic had been struck by hurricanes, floods, fires, diseases, and all sorts of other destructive events that today would qualify as disasters, no one asked the federal government for relief from a disaster until 1811, when a massive earthquake struck New Madrid County in Missouri. Some scientists claim this quake was the largest ever seen in North America—Otto Nuttli at St. Louis University estimated it reached Richter scale proportions of 8.7, or almost two points higher than the San Francisco quake of 1906.[2] Yet there was no organized relief by the state. Instead, so-called earthquake Christians, church groups who heard about the quake, marched in to provide assistance. However, in 1814 (notably three years after the earthquake hit), a petition was presented to Congress for relief of the victims, based on a bill that had passed in 1812 granting Venezuela $50,000 for relief of an earthquake. The Missourians were sure Congress would be "equally ready to extend relief to a portion of its own Citizens." After a year, Congress provided grants from public lands to relocate people whose farms or businesses were destroyed.

Speculators moved in like locusts, and over the next thirty years, courts attempted unsuccessfully to sort out the claims. A "New Madrid claim" became "a synonym for fraud."[3]

Out of this example, a clear picture emerges of the superiority of private sector and local responses to those of the federal government in the area of disaster relief. Subsequently, the Johnstown Flood of 1889, the 1900 Galveston Hurricane, the Dayton Flood of 1913, and the 1906 Great San Francisco Earthquake help solidify this picture, especially when compared to the sheer disaster that ensued after Hurricane Katrina struck New Orleans in 2005. In the first four cases, communities and individuals rose to the occasion and not only provided immediate relief, but organized short-term security and then undertook long-term planning to prevent future calamities. In the latter case, the Founders' worst nightmares about bureaucracies—"swarms of officers," as Jefferson called them in the Declaration—became reality. There was a reason the Founders hesitated to give overt powers of disaster relief to the federal government, and it became apparent after Katrina. Yet over a century earlier, another American city saw waves crash down on it, and while the event itself was a disaster, the response was anything but.

Johnstown, Pennsylvania, was a typical steel town facing atypically heavy rains in 1889, when the faulty design of the South Fork dam, located fourteen miles away, caused it to collapse and unleash 20 million tons of water down a valley leading to the community. The destruction was near total: over 2,200 people were killed, and the waters caused $17 million in damage. It constituted the worst single loss of civilian life in America prior to 9/11. Floodwaters carried trees and other debris smashing through the city and trapping anyone caught in the torrent of steel and wire from the nearby steel plant that had wrapped around wood from fallen trees, making removal all the more difficult. The flood destroyed the railroad, along with 1,600 homes, and four square miles of Johnstown proper. After the damage had been done, at least 27,000 people needed care, shelter, and food.

The dam had burst shortly after three o'clock on Friday, May 31, condemning the Johnstown citizens to a night of hell. By noon the next day, however, the waters had receded and citizens had already started to help stranded neighbors.[4] As the finest historian of the flood, David McCullough, noted:

People on the hillsides whose houses had escaped harm and farmers from miles out in the country began coming into town bringing food, water, and clothing. At the corner of Adams and Main milk was passed out in big tinfuls. Unclaimed children were looked after. A rope bridge had been strung across the Little Conemaugh [River] near the depot. . . .⁵

Less than three hours later, every surviving able-bodied man reported to the Adams Street schoolhouse, voted to elect a "dictator" whose instructions they would all follow (Arthur Moxham, as it turned out), and, despite mind-boggling fatigue—having already struggled to survive themselves—the men organized into committees and leaped into action. They cleaned up the wreckage and removed dead bodies and animal carcasses. Some seventy-five men were specifically appointed "deputies," with tin stars cut from tomato cans, to throw up a cordon around the town's banks and recover and account for all cash lying around. Virtually everyone had lost someone they knew to the flood, yet the work continued. They grimly tagged bodies of those they did not recognize as best they could (noting sex, age, hair color, distinguishing features), writing the information on any available paper.

Moxham and his deputies commandeered every remaining intact structure, and also began erecting tents from blankets and bedspreads that had started to arrive from nearby communities. Even though it was May, the storm had brought an unusual cold to the valley, requiring people to start controlled fires for heating, cooking, and boiling water. In spite of their dogged efforts, the survivors couldn't process the dead fast enough. They transported the decomposing bodies across the river to Prospect Hill, where shallow graves were being dug as quickly as possible. George Spangler, the night watchman at the First National Bank, referred to the act in his diary as "holing the dead," noting "I hold [sic] 62 to the semitre [sic]."⁶

Flooding had cut the Pennsylvania Railroad at Sang Hollow depot, forcing rescuers to unload boxcars of food, blankets, clothes, and even medicine by hand and move them upriver—over rock falls, landslides, through water—on their backs. By the next morning they had successfully transported two carloads. Workers then methodically stretched a rope bridge across the Conemaugh. The Stone Bridge, built by the Pennsylvania Railroad, had not collapsed (it did block debris from drifting further downstream, which later caused a fire that burned thirty of the surrounding acres), and the Pittsburgh supply train arrived Sunday morning from the west, its track restored from Sang Hollow in another astounding feat of determination. It had left at four o'clock Saturday afternoon, when stunned onlookers in Pittsburgh had watched the debris-filled water flow into the Allegheny with its debris and reacted immediately. When the train arrived at the outskirts of Johnstown, men stood in the open doors of its boxcars and tossed bundles of crackers and cheese to those who lined the tracks. Without waiting for a government assessment, both the bedraggled citizens of Johnstown and their fellow Pennsylvanians sixty miles away rolled up their sleeves and addressed the problem.

There was a call to arms, though: at a meeting at one o'clock in Pittsburgh's Old City Hall, one resident, Robert Pitcairn, implored the attendees, saying, "it is not tomorrow you want to act, but today; thousands of lives were lost in a moment and the living need immediate help."[7] In less than an hour, two men standing at the front of the hall collected over $48,000 (a staggering amount in the 1800s, when a steak dinner cost less than half a dollar). As one reporter put it, there was "no oratory but the eloquence of cash."[8] Pittsburghers then dispatched wagons throughout the city to collect food, blankets, clothing, and tools, depositing the goods at Union Station, which took on the look of a Civil War depot, swarming with people loading the trains. Boats were also ferried up the line, bringing refugees back from across the river where they had been stranded, along with the ever-present army of corpses. People sent anything and everything, and Johnstowners put it all to good use. A steady stream of volunteers arrived from out of town— over a thousand by Sunday night, including fifty undertakers. Pittsburgh sent members of its fire department (who put out the Stone Bridge fire), while the Pennsy ordered in railroad workers.

Perhaps the first semblance of government on the scene came with the arrival of Daniel Hartman Hastings, the state's adjutant general, who hitched up his wagon on Saturday and watched the developments all day Sunday before speaking to Moxham and the committeemen about calling out the Pennsylvania National Guard. But the Johnstowners thought it best for the residents (and volunteers) to handle their own problems. Moxham thought the work would help people get their minds off the disaster. So when the first troops arrived from Pittsburgh, Hastings instructed them to return home. Even so, everyone began to see the need for help, especially when rumors of looting and brawling spread. Indeed, the news that out-of-town construction workers (such as the Booth and Flinn Construction Company's workers, who had a reputation for thuggery and theft) were on the way caused much anxiety. Thus, if only to keep order, the committee-men decided to draft a formal request to the governor. But this came only after the rescue and recovery operations had been going on for more than twenty-four hours.

An outpouring of relief, both physical goods and labor, arrived at John-stown. Clara Barton, who would later receive deserved credit for the young American Red Cross's efforts to help, arrived three days after the flood ended and would prove invaluable. But the rescuers had already been there for days, and none was more prominent than Captain Bill Jones, Andrew Car-negie's famous supervisor at the Edgar Thomson Steel Works, who brought three hundred steelmen from Pittsburgh to help in the effort. Jones began his career as a private in the Civil War, gaining promotion to the rank of captain by 1864. He had achieved notoriety when he rejected Carnegie's standing offer to co-opt talented leaders by making them part owners of his steel company, saying that he was not ownership material. When Carnegie asked what it would take to keep Jones, Jones replied, "A hell of a big raise."[9] Carnegie asked him for a number, and after he gave it to him Carnegie thought the amount—$15,000—was too low. Instead, Carnegie paid him $25,000—the salary of the president of the United States—making Jones one of the most highly paid managers in America. A master motivator, Jones knew how to organize, and above all he knew how to work. He paid out of his own pocket to stock a relief train, then labored for four straight days without rest until he was on the point of collapse. Just after Barton and her Red Cross showed up, Jones, exhausted, returned to Pittsburgh for sleep, praising the men who worked with him (particularly a group of Hungarians, who had been accused of looting), saying they "worked like heroes."[10] Bill Jones died just a few months after the flood when a blast furnace exploded in the Carnegie Steel plant.

By June 6 and 7, thousands of pounds of coffee, ham, cornmeal, soap, canned goods, cheese, biscuits, and candles were being unloaded by the hour from trains. Tar, pitch, building supplies of all sorts, furniture, and even embalming fluid and quicklime for the dead bodies all flowed into

Johnstown. Cincinnati meat packers shipped 20,000 pounds of ham, and a single New York butcher sent 150 pounds of bologna; Pennsylvania prison inmates bagged 1,000 loaves of bread; Wheeling, West Virginia, residents shipped a boxcar-load of nails. Commissaries scattered around town were so well stocked that all fears of food shortages had vanished by midweek. Mattresses, cots, blankets, tents, pillows, coffeepots, pipes, and over 7,000 pairs of shoes arrived, piling so high on the platforms that they obscured the trains. Enough tools came in that no worker had a reason to sit idle. Animal carcasses were thrown onto any of a dozen bonfires; graves with quicklime consumed the human dead; live plow teams pulled away debris.

Then there was the money, which was generated by newspaper accounts, pictures, and even songs of the tragedy. Pittsburgh raised $100,000 in a week, and over half a million dollars total over a few weeks. Philadelphia sent $600,000; New York, $160,000; Boston, $150,000. Boxer Jake Kilrain, scheduled to fight John L. Sullivan for the world championship a few weeks later, fought an exhibition to raise Johnstown relief funds. The New York Metropolitan Opera produced a relief performance of *Othello*, and Buffalo Bill Cody, in Paris at the time, donated the earnings from a special show attended by the Prince of Wales. Bandleader and composer John Philip Sousa staged a special relief concert in Washington, D.C. Money streamed into Johnstown from everywhere, including Tiffany's and Macy's in New York City, donors in Tombstone, Arizona, and the Hebrew Benevolent Society of Los Angeles.

President Benjamin Harrison kicked in $300 of his own money, but he also made an appeal at a meeting at the Willard Hotel that proved so emotional it raised $10,000. Pennsylvania Republican boss Simon Cameron, known for his corruption and his comment that an honest politician is one who "when he is bought, stays bought," wrote a check for $1,000. Help came from abroad too. The Irish cities of Belfast and Dublin sent money, while German donations exceeded $30,000. (Funds came from a total of fourteen foreign countries.) Total monetary contributions exceeded $3.6 million.

Others joined Jones on the scene, including H. C. Tarr of the Utopia Embalming Fluid Company, who rode two hundred miles on horseback to help take care of the bodies. Half a dozen Philadelphia churches organized wagons of medical supplies. Thousands of preachers, doctors, and, of course, the usual retinue of adventurers, thieves, and the unemployed also descended on the struggling town. Billy Flinn's construction crews, totaling roughly 1,000 men ("very few Americans among them," according to one reporter) marched in, accompanied by four more relief trains.[11] More than 7,000 outsiders came to work in Johnstown, and indeed, the appearance of so many new faces and rough men began to frighten the residents, thus leading Moxham to request National Guard troops to keep order. On Wednesday, Hastings called for an additional 500 men from Pittsburgh's Fourteenth Regiment, who were brought in strictly to act as security.

This was no small point: private philanthropy and local citizens had dealt with the "relief" efforts without the intrusion of even the state—let alone the federal—government. But the constitutional duty to protect life and secure property from pillaging had forced the federal government to send national guardsmen, an act completely in its power under the "general welfare" clause. Even before the army showed up, however, according to McCullough, "things were exceptionally well organized."[12]

The Red Cross established its reputation at Johnstown, despite arriving late to the cleanup process. Barton, then sixty-seven years old, came from Washington with a delegation of fifty doctors and nurses. Perhaps because of her frail appearance, Barton got a lot of attention from reporters. She also realized the importance of publicity for her organization and recognized that, while the Red Cross had worked in Illinois after a tornado and in Florida after a yellow fever epidemic, Johnstown presented a disaster of unprecedented magnitude. Yet Barton worked well with Hastings, who was taken aback by her aggressiveness ("the gallant soldier could not have been more courteous and kind," she said, but "I could not have puzzled General Hastings more if I had addressed him in Chinese").[13] She soon had six two-story Red Cross hospitals up and running, with volunteers working around the clock, and as one of the most recognizable figures in Johnstown, Barton served to rally the workers and encourage the victims.

Less than two decades after the Johnstown Flood, Ohio's Miami Valley experienced a similar, though much less disastrous, flood. The hero of this story, John H. Patterson, could not have had less in common with Captain Bill Jones. Patterson was an industrialist of the first order who headed the powerful National Cash Register Company (NCR) in Dayton. Early in 1913, a federal judge had found Patterson and other company officers guilty of antitrust violations and sentenced most of them to prison time (Patterson was sentenced to a year in the hoosegow, although the sentences were overturned on appeal). Only a few months after the sentences were handed down, a massive rainstorm hit Ohio, and by March, the rainfall levels had eclipsed anything the Weather Bureau had recorded. It rained for forty-eight hours straight at heavy levels, with the water pouring into the Miami River, as well as the Mad River. Flooding began on the Monday after Easter in the northern towns around Dayton, and although the levees held for a time, the Mad River levee broke on Tuesday morning, March 25, sending its contents into the Miami and Erie Canal. Within minutes, the floods surged over the canal banks and covered Dayton's streets with five feet of water.

The deluge struck before businesses and schools had opened, but the floodwaters soon reached residential areas, speeding in at 40 miles per hour and reaching a depth of up to 14 feet in some places.[14] Compromised by the additional volume, other levees, including the town of Hamilton's, failed. As it usually does, damage from the flood soon produced fires, and people who had scrambled into the upper stories of apartment houses found themselves trapped by flames. By the time snow and more rain fell that night and helped put out the fires, over three hundred Daytonians were dead and property damage was over $1 million.[15] One Dayton resident watched "houses and barns . . . torn from their foundations and float[ing] down Vine Street," and could only helplessly look on as an old man on a makeshift raft was swept away by the current.[16] Historian Judith Sealander, who chronicled the event, noted, "that several hundred rather than several thousand died was something for which the city's business community, led by John H. Patterson and the NCR, deserved a large measure of credit."[17] Patterson had written a pamphlet in 1896 called "What Dayton, Ohio, Should Do to Become a Model City," incorporating typical progressive views of the day regarding the importation of "experts" to handle specific functions. But it also involved applying business methods and common sense to city problems.

Governor (and future presidential candidate) James Cox placed the city under martial law on March 27, but by that time Patterson had already organized the relief, even taking command over elected leaders such as Mayor Edward Phillips. Part of local government's problem consisted of the fact that city hall was under water almost immediately. Nevertheless, the successful, efficient, and relatively quick disaster response and crisis management by the private sector "set a pattern that was followed for years," noted Sealander:

> Voluntary community organization, not reliance on government aid, dominated flood relief and recovery efforts. The Miami Valley business community, led by John H. Patterson, raised millions of dollars, devised new methods and associations to speed the area's reconstruction and recovery efforts, and supported a challenging new plan for permanent flood prevention. Its members repeatedly warned against dependence on outside state and federal monies, and in the enormous work of flood relief and recovery the private sector always dominated.[18]

By 1913, these business leaders, who had formed the "Committee of One Hundred" in 1889 to pave the streets, install sewers, and develop green spaces, consistently viewed the government as part of the problem. Whether federal or state, governments, they felt, imposed unnecessary delays, represented bottlenecks, and were consistently behind the curve. While the unelected Patterson organized the recovery, setting up NCR as an emergency headquarters, the mayor and the city council—none of whom were injured—meekly asked only to be notified of decisions. Indeed, many residents thought the mayor had drowned, so irrelevant was his role in the relief effort. Governor Cox's role was hardly more impressive, limited mostly to calling for relief from the secretary of war. Woodrow Wilson asked people to donate to the Red Cross. The Navy managed to arrive in Dayton from Louisville, adding experienced sailors to the boat rescues, but not for days after local Daytonians had already pulled out most of the desperate cases.

Indeed, Patterson had little time for updating the mayor because his cash register company had suddenly become a rowboat manufacturing business, replete with an army of shipbuilders who turned out a rowboat every five minutes. Three days after the flood, NCR workers had churned out 276 flat-bottomed boats and delivered them to flooded districts to rescue people who had been stranded on rooftops or clinging to light poles, augmenting the 150 private boat owners who had already started rescue efforts on their own.[19] One dynamic duo of canoeists, J. Bob Fries and Fred Nitzel, were credited with rescuing 135 persons.[20] Patterson's improvised boat-works, however, built boats capable of carrying six people plus the rower, and NCR's carpenters made two of these vessels every fifteen minutes, allowing for much more widespread rescues. NCR's Fred Oates used one of the boats not only to bring in ten to twelve people himself, but, after everyone in his zone was safe, went back out to deliver food to families holed up in upper stories of flooded districts.

After turning NCR headquarters into a housing and medical station, Patterson allowed the *Dayton Daily News* to operate there until its own offices had been cleared of mud. An entire floor was converted into a dining room, complete with waitresses (normally company secretaries or clerks) in uniforms. NCR's commissary served 2,700 meals a day, and all of NCR's staff members were tasked with some type of emergency work, including sorting and "fumigating great piles of clothing," while other NCR teams canvassed the city to seek donations.[21] Patterson even cleared out a few offices to make room for pianos and solicited musicians from among the refugees to organize hymns or play ragtime. The company paid for an entire relief train stocked with medicine, then another, then still another. NCR even handled basic law enforcement functions before the National Guard arrived, with the full acquiescence of local authorities. Suddenly the private police, who had been the bane of unions, were welcome, and the tycoons who had "oppressed" average citizens with their wealth and power became indispensable in their moment of generosity and efficiency. Motorcyclists and boaters patrolled the city, deterring vandals and delivering supplies. Yet when the National Guard arrived, it was criticized by locals for its heavy-handedness, and as one reporter noted, guardsmen "forced in some instances at the points of bayonets [sightseers] to assist in the removal of carcasses."[22]

A publication called the *Outlook* reported that "No novelist or playwright . . . ever devised anything more ingeniously dramatic—this heroic use of efficiency."[23] The *St. Louis Star* chimed in with praise of Patterson: "Patterson is the man, more than any other, who brought cosmos out of chaos," and noted that if the U.S. government had had its way, Patterson would have been entirely out of the picture.[24] For all his contributions, however, Patterson was certainly not alone in his efforts. Residents of North Dayton, Riverdale, and Dayton View all commenced their own rescue and relief plans in a short time. The isolated and wealthy Dayton View formed an association of seventy-five residents the next morning and allocated food, boats, and automobiles and dealt with sanitation issues.[25] Riverdale, the *Dayton Daily News* reported, had a "first class [organization] from the start," dispatching automobiles and wagons to the countryside to collect food and clothing immediately.[26] At the same time, both NCR and, later, R. H. Grant (who oversaw the relief effort), kept close track of what provisions were given out and watched for abuse. Grant found that money "had been carefully accounted for," and that even ruined clothing was turned over to rag dealers.[27]

The business community and individual citizens, using their own initiative, had saved the city, while government contributed little. When Army doctors arrived, they expressed stunned amazement at the "business ability . . . reflected throughout the entire community."[28] When R. H. Grant took over on March 30, he found relief networks already in place, complete with geographic delineations used by churches and schools as relief stations, leaving little for government officials to do. If anything, Maj. Thomas Rhoads of the Army's Medical Corps criticized the city government for encouraging unsanitary practices and turning "the Board of Health into just another patronage post, [whose] unqualified appointees had allowed all kinds of health dangers to persist."[29] Without question, Rhoads, who was placed in charge of sanitizing Dayton, did much to clean up the Gem City, building ten cleaning stations that offered lime and other chemicals, along with proper instructions on how to use them. Rhoads, however, did not always employ volunteer labor and sometimes ordered cleanups at bayonet point. At the same time, the private sector did not sit back: the Dayton Bicycle Club removed 2,000 dead horses and other small animals using 150 trucks.

Meanwhile, as in Johnstown, nearby communities delivered bread, ham, eggs, butter, cheese, milk, and canoes and had begun collecting those items before the water even reached its full height.[30] Preble County began relief efforts a mere two hours after the reports reached officials, and nearby towns reacted nearly as quickly by forming relief committees in Troy, Greenville, Tippecanoe, and many other communities. NCR acted as a clearinghouse for refugees, but every day citizens from Oakwood, Lebanon, Xenia, and elsewhere took in families. The Pennsylvania Railroad shipped goods free of charge, sending its own supply train of carpenters, machinists, tradesmen, and wiremen. Tracks cleared by Wednesday, when the trains began to arrive. Auto companies sent fleets of rescue trucks and cars.[31] Perhaps not ironically, the mayor of Johnstown sent a note to Patterson with "four cars of provisions and clocthing [sic] accompanied by our chief of police who is at your command," and further promised money "collected for your relief."[32]

Sealander concluded that "business planning, not luck" (nor, it should be added, government) saved the city from an epidemic that threatened to engulf a population exposed to raw sewage and freezing temperatures.[33] A weekly newspaper writer gushed with admiration for Patterson's operation: "this polished organism was turned in a twinkling without discord or hitch, into a vast smoothly working executive headquarters, hotel, hospital, and relief station."[34] Except for one political appointee, everyone on the Citizens' Relief Committee was a Dayton businessman. Members included Frank T. Huffman of the Davis Sewing Machine Company; Adam Schantz, the head of a large local brewery; John R. Flotron of the John Rouzer Company; and Patterson. Not only did Patterson and the citizens ignore government, but they used the Relief Committee to abrogate the city's health powers and assumed the duties themselves, overseeing inspections of every house in the city and isolating those with communicable diseases. Committee members inspected every grocery, bakery, restaurant, and school and disinfected them before permitting them to reopen. NCR's tent city had electric lights, sewer lines, flush toilets, and showers, and the committee provided flooded regions of Dayton with lime and disinfectant chemicals. The Dayton Bicycle Club handled the removal of animal carcasses (they carted off more than two thousand large animals and three thousand cats, dogs, and birds, often pulling them from rooftops or flooded basements).[35]

Once again, the Red Cross got involved, donating almost $1 million for Dayton flood relief, while local Ohio contributions exceeded half a million dollars. Naturally, the Red Cross set up its local headquarters in the NCR building, where officials "became the company's pupils and used lessons learned during national disasters for decades to come."[36] Patterson set up officers to review the relief requests and process them for the Red Cross, although most assistance came in the form not of cash, but of "sweat equity," in which teams of burly men arrived to rebuild a house. If citizens owned their residence, the Relief Committee provided bridge loans until the banks could reopen to more than one thousand families. In addition, the Relief Committee created a department specifically to help reopen businesses, and within a year, more than five hundred firms received basic assistance grants to help them get started. Bakers used the funds to buy new ovens, seamstresses and tailors new sewing machines, and so on.

Patterson paid some seven thousand NCR employees their full salary for two weeks in April while they did absolutely no business at all for the company. His managers worked fourteen-hour days arranging, procuring, and organizing everything from the placement of latrines to the qualifications for cash assistance. All their contributions were made at a time when neither U.S. tax law nor Ohio's tax code rewarded them with deductions for such philanthropy. Nor did it end when the floodwaters receded and Dayton returned to "normalcy." Those same business leaders joined in development of the Miami Conservancy District, a massive effort at water control and flood relief undertaken on a topography only slightly less daunting than that of the Panama Canal. The Miami Conservancy District purchased thirty thousand acres of farmland spread over nine counties using eminent domain, but also employing their own cash. As Sealander pointed out, "the Flood Prevention Committee and the Finance committee . . . would waste little time begging either the federal or the state government for financial assistance for flood control."[37] Not only would it take too long, but the businessmen wanted no restrictions on their planning. Raising their own financing—Patterson directed a subscription campaign that raised $2 million in a month, using NCR employees, again, to solicit contributions—involved ribbons, rallies, slide and movie shows, all generating enthusiasm for the "Two Million Dollar Fund."

At that point, Patterson gained the assistance of another Dayton businessman, Arthur Morgan, who ran a local engineering business and had worked as a drainage engineer for the U.S. Department of Agriculture. Morgan was self-taught and did not have a formal engineering degree. Just like noneconomist George Gilder, who, in the 1980s, would be able to reshape economic thinking away from Keynesianism because he was not tied to existing "monetarist" schools, Morgan was "a man interested in untried methods, in unconventional techniques. . . ."[38] Like Patterson and another Dayton legend, Colonel Edward Deeds, who had worked at NCR and who built the Shredded Wheat factory, Morgan wanted to avoid a quick fix and create a plan for the district that would endure for hundreds of years. They all recognized that the trouble was not in local bridges or canals, but higher up in the valley, and that a series of earthen dams—or, more appropriately, hills—would have to be erected to control flooding. The plan called for large retarding basins, four situated north of Dayton and one to the south, each allowing for normal water flow through canals, slowing down the torrent during storms. Ultimately, the system was built to sustain water at *double* the 1913 flood levels. Meanwhile, farmland within the thirty thousand acres would be leased in dry times. Overall, the plan protected everyone in the Miami Valley, not just Daytonians, and never again did a flood damage the valley. In 1937, a flood of nearly equal magnitude struck the Miami Valley and was easily controlled, even as other states in the Midwest and along the Atlantic coast were ravaged by the storm.

Of course, opponents railed against "big business," Colonel Deeds, Patterson, and their friends. Despite the fact that there was virtually no money in the relief effort for any of the Dayton companies, critics complained that it was all a money-grab, and accused them of using the effort to set up large electric power plants. Morgan responded by organizing the support of academics and engineers who endorsed the plan, and who testified on its behalf in state hearings. When it was approved, and when construction started, the business leaders involved in the Conservancy District remained committed to humane working conditions, building camps for both single and married workers near the dam sites. They provided adult education, including industrial arithmetic, math, and English. From 1914 until 1922 when the system was completed, the district paid lower wages than most other sectors, but never wanted for employees because of the exceptional working conditions. Dayton's business leaders weren't perfect—they misjudged the total cost of the effort by about $11 million (the final price tag was $34 million)—but they protected the citizens and lived up to their promise that Dayton would never again suffer from a major flood. Looking back in his 1951 memoir, Morgan wrote that "the extremely small loss of life in proportion to the numbers caught in the flood did not mean that there was not a great danger, but rather that a practical-minded, competent, and resourceful people met an unprecedented situation with stamina, inventive genius, and a fine sense of mutual responsibility and neighborly sharing of tasks."[39]

Morgan, of course, gave himself no credit even though he and fellow business leaders went above and beyond to save the city, then got it back on its feet. This has led one historian to complain that the Dayton planners accomplished their grand plans "'for' the people, not, by and large, 'with' them," which, of course, would be a characterization of almost every "great man" in the nineteenth or early twentieth century, in that few consulted "the people" when they did anything. Nor should they have.[40] When "the people" were sitting on rooftops or running from floodwaters, it wasn't "the people" or "the government" who came to their rescue but *individuals*. In fact, the most effective relief efforts were conducted by units of heroes directed by one man (or, in the case of the Red Cross, one woman). Even government-sanctioned organizations originated in the will of the individual. For instance, the Miami Valley Conservation District was the embodiment of the intentions of Patterson, Morgan, and Deeds, not a government body created by elected officials. Throughout history, all inventions, all major decisions have come down to a single person, no matter how many outside pressures or "social factors" provided influence. The simple fact is, had Patterson's NCR not existed, it would, in all likelihood, have taken Dayton years to recover, and the death toll and suffering would have been higher by several orders of magnitude.

More important, however, the people of the Miami Valley, just like those in Johnstown, not only accepted private philanthropy, they accepted and welcomed the "strings" that accompanied it. It was understood that as soon as possible people had to pitch in and help other victims; that it was not permissible to take handouts without attempting to repay them, either directly to the giver, or indirectly by helping others in similar circumstances. *No one* expected government at any level to provide any amount of relief at all, save basic police protection. *Everyone* knew that if they had to rely on government, instead of friends, neighbors, and fellow citizens, not only would relief take longer, it might never come at all.

In 1900, when a massive hurricane slammed into Galveston Island, Texas, it put one-third of Galveston under water and killed six thousand. Although Mayor Walter C. Jones created the Citizens Relief Committee (CRC) to organize the short-run recovery, the committee members did all the work of setting up relief stations, acquiring goods, and enlisting local workers to clear wreckage and retrieve bodies.[41] A building committee built 483 houses at a cost of only $350 each, while railroads gave free passes to those seeking to relocate. As in other disasters, money poured in, and, of course, the Red Cross arrived. Galveston's consumer economy began to return in less than three weeks. Except for the involvement of Jones, the private sector had handled the recovery and cleanup.

A disaster of a different sort—but met with quite similar public response—occurred seven years earlier on the other side of the United States. At 5:12 in the morning on April 18, 1906, the ground under San Francisco shook violently from a massive earthquake (today estimated to be in the range of 7.8 on the Richter scale). Its epicenter lay only two miles offshore, and as entire sections of city buildings collapsed, more than 3,000 people died. A quarter of a million people became homeless as 80 percent of the city was destroyed directly in the quake or shortly thereafter in the ensuing fires, which consumed 25,000 buildings and covered almost 500 city blocks. Unlike in Johnstown or Dayton, in San Francisco the U.S. Army under Maj. Gen. Adolphus Greely moved in rapidly and provided valuable services, guarding all the banks and city offices and helping to feed, clothe, and supply the thousands of victims. The Army also constructed over 5,500 relief houses, grouped in eleven camps and rented to the refugees for $2 a month until their homes were rebuilt.

Perhaps the greatest story of San Francisco heroism, however, came in the form of an Italian banker, Amadeo Peter Giannini, who had founded the Bank of Italy two years earlier. Giannini, asleep in his home in San Mateo, was thrown out of bed by the force of the quake. He dressed, took a commuter train some of the distance to San Francisco, then "ran, walked and hitched the rest of the way."[42] An employee had opened for business as usual at 9:00, and the bank held $80,000 in gold, silver, coins, and paper National Bank notes when Giannini arrived there. He figured he had "about two hours to get out of there [and] no place in San Francisco could be a safe storage spot for the money."[43] The banker assembled two teams of horses and two wagons from his stepfather's produce company that were loaded with orange crates, emptied the oranges and filled the boxes with gold, and waited until nightfall to attempt to leave. He found the streets clogged with refugees and firefighters, and expected to be robbed at any moment. Somehow, Giannini reached his home and stored the gold in the ash trap of his living room fireplace.

When he returned to the city, much of it had burned down and the Italian residents of North Beach had been badly hit. There was no Bank of Italy building left, and all the assets that remained were the $80,000 Giannini had to cover deposits of over $840,000. Yet Giannini correctly perceived that it would be not only a bold statement of confidence, but also good business for the bank to reopen. Despite a government prohibition and bank holiday, Giannini stretched a banner across some barrels to create a makeshift sign and opened the Bank of Italy in a temporary headquarters before any other banks were doing business. Typically, the government stood in the way of progress, but Giannini would have none of it: he announced in a booming voice to anyone who would listen, "We're going to rebuild San Francisco, and it will be greater than ever."[44] He placed a big bag of money conspicuously in the open and by his—and the bank's—presence stated that he believed in San Francisco. Although he only gave depositors half of what they said they needed, he reckoned, correctly, that many people were hoarding gold and that his confidence would help bring that into circulation. In a mere six weeks after the earthquake and fire, deposits exceeded withdrawals. The North Beach Italians stunned the rest of the city by rebuilding faster than anyone else, and within two months, Giannini announced plans (plus a $500,000 stock offering) to build a new office.

The larger story, of course, was that Giannini went on to reshape American banking with his massive system of branch banks and through his innovative approach to lending in which he focused on smaller borrowers. "A retail bank for the many," he would later call the Bank of Italy. It never could have happened, though, without his daunting rescue of San Francisco when the government said "No!"

Downtown, the city hall was in ruins after the earthquake, so Mayor E. E. Schmitz proceeded to the Hall of Justice. The earthquake rendered the jails unsafe, so Schmitz ordered the release of petty offenders and sent the serious felons to San Quentin State Prison. In the subsequent looting, police were so busy helping with the rescue of those crushed and wounded that they could do little. Other than that, and closing the saloons, the city government commandeered several ships in the harbor which had provisions. Yet Schmitz also quickly sent telegrams to architects, draftsmen, and builders in several major cities, causing an army of architects to arrive while the rubble was still smoldering. As the *American Builder's Review* sarcastically noted:

we are literally swamped with architects and draftsmen. Hundreds have come here and hundreds more are coming. In face of all this it is safe to say, and we know what we are talking about, that our architects are on the whole less busy than they were before the 18th of April.[45]

One of the best memoirs of the San Francisco earthquake, "Man at His Best," was written by Robin Lampson, who recalled his childhood experience of feeling the buildings shake in Geyserville, California, located in Sonoma County, some seventy-five miles north of San Francisco.[46] As word spread farther south that survivors of the calamity needed food, Lampson recalled that a freight train shunted a boxcar onto a siding in Geyserville (as it did at every way station along the route). The town, with a population of four hundred, responded with remarkable generosity: within a couple of hours, "men, women, and children began coming to that boxcar with baskets and packages and armloads of food . . . [bringing] homemade bread, mason jars of home-canned fruits and vegetables, sacks of potatoes, bags of dry beans, rice and sugar, and jars of fresh milk and freshly churned butter."[47] Without radio or television—relying only on postal carriers and bicycles to carry information—people kept delivering food. Meats arrived later that day, Lampson recalled. Even though families traditionally put away most of their canned food for the winter, his parents quickly agreed to share half of what they had. But the most remarkable thing was what followed: "the next morning the northbound freight left another empty car on the siding—and the amazing spontaneous process of filling it began all over again. And from the report I remember hearing at the time, the same sort of response was happening at all the other stations of the railroad."[48] This went on, he wrote, for almost two weeks. None of the people in the community were wealthy, but all shared.

In each of these cases, and others (such as nineteenth-century strikes), consistent with the Constitution, the federal government only became involved in disaster relief when there was a threat to public order that affected national interests. From 1886 to 1900, the "most deadly weather ever to hit the United States," including six hurricanes, a flood, an earthquake, and wildfires, battered the country, but there was no federal response because in no case was the *national* security issue involved.[49] When disaster relief was deemed of national import, the militia (later the National Guard) was the primary coordinator and source of manpower, since it was considered a security issue, not philanthropy. Hence, administrations used the 1807 Insurrection Act, which empowered the president to deploy troops to put down insurrection and rebellion and to crush strikes at steel plants.

In 1917, the War Department's Special Regulation Number 67 first federalized disaster coordination in its "Regulations Governing Flood Relief Work in the War Department."[50] Even then, and until the Cold War, citizens did not expect the U.S. government to contribute to relief efforts, and both Democratic and Republican administrations followed Article II, Section 2, clause 1 of the Constitution (i.e., the presidential "commander in chief" clause) to govern their responses to natural disasters.

During the pre–Cold War period, administrations were careful not to tread on the rights of states following the Posse Comitatus Act of 1878 in which the Congress, responding to the deployment of federal troops in the South to maintain civil order following Reconstruction, stated that the use of federal troops for law enforcement within the United States was prohibited except "in cases and under circumstances expressly authorized by the Constitution or Act of Congress."[51] There were deep and widespread concerns that the use of federal troops to conduct law enforcement on home soil would lead to the politicization of the military and possibly dictatorship. While the Cold War became the mechanism by which the federal government incorporated disasters into the catalogue of occurrences over which it had authority, the change in public attitudes toward government help had come more than a decade earlier, under the New Deal.

Although, as so many scholars have pointed out, the New Deal had its programmatic origins in the administration of Herbert Hoover, conceptually Franklin Roosevelt broke with all previous American attitudes toward relief by tying national security to the economy, and tying the economy to confidence. When he proclaimed, "The only thing we have to fear is fear itself," he had subtly bundled public confidence with policy, thus giving him the authority to do whatever was necessary (including lie) to restore a positive view of the future. As Amity Shlaes wrote of the moment, "The country was in no mood . . . to put Roosevelt's concepts up to a microscope. What mattered was change: like an invalid, the country took pleasure in the very thought of motion."[52] Will Rogers, a comedian and social critic, observed, "The whole country is with him. . . . If he burned down the Capitol, we would cheer and say, 'well we at least got a fire started anyhow.' "[53] The purpose here is not to review the New Deal. Amity Shlaes and Burton Folsom have done so in detail, explaining convincingly how FDR's programs prolonged and deepened the Depression by squelching capital formation, innovation, work, and invest-ment.[54] An entire cohort of Americans moved from self-sufficiency to govern-ment dependency. It was irrelevant if they *thought* their work was legitimate and productive. In the absence of a war, virtually all make-work created by the government is by definition unnecessary or unwanted, or market forces would have already addressed it. A small group held out—the "Forgotten Men"—who still tried to "get along without public relief." But in the meantime, noted one Muncie, Indiana, paper, "the taxpayers go on supporting many that would not work if they had jobs."[55] Roosevelt's "revolution" had the dual effect of convincing ordinary Americans that welfare was not a badge of shame, while at the same time encouraging more and more Americans to accept it even when they could work. Thus Americans began to see government as a savior that addressed life's inequities.

And nothing was more unfair than a natural disaster. The Cold War pro-vided the final impetus toward transferring disaster response to the federal government with the Disaster Relief Act of 1950, which sought to provide "orderly and continuing . . . assistance to the state and local governments [suffering] from a major *peacetime* disaster. . . . [emphasis mine]"[56] By in-cluding peacetime disasters, the act opened the door for the federal govern-ment to act in the case of non-war-related events, and as one historian of the bill noted, it "was a logical expansion of the New Deal social policies."[57] Andrew Mener, a student of government disaster response bureaucracy, ob-served that by assuming those powers, "the federal government became the subject of intense criticism every time disaster relief was less than ideal."[58] Authority was batted around different agencies until it finally landed in the Department of Defense, and within the DoD it continued to be transferred repeatedly.[59] Control of the program jumped from the Housing and Home Finance Agency (1951–52) to the Federal Civil Defense Administration (1952–58) to the Office of Civil Defense and Mobilization (1958–62) to the Office of Emergency Planning (1962–74) to the Federal Disaster Assistance Administration (1974–79) before Jimmy Carter created the Federal Emer-gency Management Agency (FEMA). Relief efforts after Hurricane Agnes in 1972 were "characterized by mass confusion."[60] The National Governors Association began lobbying for better preparedness and more aid.

In 1979, the radiation leak at Three Mile Island nuclear power plant set in motion many of the Cold War preparedness procedures, once again deemed inadequate by critics.[61] Similarly, the Commonwealth of Pennsylvania found its own emergency preparedness inadequate in the situation.[62] One could make a national security case, on a number of levels, for the difference between a leak at a nuclear facility (with its potential radiation clouds that might imperil dozens of states) and a "contained" flood or hurricane, but what did not change was the hysteria and sensationalism the media brought to the event.[63] Walter Cronkite, whose inflated reputation seemed to shrink after more careful examination of his reports, intoned that "The world has never known a day quite like today," suggesting that "the horror tonight could get much worse" and that the radiation release was second in scale only to an atomic explosion.[64] Such comments, when examined today, seem shockingly similar to the unproven reports of snipers in New Orleans in 2005.

Three Mile Island prompted Carter to create FEMA, which clearly focused on preparedness, not relief, and which was justified almost entirely in terms of civil defense. Almost no new emergency response functions were added, and it "did not overhaul the way disasters are handled in the United States."[65] What had changed was the underlying assumption that the federal government could, and should, get involved in any and all calls for help.

Nevertheless, the burden of responding to an emergency began with the states, which developed their own emergency plans. The federal government was to provide manpower, but the states, in theory, were to coordinate all efforts. FEMA had no trucks or planes of its own, but had to rely on a wilderness of agencies (some twenty-nine, total) to provide equipment and transportation. Yet in its first major test (Hurricane Hugo in 1989) FEMA proved sluggish, and, more important, in a preview of Katrina, the states failed to make timely requests.[66] Governors and federal authorities maintained separate emergency management offices, with little communication between the two. A second hurricane, Andrew, which struck in 1992, revealed that little had improved, only this time the blame was laid at the feet of Florida officials, who were late in requesting aid.[67] After reviewing the effort in Hurricane Andrew, the General Accounting Office recommended to Congress that still more power be handed to FEMA.

But it was a genuine national security threat, the 9/11 attacks, that pro-

voked President George W. Bush, succumbing to calls that he "do something," to establish the Department of Homeland Security in 2002. The act
establishing DHS grouped 170,000 employees from twenty-two different
federal agencies (including FEMA) into a cabinet-level agency. The potential for uncoordination and chaos was extreme: a study at the American
Enterprise Institute found that some thirteen House and Senate committees and sixty subcommittees exercised some level of authority over DHS.[68]
When an analyst concluded that the department's senior officials were "so
buried under the pressing day-to-day operational issues" that they had no
time to resolve management conflicts or coordination problems, it was an
indictment across the board of big government and its likelihood of achieving effective disaster response.[69] Moreover, by lumping in natural disasters
with national security threats, such as terrorism or sabotage, DHS virtually
ensured that it would be poorly prepared for either.

Despite massive planning, including a hurricane "war game" in 2004,
Hurricane Katrina once again overwhelmed the system. Certainly there
was some degree of media bias that sought to indict President Bush and
anyone in his administration, so much of the carping about FEMA can
be reduced to little more than Bush bashing. One thus has to use cau-
tion when reading headlines such as "FEMA, Slow to the Rescue, Now
Stumbles in Aid Effort" (*New York Times*, September 17, 2005) or "FEMA
Was Unprepared for Katrina Relief Effort, Insiders Say" (ABC News, September 8, 2005).[70] The real evaluation of Bush and FEMA was far less
damning, but overall, the majority of successes from Katrina came from
individuals and businesses, and the worst failures came from government
at every level.

Hurricane Katrina hit the American Gulf Coast in August 2005 and
was estimated by the National Hurricane Center as a Category 5 hurricane
(categorized by "winds in excess of 155 miles per hour," including total roof
failure on many residences and industrial buildings and major evacuation
of residential areas within five to ten miles of the shoreline). After flattening
the entire Gulf Coast beach area and smashing into New Orleans, Katrina
generated such stresses on the waterways that the levees failed. Over 1,800
people died from either debris or drowning. Historically, in terms of loss of
life, this was nowhere near some of the other hurricane disasters: Calcutta,
in World War II, lost 35,000 to a storm; the Galveston hurricane in 1900

killed between four and five times as many; and a cyclone in East Pakistan in the early 1960s wiped out over 22,000 people. But because Katrina became a political issue—a club with which to bash the Bush administration's "poor response"—it took on the aura of one of the worst disasters ever to strike America.

Yet the oft-overlooked story of Katrina tells of the utter incompetence of local government and, overall, of government at any level to do what people, individually or in groups, could and did accomplish. New Orleans, in fact, had a "Comprehensive Emergency Management Plan," which outlined evacuation procedures. It recommended "long range planning," which was never implemented by then-mayor Ray Nagin. Not only did the city follow "virtually no aspect of its own emergency management plan" when Katrina struck, but New Orleans also "failed to implement most federal guidelines."[71] For example, the Federal Emergency Relief Administration had tasked the mayor's office with coordinating the use of school buses and drivers to support the evacuation of 100,000 citizens who did not have personal transportation. No such effort was made. As one well-reviewed history of Katrina put it, "Direct action was necessary on a dozen fronts and Nagin was hesitating like a schoolboy afraid to receive his report card."[72] As the deadly storm bore down on New Orleans on Saturday afternoon, Nagin—who should have been ordering a mandatory evacuation—was consulting with city attorneys about possible legal ramifications from the hotels, which stood to lose considerable revenue when guests were forced out. Most of the tourists could have gotten out, but by the time Nagin made the evacuation official, he could only "hope they have a hotel room and it's at least on the third floor up."[73]

The federal government did its job in providing proper warning to Louisiana and New Orleans when the National Weather Service issued a 10:11 a.m. advisory on Sunday, August 28, that said:

DEVASTATING DAMAGE EXPECTED . . . HURRICANE WITH UNPRECEDENTED STRENGTH . . . RIVALING THE INTENSITY OF CAMILLE OF 1969 . . . MOST OF THE AREA WILL BE UNINHABITABLE FOR WEEKS . . . POWER OUTAGES WILL LAST FOR WEEKS . . . DO NOT VENTURE OUTSIDE.[74]

Not only did the National Oceanic and Atmospheric Administration (NOAA) issue this dire warning, but President Bush issued a disaster declaration before the hurricane even reached landfall, which was extremely rare. Moreover, the director of the National Hurricane Center personally called Governor Kathleen Blanco to warn her that New Orleans should be evacuated, "the only time he had made such a call in his 36-year career."[75] The fault lay first and foremost with Mayor Nagin's failure to evacuate New Orleans and with Governor Blanco for not superseding him and ordering the evacuation herself. Had that been done, even when the levees were breached, the near-term human losses would have been a fraction of what they eventually were.

Although Governor Blanco rightly requested that President Bush declare a state of emergency on Saturday, her formal request did *not* include any provision for help in *advance of the storm*, either in terms of additional transportation or rescue boats. Her nonchalance contributed to the view in Washington that state and local officials had the effort under control, in contrast to similar actions by governors in New York, Oklahoma, and California in other disaster scenarios.[76] This also influenced the actions of FEMA director Michael Brown, who was universally assailed for his incompetence after the fact, because he had concluded the request was not urgent. Yet even as they dithered (in Nagin's case) or filed boilerplate reports (in Blanco's case), both the mayor and the governor had time to criticize the federal government for inaction, leading historian Douglas Brinkley to observe, "the blame game had begun even before Katrina made landfall."[77] Later, Blanco swung to the other extreme, issuing such emotional appeals that they came across as near-hysterical but ineffectual, leading her to conclude, "I should have screamed louder." In neither case did her appeals strike the right tone to achieve action or deliver information.

Meanwhile, Nagin's incompetence seemed to grow by the hour. He did not assemble or employ the city's hundreds of public buses or school buses, which sat in massive parking lots while citizens struggled to get out of town. The Regional Transit Authority alone had 360 buses, each capable of holding 60 people, meaning on a single trip they could have evacuated over 20,000 people. If the city government had mobilized the RTA buses, it could have evacuated New Orleans in four trips—a total evacuation time of less than twelve hours. But on top of the failure to use the buses, the city had no clearly marked signs for bus evacuation pickup. Even at that, Amtrak officials "repeatedly tried to offer seven hundred seats on an unscheduled train" leaving on Sunday, and Nagin's office "would not accept their telephone calls."[78] Ultimately, Amtrak took five empty trains, which could have evacuated 3,000 people total, out of New Orleans. Five months later, the remorseless Nagin said, "If I had it to do again, I would probably go to the school board, cut a cooperative endeavor agreement with them, and move all the city-controlled buses to another section of the state," leading former mayor Marc Morial to say Nagin didn't have a disaster plan "because *he* was the disaster."[79] These comments prove that even five months after the fact Nagin still did not understand that buses were needed to be involved in the *evacuation process itself.* Not that it mattered after a while because, by the time FEMA was called in, the streets were flooded and it was too late for the buses to have any impact. Not until Sunday at 10:00 a.m. did Nagin order the first mandatory evacuation in New Orleans's history—at which point it was unenforceable. About 100,000 residents remained in the city, and no one at City Hall even knew what the term "mandatory" actually meant. The police were unable to arrest transgressors, and as Douglas Brinkley reported in his book *The Great Deluge,* up to 200 NOPD had already left the city.

FEMA director Michael Brown convened a videoconference at noon on Sunday with emergency officials from every state in the Gulf, plus President Bush and Homeland Security director Michael Chertoff. Under less dire circumstances, FEMA and the federal government's preparations would have been considered adequate. The National Guard had helicopters on twenty-four-hour alert throughout the Gulf Coast, and began rescue missions only four hours after the hurricane made landfall (the Coast Guard alone rescued 33,000 people). National Guard troops totaled over 36,000 by Tuesday, while virtually all of FEMA's national Urban and Rescue Incident Support Teams were sent to the Gulf.[80] When trying to save the levees on Tuesday, government helicopters dropped 3,000-pound sandbags, and within an hour of Governor Blanco's decision to evacuate the Superdome, FEMA had the U.S. Department of Transportation assemble over 1,100 trucks and vehicles to get people out, even as the city's own buses sat idle thanks to its myopic mayor.

FEMA itself was a large, Carter-era agency created in 1979 and staffed with 2,600 full-time employees overseeing twenty-seven other federal agencies. It has responded to more than nine hundred declared disasters since 1990, including Hurricane Andrew in Florida and Louisiana in 1992, the Northridge, California, earthquake in 1994, and the 9/11 attacks. As with many federal bureaucracies, it was formed to coordinate . . . all the other bureaucracies. Planning for a Katrina-type event had resulted in a 2004 weeklong meeting that concluded that a severe hurricane striking New Orleans needed to be met with an immediate evacuation. Even so, FEMA had astounding resources prepositioned, including millions of tons of ice, millions of MREs (meals ready to eat), and millions of gallons of water, all contained in nearly one thousand tractor-trailers. Yet it took five days for FEMA trailers to roll toward New Orleans, and when they did, it was a *local* New Orleans Fire Department contact at the Emergency Operations Center inside the city who radioed the FEMA caravan to "vector" to Metairie—*not* the Superdome![81] Moreover, it was later confirmed by the FEMA representative on site that "the fire department made the [unwarranted and unnecessary] decision to change the destination."[82]

By the time people huddled in the Superdome, the Louisiana National Guard had sent in a 46-member Special Reaction Team specifically trained in emergency law enforcement, followed by 220 more crowd control soldiers and more than 100 other military personnel. However, the Superdome constituted an entirely inadequate shelter of last resort, even with the staff and security in place. One of the Superdome managers, Doug Thornton, observed, "We can make things very nice for 75,000 people for four hours. . . . But we aren't up to really accommodate 8,000 for four days."[83] Even before the hurricane actually hit land, more than 40 Superdome refugees were in life-threatening situations, not counting the gangs and thugs that had taken refuge there. Within twenty-four hours, the masses had become "a community of beggars, crowding the sports arena as the Hebrew cripples at the pool of Bethesda. . . . Hallways and corridors were used as toilets, trash was everywhere. . . ."[84] "Nagin's folly," as the mess was called, had turned into a scene out of Dante's *Inferno.*

Both the federal government and, to an extent, the state government succeeded at some of those things governments do well: they issued warnings and assembled troops. The Coast Guard performed brilliantly, leading Sheriff Jack Stephens of St. Bernard Parish, when asked how he would improve FEMA, to answer, "I would abolish it. I'd blow up FEMA and ask the

Coast Guard what it needs."[85] Government failure manifested itself in the civilian leadership of Blanco and Nagin, and in the sense that government asked military forces to step outside their primary role of war-fighting in order to provide charity. It was also incorrect to say, as did Marsha Evans of the Red Cross, that "Louisiana had a plan. It's New Orleans and FEMA that really didn't have much of one."[86] (The Red Cross, it should be noted, had something of a black eye after 9/11, when millions of dollars donated specifically for New York City and Washington, D.C., for relief and rescue efforts related to the terrorist bombings were instead set aside for other future disasters by the aid agency.)[87] FEMA was required to work *through* states, and did have a plan—which was ignored—while the state of Louisiana had authority and the obligation to evacuate New Orleans over Nagin's own incompetent intransigence. That made Blanco equally culpable.

But there is no question that the federal government heaped more incompetence upon previously astounding incompetence. Even the Army Corps of Engineers, involved in a road-building operation to try to buttress the levees, slowed down the actual road work with "long waits between dumps, because dozens and dozens and *dozens* of trucks . . . were traveling in convoy to their distant supply source."[88] A local supply depot that had been established was much closer, but was ignored. Finally, by Saturday night, the Corps of Engineers went back to the original system. Criticisms of the Corps of Engineers, while valid in regards to its failure to maintain the levees, must be viewed in light of similar praise for the Corps, which had constructed the almost invincible Mississippi River spillway systems, which had not flooded seriously since 1927. Rather, a narrow task given to the Corps had become politicized as each local group sought to use the levee funds from the federal government for its own projects, and the result was predictable. And while FEMA was a useful punching bag, the evidence is incontrovertible that FEMA was disorganized, unprepared, and grossly late in arriving. It is also true that FEMA had done a good job after 9/11, and that the "enormity of the challenge . . . with Hurricane Katrina . . . was an immensely more complex job" than in New York and Washington, but that event came as a complete surprise, while Katrina's track was known for days.

Of course, the sensationalist press didn't help either. In part, reporting on a twenty-four-hour basis (something the residents of Johnstown, Dayton, San Francisco, and Galveston did not have to worry about) dampened relief efforts. The reports were so commonplace in the hours after the levees broke that it brought a halt to rescue operations already under way. This led Tucker Carlson on Fox News to say, "If this had been Palm Beach, the 82nd Airborne would have been there Monday afternoon," but upon hearing that remark, even one anti-Bush writer acknowledged that "most Americans immediately thought, 'If this had been Palm Beach, there would have been no need for the 82nd Airborne because there would not have been any looters.'"[89] And although there was an element of covering one's rear in the government's own report on Katrina, nevertheless there was also some truth to the claim that "If anyone rioted, it was the media."[90] *USA Today* called the Superdome the "epicenter of human misery," and wild reports of up to one hundred deaths circulated, but in fact only six died (four of natural causes, one overdose, and one suicide): there were no murders inside the dome.[91] There were implications and speculations by otherwise reliable historian Douglas Brinkley that multiple rapes occurred inside the dome, but little real evidence of that exists. Similar media reports spread through Baton Rouge of rampant gunfire, fistfights, and auto theft—all false. But some gross and reprehensible behavior was documented, and could not be explained away. Looters not only stole with abandon, but broke into world-famous restaurants and defecated on tables and cooking surfaces. One Shell mini-market operator returned to find his store robbed blind, with feces deposited throughout his refrigerators: "They behaved like animals," he said of the vandals.

Michael Brown arrived in Baton Rouge on Monday morning and was briefed extensively. Brown himself would come in for massive criticism later. He had a spotty résumé with big question marks (as do almost all political appointees), knew little about disaster relief, but had performed well during the 2004 hurricanes in Florida. Democrats whined that federal money had also gone to counties that were not severely damaged—again, a common occurrence for money drifting out of Washington. The picture Brown got in Baton Rouge, however, was false, indicating the worst was over just as the levees had started to break. Poor communications from both local people and the FEMA contacts inside New Orleans had failed to deliver this news on a timely basis to Baton Rouge. And while Brown would tout his success in Florida, the hurricanes there came and went, and the state was well prepared. In the Gulf Coast, not only would New Orleans be under water, but virtually every state in the region would be smashed. Worse still, the difficulties of Washington bureaucrats showing up at a disaster site were magnified by their lack of knowledge of the local terrain. FEMA workers didn't know local wards, place names, or even the course of the Mississippi River. Consequently, they routinely over- or underestimated the time it took to deliver materials.

Somewhere in history, Americans got the foolish notion that just because they wanted to live in a warm climate by the ocean, their fellow citizens and neighbors should subsidize their risk when storms hit. This was as true for California, with its perpetual wildfires, earthquakes, and mudslides, as it was for the hurricane-riddled Gulf Coast. Philip Hearn, who has written about Hurricane Camille, observed in 2005, "New U.S. census figures show that nearly 90,000 people, pursuing warm climate, job opportunities, and southern hospitality, moved into Mississippi's three coastal communities" in the late 1990s, a migration made possible in part by the federal government's program of offering insurance for those living in high-risk coastal areas.[92]

A more disconcerting trend had also become evident, not just in New Orleans, but in many of America's cities, where for generations Democrats have ruled the structure of city government. The increasing levels of welfare, debt, and deterioration of schools have been accompanied by cries for still more aid, more welfare, and more spending on schools. New Orleans thus had a higher proportion of poor (almost 28 percent below the poverty line) than similar-sized cities such as Portland (13 percent) or Tucson (18 percent), but well below that of some large Democrat-dominated cities such as Detroit (almost 48 percent) or Los Angeles (40 percent), making the Crescent City merely one of the worst examples of a Democratic fiefdom, but hardly unique. The long-term effect was to create a population often entirely dependent on the city government for almost every element of daily life, from transportation to education to welfare. Ruggedly individualistic responses to a disaster, such as those in Johnstown and Dayton, became rarities. Instead, people merely started to wonder, "Who will help me?"

The fact that there were far fewer able-bodied young males available to help in New Orleans who were not criminals (another legacy of Democratic policies of crushing taxes, union favoritism, and deteriorating publicly funded school systems over the years) exacerbated the dependency mentality. With a New Orleans arrest rate of almost 25 percent of the population (or, more chillingly, nearly 50 percent of the *male* population), one was as likely to be mugged as to receive help from the typical New Orleans citizen during an emergency.[93] (The city was the nation's second leading murder capital in 2004.) In both Dayton and Johnstown, some sporadic looting occurred (mostly after rescuers arrived, bringing with them some opportunity-seekers), but both areas handled their own security until National Guard troops took over. As noted, in the case of the Dayton flood, NCR's own private security patrolled flooded streets. While a large number of New Orleans police simply vanished—some looking after their own families in contravention of their oaths, others simply running—as in Dayton and Johnstown, individuals such as the men guarding the Mardi Gras floats under the supervision of seventy-nine-year-old Blaine Kern fired at looters and chased them away. "If you come on my property," Kern said, "you're going to get shot."[94]

As in Dayton and Johnstown, a successful response came not from government at any level, but from individuals and businesses. Wal-Mart opened its stores to emergency workers, who were allowed to simply take supplies; gave cash to employees who had to relocate; and, as the *Pittsburgh Tribune-Review* concluded, "stepped over or around the confused, floundering and sluggish bodies of federal, state and local government relief agencies and sprang into action."[95] The company also gave $15 million to the Red Cross or other aid funds, and the Walton Family Foundation kicked in $8 million. Individually, companies such as American Airlines and Coca-Cola set aside significant sums to help their employees, and Coke used its own trucks to distribute materials. Skip O'Connor, the sixty-two-year-old owner of six hotels in the New Orleans area, left the Marriott Courtyard on St. Charles Avenue open as a shelter. After the evacuation, one dweller left a note saying, "I'm writing to say thanks. . . . We did not destroy anything, but did find food to eat and water. . . . I will send something back finance-wise to compensate the use of your facilities."[96] American Airlines also flew out one thousand evacuees after landing planeloads of emergency supplies. A specific musicians' relief agency was set up to replace local musicians' instruments. Individual acts of heroism, such as that of Steve Snyder, who was floating by a nursing home in his boat when he heard screaming, and pulled out a trapped resident incapable of walking, were common. The so-called "Cajun Navy" of volunteers took it upon themselves to drive to New Orleans, organize the launches and rescues, and plunge into the infamous "toxic soup."

Another group, bar patrons known as the NOLA Homeboys, used make-shift rafts, canoes, and anything else that floated to stage rescues.

While Blanco, Nagin, and FEMA all seemed utterly incapable of organizing publicly owned buses to get the Superdome refugees out, one of Blanco's state employees contacted the private Travel Industry Association, which immediately began rerouting sightseeing buses to the rescue.[97] Blanco had the authority to force local parishes to yield their (unused) buses, and there were eighty such vehicles in the Baton Rouge Capital Area Transit System that sat idle the entire time.

Katrina does not teach us that government aid can't help with disaster relief in some ways, or that proper military and police functions of government aren't useful (although in New Orleans, Homeland Security repeatedly held up relief and evacuation by civilians out of concern for their safety, delaying the rescues still further). Rather, the lesson in all these cases is that government will always lag behind the efforts of private individuals, and the more towns and communities know they need to rely on themselves, and not Washington, the more rapid and compassionate the response will be. And what *is* the constitutional role for the federal government in such natural disasters? The Founders did not mention one. Did they not ever experience hurricanes, storms, blizzards, and a host of other natural calamities? Of course. The stories of Caribbean storms were oft-told: Alexander Hamilton wrote his famous 1772 "hurricane letter" in which he said he saw "scenes of horror exhibited around us [which] naturally awakened such ideas [about death] in every thinking breast." At no time did he contemplate any government assistance to any of the victims, even though he wept at the sight of mothers with infants ("Her poverty denies relief . . . her heart is bursting, the tears gush down her cheeks"). Yet he did not appeal to government but to "ye, who revel in affluence, [to] see the afflictions of humanity and bestow your superfluity to ease them."[98]

As was clear after the practice of declaring national emergencies became common, virtually any and all hardships could fit the definition. But only recently have presidents willingly and eagerly declared "disaster areas" or used emergency powers. When, in 1887, Congress tried to push through a "compassionate" Seed Corn Bill, which would have given Texas farmers—the victims of a drought—a small amount of money for new seed, President Grover Cleveland vetoed it, writing in his message:

I can find no warrant for such an appropriation in the Constitution; and I do not believe that the power and duty of the General Government ought to be extended to the relief of individual suffering which is in no manner properly related to the public service or benefit.[99]

To "indulge a benevolent and charitable sentiment through the appropriation of public funds" was wrong, as Cleveland wrote when he vetoed the bill. He ended his veto message with an astounding admonition for modern politicians to consider: "A prevalent tendency to disregard the limited mission of this [the government's] power and duty should, I think, be steadfastly resisted, to the end that the lesson should constantly be enforced that, *though the people support the Government, the Government should not support the people* [emphasis in original]."[100] Insisting that "the friendliness and charity of our countrymen can always be relied on to relieve their fellow citizens in misfortune," he called on members of Congress to personally donate to the suffering farmers by using seed regularly given to members for distribution to their constituents (at ten times the Texas Seed Corn Bill's cost), or send money to the farmers.[101]

Cleveland only echoed a long line of Founders who had believed in such a principle. In the *Federalist* No. 44, James Madison wrote, "No axiom is more clearly established in law or in reason than that wherever the end is required, the means are authorized."[102] Much mischief has been undertaken through the so-called "elastic clause" of the Constitution, Article I, Section 8, clause 18, which says, "The Congress shall have Power to make all Laws which shall be necessary and proper for carrying into Execution the foregoing Powers, and all other Powers vested by this Constitution in the Government of the United States, or in any Department or Officer thereof." When Alexander Hamilton, as secretary of the treasury, sought to use the clause to establish a national bank and subsidize manufacturers, Madison responded, "If not only the *means*, but the *objects* are unlimited, the parchment had better be thrown into the fire at once."[103] Hamilton increasingly sought to make the "general welfare" clause a tool for Congress to take under its management anything it should deem "for the *public welfare*."

Katrina and Johnstown were opposite examples of how natural disasters have been handled. Johnstown's flood was a pivotal event in our history because it was the clearest (but not the only) demonstration of private charity combating the effects of natural disasters. The Founders knew that government did have a role to play in natural disasters, namely, keeping order. That was a military function.[104] But relief and disaster response by the federal government would always come up short compared to the compassionate efforts of communities and neighbors.

4.

IKE HAS A HEART ATTACK, TRIGGERING DIETARY NANNYISM

Was the government to prescribe to us our medicine and diet, our bodies would be in such keeping as our souls are now.

THOMAS JEFFERSON

In a chapter dealing with food, it's appropriate to start with a recipe: begin with two parts unsettled science; add three parts anticapitalism; stir in four parts big-government nannyism and vegan extremism; then sprinkle generously with overpopulation hysteria and top with a healthy dollop of global warming. Your dish? A disastrous war on meat whose initial objective—to reduce the rate of heart disease among the population—led to the politicization of the American diet in the name of public health, while providing cover for every crackpot food fearmonger and free-marketophobe in the United States. The heartburn you feel after ingesting this dish is just the first sign of something much harder to swallow: the idea that pseudoscientists can dictate, via the government food police, what you are supposed to eat. This

malignant yeast of junk science has subsequently laid waste to entire industries, diverted AIDS research in unproductive directions, and most recently
spawned the Lysenkoist "man-made global warming" nonsense that earned
Al Gore a Nobel Prize. And it all began a half-century ago on a Colorado
golf course, when President Dwight D. Eisenhower was on vacation.

After playing twenty-seven holes of golf on September 23, 1955, at
Cherry Hills Golf Club in Denver, Eisenhower complained about an upset
stomach. His physician, Dr. Howard M. Snyder, treated him for heartburn
and Ike returned to the nearby home of his mother-in-law, Elivera Doud,
where Ike and his wife were spending the evening. After midnight, he woke
up with severe chest pain, and his wife, Mamie, summoned Snyder back
around 2:00 a.m. The doctor gave him some injections, one of which was
later discovered to be morphine, but he did not take Eisenhower to Fitzsi-
mons Army Medical Center until twelve hours later. When Ike was finally
admitted, local doctors disagreed about the proper treatment. Meanwhile,
Thomas Mattingly, chief cardiologist at Walter Reed Army Hospital, who
had arrived the day after Ike had been admitted to the hospital, was convinced Ike had suffered a previous myocardial infarction (or heart attack) but
had been misdiagnosed with an attack of inflammatory bowels. This block-
age had caused an aneurysm. Mattingly quickly contacted Dr. Paul Dudley
White, a Harvard cardiologist and one of the nation's top heart surgeons.[1]

Though it's often overlooked in history books, Ike's heart attack was
probably the most important single medical case of the twentieth century,
as it fundamentally changed the way Americans viewed food. The "science"
surrounding Ike's treatment and recovery eventually instigated a war on meat
that continues to the present. Whether Ike meant to or not, he soon became
a role model for "heart-healthy" living, becoming an "exercise freak," instituting a strict postattack diet of more fruit, fewer meals, and fewer calories.
In the words of Dr. Snyder, "He eats nothing for breakfast, nothing for
lunch, and therefore is irritable during the noon hour. . . ."[2] Yet instead of
reducing cholesterol—as the experts predicted would happen—Ike's low-fat
diet *increased* his cholesterol the more he cut back on fats and cheese. If those
foods were bad for you, as some suggested, Eisenhower's "metrics" (to use a
modern buzzword) should have improved.

The media, as ever, jumped on the news of Ike's heart attack and recovery. Because of the media's uninformed sensationalism around the event,

and the medical profession's activism, Americans began to believe the government should play a role in individuals' health. After all, if the president's diet was a matter of public record and could be manipulated to improve his health, shouldn't the same dietary guidelines be available to everyone? And if they were good for everyone, shouldn't the government require Americans to follow these guidelines? More important, if government could now determine what made a diet healthy, did that not place incredible power in the hands of those who defined healthy diets? Ultimately, the events on that Denver golf course started a long, but uninterrupted, march toward dietary nannyism. But the more frightening problem came when the government—never heralded as a bastion of scientific knowledge—began to take advice from so-called experts based on preliminary and incomplete studies and to give the public potentially dangerous and very unhealthy guidelines.

In twice-daily press conferences, the news media eagerly followed the president's recovery, in the process instructing Americans on the dangers of coronary disease. A new word crept into the everyday vocabulary: cholesterol. It had dark, evil overtones. *Cholesterol.* This was the monster Americans must defeat! A healthy person must keep his or her cholesterol low! High cholesterol portended to be the new polio, and Americans quickly embraced any maxim to lower cholesterol: quit smoking, exercise, and eat right. Ike had quit smoking in 1949, exercised, kept an optimal weight, and his cholesterol was below normal just prior to his attack. Afterward, Eisenhower began a strict, low-fat diet. . . and his weight began to rise. He cut out breakfast entirely, after first switching from oatmeal and skim milk to melba toast and fruit, but his weight still inched up. At that point Dr. Snyder was mystified: how can a man eat so little, exercise regularly, and still gain weight? After the president read about a group of New Yorkers who were battling cholesterol by cutting margarine, lard, cream, and butter out of their diets (and replacing them with corn oil), he followed suit.

Finally, his weight stabilized . . . but his cholesterol *rose.* Snyder grew so conscious of Ike's fretting—his obsessing—about cholesterol that he began lying to him about the real cholesterol levels, understating them so Ike wouldn't worry. Despite the fact that Eisenhower had essentially eliminated all supposedly high-cholesterol foods from his diet, his readings dramatically soared to what some physicians would call dangerous levels. History has a way of shining the spotlight on the ironic: at the very moment Ike's physician was concealing cholesterol reports from his patient under the assumption that cholesterol caused heart ailments, *Time* magazine heralded Ancel Keys, a physiologist from the University of Minnesota whose research "proved" that a low-fat, low-cholesterol, carb-heavy diet would prevent heart disease.[3] Two weeks later, the American Heart Association endorsed the Keys analysis, calling for low-fat/low-cholesterol diets. "Diet Linked to Cut in Heart Attacks," proclaimed *The New York Times* in May 1962. And Ike? He lived for another fourteen years after his first heart attack.

Eisenhower's own cardiologist bought into the dietary fat hypothesis, claiming a "great epidemic" of cardiovascular disease had struck America in the post–World War II period.[4] Similarly, Jean Mayer of Harvard claimed in 1975 that the rise of heart disease was an epidemic as dire as the "arrival of bubonic plague . . . in fourteenth-century Europe, syphilis . . . at the end of the fifteenth century, and . . . tuberculosis at the beginning of the nineteenth century."[5] At the same time, medical "experts" and government officials began claiming that Americans had changed their diets to eat more red meat and fats in the twentieth century. In fact, both claims were false, and, as in the case of AIDs some thirty years later, one could make or break an "epidemic" simply by fiddling with definitions. And, as would be the case with global warming fifty years later, one could prove virtually anything based on where one started the trend line.

It is true that coronary cases seemed to increase dramatically between 1940 and 1970—but this was entirely because other diseases were being conquered and thus were not as rampant. A quarter of all men died of coronary disease in 1910, for example, and another quarter died from infections, parasites, flu, pneumonia, bronchitis, or tuberculosis, virtually all of which were eliminated or greatly suppressed by 1970. Cancer, meanwhile, went from eighth on the list to number two, and the rate of heart disease "doubled."[6] Simply put, modern medicine had conquered so many diseases over the previous century that people lived long enough to encounter (and die from) new or rare diseases.[7] Cancer and heart disease, which took longer to manifest themselves than, say, smallpox, became the leading killers.

At the same time, improvements in technology made it possible to more accurately diagnose the cause of death, hence, unexplained or sudden deaths that had once been mysterious were finally, correctly, attributed to heart disease or cancer.[8] Even the American Heart Association admitted that the "new" classification of arteriosclerotic heart disease in 1949 made a "great difference," and that the "remarkable increase in the *reported* number of cases of this condition" lay almost entirely in the use of the electrocardiogram in confirming clinical diagnoses (emphasis in original).[9] Predictably, when the International Classification of Diseases (ICD) added a second heart disease category (ischemic heart disease), the percentage of heart-disease deaths shot up dramatically. Even the World Health Organization acknowledged that "much of the apparent increase in [heart disease] mortality may simply be due to improvements in the quality of certification and more accurate diagnoses. . . ."[10]

Around the same time, the false notion that the United States used to be a vegan society began to gain traction, thus further contributing to misconceptions about meat. Proponents of this myth argued that the late 1800s had been some "idyllic era free of chronic disease," which was ruined after the rise of meat and fat consumption consigned Americans to heart attacks.[11] Americans, according to this legend, got away from eating as they did in the old days, when they consumed more cereals. Jane Brody's 1985 *Good Food Book* claimed that "Within this century the diet of the average American has undergone a radical shift away from plant-based foods such as grains, beans and peas, nuts and potatoes, and other vegetables and fruits and toward foods derived from animals. . . ."[12] Two factors contributed to this perception. First, the publication of *The Jungle* by Upton Sinclair in 1906, which demonized the meat industry, cut American meat sales by half, and by the time of the Great Crash in 1929, meat packers had still not recovered.[13] Second, there were flawed estimates by the United States Food and Drug Administration, which used "food disappearance" methods to calculate what people ate. Not only did the data go back no farther than the 1920s—one scholar described the data as "lousy" and said "you can prove anything you want to prove"—but most historical records show that Americans were voracious meat eaters in the 1800s.[14]

Some studies show that nineteenth-century Americans ate forty to sixty pounds of meat more per capita per year than in the twentieth century—but such evidence did not fit the "meat-makes-us-unhealthy" argument so it was largely ignored.[15] Moreover, the farther back one goes, the clearer it becomes that hunter-gatherer (i.e., heavy meat-eating) societies were healthier than farmer societies (whose diets were high in carbohydrates—grains, corn, and rice). Tom Standage, in his *Edible History of Humanity*, noted that

> farmers suffered from various diseases of malnutrition that were rare or absent in hunter-gatherers. . . . Farmers were also more susceptible to infectious diseases such as leprosy, tuberculosis, and malaria as a result of their settled lifestyles. . . . As the farming groups settle down and grow larger, the incidence of malnutrition, parasitic diseases, and infectious diseases increases.[16]

Brody reflected the new trend in which "specialists in popularizing, chiefly journalists, increasingly took over the function of presenting science to lay audiences."[17] This process involved "simplification" and "translation" of science, both of which were fraught with danger, usually sensationalizing the prevalence or danger of certain diseases or conditions untethered to the real science. And this development coincided with a decline in science education throughout the United States. "The problem," historian John Burnham noted, "was that science required tedious memorizing and thinking that no pedagogical innovation, from the laboratory exercise to the discovery method of the Deweyites . . . [could] ever succeed in easing."[18] Researchers complained that journalists took liberties "with the substance and perspectives of science," ultimately arriving at the trivialization of science.[19] In the television era, this meant that the media winner of the "authority" designation went to the most articulate, photogenic, or cooperative person—and more recently, the source who shared the press's views.[20]

Ancel Keys was exactly such a source for the media. He was well-spoken, carried the mantle of authority well, and above all, cleverly deflected questions or criticisms of his research.

He had a powerful personality and an apparently novel argument, namely, that fats and meat were linked to cholesterol, and cholesterol to heart disease. His theory dated to a visit to Italy in 1951, where on the basis of noncontrolled (that is to say, unscientific) blood-serum measurements taken on a few hundred workers and Rotary Club members, he concluded that rich people had more heart disease simply because they ate more meat.[21] Even then, he had to admit, "Direct evidence on the effect of the diet on human arteriosclerosis is very little. . . ."[22] Over the next decade, Keys assembled his famous "six countries" study (later expanded to seven), claiming a consistent relationship between fat calories in the diet and heart disease. When other researchers examined his work, however, they found he had left out sixteen other countries, whose inclusion would disprove his hypothesis.[23] Similarly, in 1957 the American Heart Association sharply criticized Keys's findings as "uncompromising stands based on evidence that does not stand up under critical examination," and concluded that there wasn't enough evidence to link food, especially fat, and heart disease.[24] Only four years later, in 1961, the AHA made a U-turn, directed by a six-man committee including Keys and his chief supporter, Jeremiah Stamler, by issuing a report that contained only half a page of "recent scientific references," many of which actually contradicted the 1957 report's conclusions. The new AHA report cited the "best scientific evidence of the time" to link dietary fat and heart disease. *Time* quickly enshrined Keys as the heart guru of the age.

From 1961 to 1977, a tidal wave of research appeared on the causes of heart disease, diet, and cholesterol, yet none of it arrived at any clear conclusions. At best, two camps appeared—the Keys school, arguing that a high-fat diet led to heart disease, and a completely opposite school of thought comprising researchers who claimed that, in fact, fats and meat were not the problem, carbohydrates and insulin were. One protégé of Keys at Minnesota, Henry Blackburn, observed in 1975 that two "strikingly polar attitudes persist" while Thomas Dawber, who pioneered the Framingham Heart Study, flipped back and forth, admitting in 1978 that "the diet-heart relation is an unproved hypothesis," then in 1980 insisting that the Framingham Heart Study proved the Keys hypothesis, before adding the caveat, "many physicians and investigators of considerable renown still doubt the validity of the fat hypothesis . . . [and] some even question the relationship of blood cholesterol level to disease."[25] Research was showing fairly consistently that low-carbohydrate diets were optimal for losing weight, at which point the arguments usually shifted to the impact of high-fat diets on cholesterol, not weight.[26]

Despite the debate, the science was *never* settled. But there was a difference: the dietary-fat-equals-death group became utterly convinced of its certitude and acted like *activists*, while the other half of the researchers continued to act like *scientists* by suggesting nothing was proven on either side. Claude Bernard, in his *Introduction to the Study of Experimental Medicine* in 1865, warned that men who have excessive faith in their theories or ideas are not only ill prepared for making discoveries; they also make very poor observations [because] they observe with a preconceived idea, and when they devise an experiment, they can see, in its results, only a confirmation of their theory. . . . it happens further quite naturally that men who believe too firmly in their theories, do not believe enough in the theories of others. So the dominant idea of these [men] is to find others' theories faulty and to try to contradict them.[27]

Meyer Friedman, in 1969, labeled this tendency the "tyranny [of a] hypothesis once formulated," noting that "to enthuse about one's own theory or hypothesis is legitimate and even beneficial, but if presentation gives way to evangelistic fervor, emphasis to special pleading, and enthusiasm to bias, then progress is stopped dead."[28] Thomas Jefferson said it only slightly differently: "He who knows best knows how little he knows."

Even as massive studies by the National Institutes of Health and the American Heart Association involving fifty thousand test subjects were being prepared in 1961—studies that would provide abundant evidence when the conclusions came in—the AHA was already preparing booklets emphasizing the importance of lowering cholesterol. Some of the researchers were already spinning the results in favor of the Keys hypothesis before the study was even under way. It made good press to say that fat caused heart disease, reinforcing the "truth" of the original hypothesis. Albert Einstein had categorically dismissed such an approach when, in 1919, two of his required three experiments proved his theory of relativity, saying only that until the "redshift" condition had been met, "the whole theory would have to be abandoned."[29] After the redshift was in fact confirmed empirically, philosopher Karl Popper remarked, "What impressed me most was Einstein's own clear statement that he would regard his theory as untenable if it should fail in certain tests."[30] This was merely the theory of the universe, not a minor point about dietary fat—and yet Einstein was anything but dogmatic or proselytizing. Forty years later, not only did a large segment of heart researchers fail to wait for the results of a dietary/cholesterol version of a redshift, but there was no acknowledgment that the absence of such data would matter anyway!

Data that didn't fit the Keys hypothesis was arbitrarily dismissed. This included evidence of Japanese men in California who had low cholesterol levels and still had higher rates of heart disease than relatives living in Japan. As the insightful historian of the diet debate Gary Taubes noted:

> Any research that did not support their hypothesis was said to be misinterpreted, irrelevant, or based on untrustworthy data. Studies of Navajo Indians, Irish immigrants to Boston, African nomads, Swiss Alpine farmers, and Benedictine and Trappist monks all suggested that dietary fat seemed unrelated to heart disease. These were explained away or rejected by Keys.[31]

Among the various subgroups that began to stand out as more studies were conducted, the Masai nomads of Kenya had incredibly low blood-cholesterol levels, despite an almost exclusively fat/meat/milk diet; and other African tribes disproved the Keys hypothesis, despite his claims that they supported his conclusions.[32]

Supposedly, the Framingham Heart Study would provide definitive answers. Begun in 1952 in Framingham, Massachusetts, with 5,100 volunteers who were subjected to regular physicals and blood work—then reexamined every two years—the study initially included cholesterol among its risk factors, but as the evidence unfolded and as the participants in the study aged, low cholesterol was more closely linked to heart problems than high cholesterol![33] More important still, the Framingham dietary research disproved Keys, yet it was not published with the rest of the Framingham data until researchers dug it out in the late 1960s and it was finally included in the twenty-fourth volume of the study released in 1968. This data found no difference at all between the diets of high-cholesterol men and low-cholesterol men.[34] In short, there was a significant amount of evidence that the fat-cholesterol–heart disease links either did not exist or, in fact, were the opposite of what was being sold to the public by the American Heart Association and the government.

Over the next few years, studies examining the amount of fat consumed and correlating it with either cholesterol or heart disease proved remarkably *un*supportive of the Keys hypothesis. (Within particular populations in Puerto Rico, Honolulu, Chicago, Michigan, and Israel the results were the same, which is to say that there was no correlation.[35]) Then came the 5,400-strong Western Electric study in which, out of the 88 coronary cases,

14 were in the high-fat-intake group, 16 in the low-fat group. In 1977, re-searchers revisited the subjects and examined the cause of death, discovering that the "amount of saturated fatty acids in the diet was not significantly as-sociated with the risk" of heart disease, and found no significant association of fatty acids in the diet with coronary disease.[36] Despite a serpentine ratio-nalization, the authors admitted that "most attempts to document the rela-tion of dietary cholesterol, saturated fatty acids, and polyunsaturated fatty acids to serum cholesterol concentration . . . have been unsuccessful."[37]

What followed is a case study in how data can be manipulated, regur-gitated uncritically by the press, and turned into public policy. The update of the Western Electric study provided contrary evidence to the fat–heart disease hypothesis, so the authors of the study included four *other* studies whose evidence seemed to disprove their own results. Thus, they concluded that in fact a fatty diet affected serum cholesterol and long-term risk of death, and published this result in the *New England Journal of Medicine* in 1981. Jane Brody in *The New York Times* and *The Washington Post* slavishly reported these findings, which were then echoed in a report by the Ameri-can Heart Association. To repeat: the Western Electric study did *not* show a correlation between risk of heart disease and a high-fat diet—it showed the opposite. Yet within four years after the publication of the study, virtually every major heart-related association had endorsed the false position.[38]

In fact, the only reliable method of arriving at medically and scientifi-cally valid conclusions is to conduct double-blind, placebo-controlled clini-cal trials, and in fact, such trials are virtually impossible with food. Meat, butter, and cream, for example, have certain tastes that cannot be faked. Moreover, changing one aspect of a diet—fats—tends to change overall calories as well. Between 1950 and 1975, only about a dozen truly scientific trials of diet and heart disease were conducted. Only two of these actually examined low-fat diets and heart disease as opposed to cholesterol-lowering diets; and the two studies arrived at completely contradictory results.[39] Or how about the New York Anti-Coronary Club, which examined 1,100 males beginning in the late 1950s? The researchers were so convinced that the fat/heart disease link existed that as early as 1962 they leaked the interim results to *The New York Times*, which dutifully ran the headline "Diet Linked to Cut in Heart Attacks."[40] But there was a problem. The longer the study went, the more the data disproved the fat/heart disease link. In November

1966, another interim article appeared showing that 26 men on the low-fat diet had died, compared to only 6 on the high-fat diet. Seymour Dayton, in 1969, gave half of his test group a cholesterol-lowering diet and the other half a placebo: while only 66 of the lower-cholesterol group died from heart disease (compared to 96 in the placebo diet), the low-cholesterol group had higher death rates from cancer! A large study in Minnesota (the Minnesota Coronary Study) in 1968 found a cholesterol-lowering diet *increased* the risk of heart disease—but the results went unpublished for sixteen years, because, as one of the researchers said, "We were just disappointed in the way it came out."[41] In other words, the researchers were convinced that the science was "settled," so their own results could not be valid.

Beneath the surface, those at the American Heart Association and the National Heart Institute knew there was a lack of support for their hypothesis in the data. In 1968, after six researchers had received large grants to confirm the fat/heart disease link, Pete Ahrens of Rockefeller University was tasked to examine the evidence of the studies. Even in 1968—six years after the AHA had already gone on record as touting the benefits of a low-fat diet—the report concluded, "it is not known whether dietary manipulation has any effect whatsoever on coronary heart disease."[42]

At that point, the science—which was completely unsettled—became politicized by hysteria over population growth, exacerbated by the fear-mongering (and utterly wrong) book by Paul Ehrlich, *The Population Bomb* (1968). Concerns about growing worldwide population, along with the flawed notion that "not cleaning your plate" somehow caused "kids in China to starve," allowed the antimeat activists to gain a foothold in policy making. This illogical association, used at countless dinner tables, took another turn when the diet radicals linked it to the production costs of meat as opposed to vegetables and fruits. Hence, the aforementioned Jean Mayer claimed in 1974 that the "enormous appetite for animal products" had caused more grain and soybeans to go into feeding cattle and hogs, "decreasing the amounts of food directly available for direct consumption by the poor."[43] In reality, it was the opposite: the more grain and soybeans that were needed for animals, the higher the demand, which meant the more likelihood farmers would grow even more—which they did. Such free-market logic didn't faze Mayer, who concluded we needed "a shift in consumption in developed countries toward a 'simplified' diet containing less animal products, and, in particular, less meat." (Though of course he failed to acknowledge that our predecessors ate a "simple" diet as well, but theirs was full of meat.) This view fit well with the new vegan movement, as argued in *Diet for a Small Planet* by Frances Moore Lappé.

One characteristic of all these works is the obsession with limits on resources, an economic zero-sum approach developed by Thomas Mun and the mercantilists, and proven wrong by two centuries' worth of growing economies and vast new discoveries of resources. The buzzword was "small," emphasizing the absence of a capacity for growth, only constant entropy to, presumably, a single pair of humans huddled around the last berry bush. Similarly, *Appetite for Change* by Warren James Belasco warned that shoppers in Indiana would affect food availability in India. The fact that the Left glommed on to the antifat/meat-kills mantra should not be surprising, nor should the notion that "Big Food" was somehow behind the fat-heavy shift in eating.

Government had already started to insert itself into Americans' diets long before Ike's heart attack, but with nowhere near the same levels of intensity or control. Uncle Sam's first foray into the regulation of food, of course, was the Pure Food and Drug Act of 1906. Using the enforcement powers of the FDA, one of the first products the government set its sights on was that grave threat to humankind, Coca-Cola! For many years, the FDA had pursued Coke on the grounds that it had cocaine in it, even though Asa Candler, who had taken over the manufacturing of Coke, came up with a "Secret Formula" that so diluted the coca leaf in the Coca-Cola ingredients that it virtually disappeared.[44] Nevertheless, the government under the zealous Dr. Harvey Wiley continued to investigate. Upon finding *no* cocaine in Coke, Wiley then charged the company with "misbranding" and false advertising. The case collapsed and Coke was finally free of the strong arm of government. But the public was just beginning to see government's hand in its dietary affairs.

Even before the creation of the FDA, in 1894, the U.S. Department of Agriculture published dietary recommendations and in 1916 released the first food guide, *Food for Young Children*, written by Caroline Hunt, who came up with the "five basic food groups." Franklin Roosevelt called a National Nutrition Conference in 1941, which came up with the recommended daily allowances (RDA) of calories for Americans to observe. These included caloric intake, nutrients, vitamins, and other guidelines, revising the original five basic food groups down to four: milk, meats, fruits and vegetables, and grains. In the 1970s, a fifth category of sweets, fats, and alcoholic beverages was added. By the 1980s, the famous "food pyramid" was established, and in 1988, a graphic was added to convey the goals of variety, proportionality, and moderation based on the sizes of the food group depicted. In 1994, the Nutrition Labeling and Education Act forced food companies to put nutritional and caloric information on cans and boxes. The impact was hardly what the government anticipated: a 1996 USDA poll found that over 40 percent of Americans thought that the information only confused them.[45] Yet the information was of little use if the recommendations and guidelines were wrong to begin with. It all depended on a politicized "consensus" about what constituted acceptable levels, and all of that was determined by which of the previous studies one thought was correct. It all came down to someone in government making a decision about *contested* science, which meant that the decision of which side to accept was determined by politics, power, and money, not science.

The government/science/advocacy link was greatly strengthened in 1977 with the McGovern Committee's release of *Dietary Goals for the United States*.[46] That the government should be involved in telling people what to eat spoke volumes about how far from the Founders' vision the United States had strayed. When Franklin said, "Those who would give up essential liberty to purchase a little temporary safety deserve neither liberty nor safety," he likely meant tyranny from the British—not the food police—but the principle was the same. Adams agreed: "Liberty once lost"—even to eat as one chooses—"is lost forever." Formed in 1968 as a part of the War on Poverty and the drive to end hunger, the committee had originally supervised food-assistance programs. Like all good Washington committees, though, rather than go out of business, the members looked for more work. George McGovern himself was a low-fat believer—having attended the Pritikin Longevity Research Institute in Santa Barbara—but most of the staff were shallow in their knowledge and, according to Gary Taubes, thought "relevant nutritional and social issues were simple and obvious."[47] Having gained most of their knowledge about the subject from newspapers (as one admitted), it was no surprise that they had the viewpoint of *The New York Times*, which is to say, the viewpoint of Jane Brody, who was already in the antifat/antimeat camp. After hearings in which the committee members heard testimony about how the American diet had changed to a higher intake of meat and fat since the turn of the century, the results were predictable. The first goal the committee listed was to increase carbohydrate consumption and decrease fat consumption, all on the assumption that this would help Americans lose weight. Buried inside *Dietary Goals* was the admission that the evidence was not clear or compelling. Many of the witnesses had testified that the recommendations were either premature or flat-out harmful.

Empowered by the McGovern Committee, administrators at the Department of Agriculture, particularly Carol Foreman, the assistant secretary under Jimmy Carter, used the agency to turn the guidelines into policy. Foreman believed "people were getting sick and dying because they ate too much," and worked with the surgeon general to support more dietary guidelines.[48] Immediately, the science behind the war on meat began to "support" the guidelines, as researchers who failed to support the new government position found their work suddenly unfunded. The peer-review system intended to ensure quality scholarship instead excluded any dissenters.[49] Another researcher admitted, "If you say what the government says, then it's okay. If you say something that isn't what the government says . . . that makes you suspect."[50] Nor did the government note that one of its chief sources of the diet-heart interpretation, Jeremiah Stamler, was a consultant for the radical Center for Science in the Public Interest—the organization that would later attempt to ban buttered popcorn and attack ice cream as a "liquid heart attack." Yet the more research that came in, the less solid the fat/cholesterol/heart links looked. A massive Multiple Risk Factor Intervention Trial, which followed twelve thousand middle-aged men with high cholesterol for a seven-year period, discovered that there was a *higher* death rate among men who had quit smoking and eaten a lower-cholesterol diet than among those who hadn't. *The Wall Street Journal* summarized the stunning results in 1982 with the headline "Heart Attacks: A Test Collapses."[51] That did not dissuade *Time* magazine, however, from touting the evils of cholesterol on its March 1984 cover with a "frownie face" made up of two eggs and bacon.[52]

By the mid-1980s, when the National Institutes of Health joined in with its Cholesterol Education Program, then supported by Surgeon Gen-

IKE HAS A HEART ATTACK, TRIGGERING DIETARY NANNYISM 109

eral C. Everett Koop, it seemed clear that Americans should "cut out the fat." Foods high in fat, warned the surgeon general, could account for two-thirds of U.S. deaths in 1988.[53] Upon closer examination, however, the incest of the whole process revealed that the recommendations had come from the same people who had produced the questionable science in the first place. J. Michael McGinnis, for example, oversaw the surgeon general's report, yet he had been Mark Hegsted's liaison to the Surgeon General's Office when the original *Dietary Goals* were issued. In 1977, Hegsted had headed the drafting of the first dietary guidelines, relying on a report from the American Society of Clinical Nutrition that instructed "*not* to draw up a set of recommendations" based on the findings.[54] All these "new" reports relied heavily on researchers who had been involved in the dietary-fat controversy earlier and shared the same viewpoint as one another. In a stunning foreshadowing of the global warming debate, once the new guidelines came out, antimeat advocacy groups, such as the Center for Science in the Public Interest, drove the public discussion so as to eliminate all skeptical reports by dismissing any research that contradicted theirs as an irrelevant anomaly to the "broad scientific consensus." What followed was predictable: now that the "science was settled," all subsequent research challenging the fat-equals-heart-attack thesis was not just questioned, it was blocked altogether. When Warren Browner conducted a study at the University of California, San Francisco, and found minor benefits to cutting out *all* fats during a lifetime, McGinnis tried to block publication.[55]

Indeed, what was becoming obvious to everyone was just how difficult it was to come to *any* conclusions about the relationship of fat, cholesterol, diet, exercise, and heart health. A significant problem with any diet study is that because of the taste and texture of food, it is impossible to substitute one food for another. The calories might match up, but the person might eat more fruit instead of a donut, seeking to replace the sensation and "filling-ness" of fat, for example. As a result, the participant might ingest more sugar and less fat but would still be credited with a shift from "junk food" to fruit. Conducting long-term, double-blind, placebo-controlled diet research was nearly impossible (as admitted in a study touted by *USA Today* in 2009, whose fine print pointed out that as the period of time analyzed increased, the researchers found that the benefits of the diets declined sharply).[56]

Worse still, the playing field steadily shifted. Recall the sequence of events that started it all: Ike had a heart attack and people became concerned that cholesterol influenced heart health; then they started demonizing fat as a high-cholesterol food; and finally they began to blame heart disease on meat. By the 1970s, however, even Ancel Keys admitted there was "no basis" for the claim that there was a heart attack "epidemic" in the first place, and by 1987, he further admitted that "cholesterol is not as important as we used to think it was."[57]

The stage was thus set for Dr. Robert Atkins to spark a firestorm with his book *Dr. Atkins' Diet Revolution*, published in 1992. He noted that the human diet had changed dramatically beginning in the last decades of the 1800s, when white flour and refined sugar were introduced on a regular basis to the kitchens and dinner tables of average people. Sugar intake, which "averaged 12 pounds a year per person in 1828, was nearly ten times that in 1928," he noted. Between 1910 and 1970, "the intake of animal fat and butter dropped . . . [while] the intake of refined carbohydrates (mainly sugar, corn syrup and white flour) escalated by sixty percent."[58] Between 1975 and 1999, the average American increased his consumption of sugar and corn syrup by 34 pounds annually (750 calories a day from sugar increases alone!).[59] That amount constituted one-third of all calories an adult put into his body per day, and alone should have been cause for deep concern about its connections to diabetes and hyperinsulinism. The French, by comparison, until very recent years lived on a high-fat diet that contained an average of four times the butter of Americans, but they suffered 60 percent less heart disease because they consumed five times less sugar than those in the United States. Since high-sugar and heavy-flour fast foods have become more common overseas, however, the French have begun to catch up with us.

Atkins relied on plenty of research that was largely disregarded by the fat-is-evil community, including a study at the Oakland Naval Hospital by Frederick Benoit and others who found that a low-carb diet actually caused subjects to lose weight twice as fast as when they ate nothing![60] Since Atkins published his high-fat, meat-heavy, low-carb diet, numerous other studies have confirmed his observations. A conclusive study in the *New England Journal of Medicine* that evaluated data on over 82,000 women found "diets lower in carbohydrate and higher in protein and fat are not associated with increased risk of coronary heart disease in women . . . [and] may moderately reduce the risk of coronary heart disease."[61] The study failed to include any kind of control-group alternative with the high-carb diets, however—but the conclusions were impressive nonetheless. In July 2008, a study pitting the "Mediterranean diet" of high fiber against a low-carb diet once again found the low-carb diet superior for losing weight, as well as having the most favorable effects on lipids.[62] Another study of 447 individuals agreed that the low-carb group lost more weight than low-fat groups, but claimed there could be "unfavorable changes in low-density lipoprotein cholesterol values."[63] (We will turn in a moment to the cholesterol values.) Then there was the study at the University of Pennsylvania of 63 obese men and women who were randomly assigned to a high-fat/low-carb diet or a low-calorie/high-carb diet. Once again, the results were predictable:

> The low-carbohydrate diet produced a greater weight loss (absolute difference, approximately 4 percent) than did the conventional diet for the first six months, but the differences were not significant at one year. The low-carbohydrate diet was associated with a greater improvement in some risk factors for coronary heart disease.[64]

During the 1990s, new studies in France and Italy confirmed (and ignored) earlier evidence from Japan. Both France and Italy showed declining death rates from stroke and heart disease (with Spain only slightly behind) despite a substantial increase in meat consumption.[65] These findings were labeled "paradoxes," the name alone implying that the science was set, as it would not be a paradox unless it was thought odd or counterintuitive. One would see the same lunacy attached to global warming amid overwhelming evidence of plunging temperatures, wherein even *cooling* was ascribed to global warming. As would be the case with global warming, once purely scientific but now highly politicized journals such as *Science* weighed in on policy, warning that obesity had become an "epidemic" resulting from "improved prosperity."[66]

With each new offensive against fats and meat—and in favor of "healthy" carbohydrates—Americans continued to get fatter and to have more diabetes and heart disease. Just thirty years ago, American women ate 42 percent of their diet in fats, the same as men. By 1995, however, both men and women only consumed 32 percent of their diet in fats, even though obesity was skyrocketing. Meanwhile, women carbed up, as per the advice of the heart specialists and media, increasing the percentage of diet made up of carbohydrates from 42 percent to 62 percent, with men only slightly behind at 59 percent.[67] Meanwhile, a quiet group of researchers was debunking the fat-cholesterol-heart-disease model. Famed heart surgeon Michael DeBakey in 1964 reported in a test of 1,700 patients that he had negative correlations for cholesterol and heart problems; and researchers had already shown that the cholesterol consumed has little relevance to the amount of cholesterol in the blood.[68]

The fact that government—through its very public-health agenda— might be more responsible for the rapid rise in obesity apparently never crossed the mind of the dietary fat-equals-heart-disease crowd. Yale's Kelly Brownell, who headed the school's center for weight disorders, complained that American culture "encourages overeating and physical inactivity."[69] He never considered that Americans' work—largely relegated to the office instead of the field—was becoming more sedentary. At the same time, the Centers for Disease Control offered evidence that Americans were "no less active at the end of the 1990s than they were at the beginning of that decade. . . ."[70] More than 40 million Americans belonged to health clubs (which had revenues of some $16 billion by 2005), and as early as 1977 *The New York Times* noted an "exercise explosion" and three years later *The Washington Post* proclaimed a "fitness revolution."[71] Sporting goods sales in America topped $52 billion. Nor was it the case that Americans had "supersized" everything: from 1971 to 2000, average caloric intake only rose by 150 in the United States, while men's intake of fat decreased and women's intake increased only slightly.[72] What had changed was the nature of the foods consumed, not their caloric count.

Buried beneath the obesity hysteria was a deep hatred of capitalism and prosperity. Health problems of all sorts, especially cancer, continued to be blamed on capitalism, industrialism, and the West. The WHO and its International Agency for Research on Cancer (IARC), beginning in the 1950s, had studied cancer rates in Africa and compared them to those in the United States and some European nations, concluding that "most" human cancers were caused by environmental cancers and were preventable.[73] Precisely because the American food industry expanded worldwide, it became a target for consumer advocates and health zealots, resulting in the demonization of such fast-food companies as McDonald's. Leading the charge were polemics such as *Fast Food Nation*, aided and abetted by such supposedly public-interest firms as Michael Jacobson's Center for Science in the Public Interest. By the 1990s, tort lawyers had joined the crusade, bringing suits against food corporations for causing obesity. Congress passed legislation protecting companies from such frivolous suits before any tobacco-type pattern could set in. According to *Science* magazine in 2003, "Our culture's apparent obsession with 'getting the best value' may underlie the increased offering and selection of larger portions. . . ."[74]

This fit well with the notion that the United States consumed too much of the planet's resources, long a canard regarding the issue of energy use. In 2003, nutritionists David and Marcia Pimentel lent academic credibility to the war on meat by claiming in the *American Journal of Clinical Nutrition* that meat-eating and use of fossil fuels were inexorably intertwined, and the salvation of the planet lay in a vegan diet.[75] Basing their analysis on American *overpopulation* (at a time when the world was already reaching its population peak and most nations had a more serious *underpopulation* problem to deal with), the Pimentels gave academic cover to the radical vegan movement, which was already partly supported by the antifat, heart-disease lobby. Then came *Scientific American*, which had already signed on to the bogus global warming theories with its alarmist article "How Meat Contributes to Global Warming."[76] Cow flatulence, farms that "give rise to greenhouse gases," and the process of raising just one pound of beef for the dinner table (which requires ten pounds of plant protein), they argue, all contribute to the dangerous warming of the planet.

Researchers at the London School of Hygiene and Tropical Medicine picked up the point and in 2009 said that "Food production accounts for about one fifth of greenhouse gases," and that "moving about in a heavy body is like driving a gas guzzler."[77] Published in the *Sun* newspaper under the astoundingly honest (from the perspective of the study's authors) headline, "Fatties Cause Global Warming," the study claimed that each fat person was responsible for emitting a ton more of climate-warming carbon per year. Studies such as these merely constituted the natural convergence of the antiautomobile, anticapitalism, vegan, and environmental movements—a call to limit all human freedoms (indeed, all human characteristics) as "dangerous to the planet earth."

At the root of all this hatred of meat was a hatred for humans, for the authors of such polemics were always quick to point out that even asparagus absorbed a "CO_2 equivalent of 3.2 ounces."[78] Clearly, even mandating a meatless diet wouldn't be sufficient for the zealots, who would then attack vegan diets as "un-earth-friendly." (You can just hear the critics discussing how plants "scream" at this point.) If people were the ultimate target, "Big Food"—capitalism embodied in caloric intake—was the immediate villain. Books such as *Fast Food Nation* began the assault on "Big Food" through implausible diet regimens and selective hysteria-ridden "facts." Morgan Spurlock's 2004 documentary *Super Size Me* followed the filmmaker as he consumed only McDonald's food for a thirty-day period and gained about 24 pounds. Later, however, a college student named Jared Fogle— who weighed in at 425—developed a "Subway diet," based on the Subway sandwich chain's turkey hoagies, and lost a total of 240 pounds. When a fellow student wrote a story about his weight loss, Subway hired him as a spokesman. Meanwhile, *Fast Food Nation*, Eric Schlosser's diatribe against fast food and conservatism in general, became mandatory reading on college campuses as faculties attempted to propagandize via freshman orientations that required students to read the book. Even Schlosser had to admit that no scientific study had established a relationship between fast food and obesity, but insisted that there was a connection nonetheless.[79] Like Barbara Ehrenreich's attack on entry-level jobs in America (finally successfully challenged by none other than Adam Shepard, a college student who, after being dropped in a large southeastern city with only $25 and a sleeping bag, had a full-time job, a car, an apartment, and money in the bank at the *end of a year*), *Fast Food Nation* demonized all fast food as though it were eaten three times a day, seven days a week.[80]

Larger food giants, though, soon found themselves in the crosshairs. Food corporations marketed foods low in nutritional value, duping children into buying cereals for the toys. (Unstated in these claims that Americans were getting fatter was a fundamental contradiction, given that most of the "experts" believed in evolution: if evolution meant for people to be less active and use their brains more, weren't heavier people "natural"?) With renewed concerns about the cost of health care came a fresh assault on obesity, zeroing in on "unhealthy restaurants." In 2009 the Institute of Medicine and the National Research Council issued a report detailing strategies for local government to combat an "epidemic" of childhood obesity by using zoning and land-use regulations that would "restrict fast food establishments" near schools or public playgrounds.[81] The report, called "Local Government Actions to Prevent Childhood Obesity," naturally encouraged higher taxes on foods it deemed harmful or of "minimal nutritional value" and similarly called for caloric information on all menus from restaurants with more than twenty stores. Already, some governments had taken actions, such as Los Angeles, which placed a ban on opening any new fast food restaurants in East Los Angeles. Astoundingly, the report even discussed restrictions on advertising for "physically inactive services and goods," such as cars and video games!

Given the politicization of diet, it is not surprising—in fact, now it seems entirely predictable—that the government began to politicize climate with "global warming," one of the biggest scams in history that, conveniently, dovetailed with the war on meat. But this crusade didn't come as easily. As early as 1975, when the government was still learning how to dictate dietary choices, *Newsweek* ran a major article by Peter Gwynne called "The Cooling World."[82] Gwynne saw "ominous signs" that the "Earth's weather patterns have begun to change dramatically," with horrific consequences for food production. The "great wheat-producing lands of Canada and the U.S.S.R." were "destined to feel its impact," he predicted. Farmers had seen growing seasons decline in England, and the "most devastating outbreak of tornados" in recent memory had struck the United States. All this, readers were told, was the result of global cooling.

Were it not so sad, the hysteria generated by the media on matters so out of human control as the weather would be laughable. Yet within a matter of years after Gwynne warned of an impending "Little Ice Age," liberal environmental activists jumped ship to warn of another catastrophe, the warming of the planet due to human influences. Scientists had already identified a "greenhouse effect" as one of the results of carbon dioxide in the atmosphere. This "discovery" stemmed from efforts by regulators to control smog in the late 1960s and early 1970s by reducing auto emissions. The theory was that carbon emissions in the atmosphere would trap heat, causing the earth to warm. Yet equatorial sea surface temperatures had remained within plus or minus one degree for centuries—perhaps billions of years.[83] Studies even showed that a *doubling* of the earth's CO_2 cover would have a small effect on temperatures.

A complete history of the war on the automobile would require its own book. B. Bruce-Briggs and John Heitmann, among others, have documented the attacks on cars that have persisted for decades.[84] "Green" parties in Europe had already been formed as early as the 1970s, mostly by the Socialist Left, as a more palatable cover for opposing economic growth, and the concern in the 1980s was less a warming planet than the loss of the ozone layer over the earth. When this proved a phantom threat, the environmentalists turned to temperature variance as evidence that humans were hurting the planet.

Tom Paine once said, "He that would make his own liberty secure, must guard even his enemy from oppression." In the decades after Eisenhower's heart attack, intrusions on economic liberty were common, and during Vietnam, many claimed that their political liberty was in jeopardy. But perhaps the most insidious threat of all was the erosion of freedom in the name of "a person's own good." At the very time that some well-meaning, but myopic, Americans sought to limit everyone's freedoms—to choose what to eat, what to drink, even what to drive—under the auspices of "helping" them become "healthier," Paine would have screamed, "Someone guard them from oppression!" Edmund Burke seemed to have the government's diet police and global warming in mind when he wrote in 1784, "The people never give up their liberties but under some delusion."

In this case, the delusion was that medical science had settled on what constituted healthy diets, and that big government needed to protect us from Twinkies or Humvees. Yet in both cases—even if the science firmly established the dangers of either—no individual should surrender personal liberty to the discretion of faceless bureaucrats who can *never* have an individual's best interest at heart. Of course, in neither the case of the dietary fat hypothesis (note the key word, *hypothesis*) nor that of global warming is the science anywhere near settled. Quite the contrary; recent studies are increasingly suggesting both are wrong. But that is a matter for science, not government. When Jefferson said, "It behooves every man who values liberty of conscience for himself to resist invasions of it in the case of others," he no doubt was referring to political issues. Yet what have food and transportation in our day become but political issues? If Ike knew what he'd started, he'd likely have had another heart attack!

5.

A STEEL GUITAR ROCKS THE IRON CURTAIN

[S]ome of the most important discoveries, both in arts and sciences, have come forward under very unpromising and suspicious appearances.

JAMES MADISON TO CONGRESS, APRIL 20, 1789

As the picks and hammers began chipping into the Berlin Wall in November 1989, "People Got to Be Free" by the Rascals blasted out from nearby boom boxes.[1] The fall of the Wall was primarily the result of eight years' worth of economic and military pressure from President Ronald Reagan, with important moral support from Pope John Paul II and Prime Minister Margaret Thatcher. Yet lost amid the flying cement and cheers of onlookers was the fact that a thoroughly American institution, rock and roll music, which the Beatles had revitalized more than twenty-five years earlier, had made a significant and quite overlooked contribution to defeating communism. When, on November 9, the checkpoints opened and border guards didn't fire on the tens of thousands of East Berliners who stormed the entry points to West Berlin, the beat of a new generation behind the Iron Curtain, largely influenced by American rock, became truly audible for the first time.

Rock and roll perfectly complemented the new freedom in Eastern Europe. It was indeed the music of the people, and occasionally, the voice of protest—completely unsupported by government at any level. Rock originated in the United States, was nourished in the United States, and perfected in the United States, so it is ironic that one of the greatest events in American history came with the arrival of the English "Fab Four," the Beatles, on American soil in February 1964. That a British band would play such a crucial role in the revival of rock—which in turn would be energized, re-Americanized, and spread throughout the world—was one of those ironic twists that makes history perpetually entertaining. Just as Reagan relied on Margaret Thatcher for support, so too the American rockers mixed freely with their English cousins in the revival of rock that ensued. But ultimately it was the American record market, American producers, American audiences, and often American artists who eventually helped pry open the jaws of tyranny enveloping much of the world. In the end, whatever the British or, for that matter, the Czech, Polish, or even Russian underground rockers played or sang, it was more or less "made in the USA."

In the mid-1960s, antiwar radicals, some of them seeking a revolution that would overthrow Western capitalist society, latched on to rock icons, hoping they would provide the attractive and popular front men (and women) necessary to reel in the youth. They were disappointed. Bob Dylan, the Beatles, Mick Jagger—all sooner or later let down the leaders who sought social upheaval by refusing to become the standard bearers of their cause. Ironically, then, two decades later rock as a musical form and cultural movement would contribute mightily to eroding the foundations of the Communist system that so many of the true radicals loved.

The paradox is that rock and roll by its nature is both entertainment and social criticism, revolutionary yet extremely sympathetic to the very liberties that infuse the American capitalist and political system. Artists who complained about "the man" and sang of "takin' it to the streets" enthusiastically took—and mostly kept—large checks for their performances. One has to look no further than the concerns musicians express over music pirating; most artists had starved to get where they were, but after meeting with some success, quickly adopted the clichéd rock-star lifestyle of indulgence and luxury. At the very moment Doors singer Jim Morrison waxed romantic about "revolting against authority," he was tooling around Los Angeles in the "Blue Lady," a Shelby GT 500 (a "terrible and mean machine," as Doors keyboardist Ray Manzarek labeled it). Shelbys weren't cheap—about the price of a fully tricked-out top-of-the-line Corvette![2] Guitarist Jim McCarty, of "Devil with a Blue Dress On" fame, rolled his eyes when he recalled the fascination of Cactus bandmates Tim Bogert and Carmine Appice (formerly in Vanilla Fudge) with their Panteras.

Commentators from the Left later attempted to redefine reality, trying to claim that some of the rockers' actions complemented their own ideology. When the Beatles formed Apple Records, one writer insisted it represented "the worker seizing control of the means of production."[3] The reality that Paul McCartney deeply resented England's high tax laws and found a way around them by forming a label in the United States seemed lost on such writers. When McCartney described Apple as a "kind of Western communism," he was talking a good Karl Marx but his actions were 100 percent Adam Smith: Apple launched a blizzard of new products and divisions—books, electronics, clothing, films—all at a profit.[4] Rock's revolutionary character came from the quite capitalistic spirit of creativity itself, a point leftist interpreters frequently missed. While rock may have "fought the system," it fought *every* system! The same undefined craving for freedom that infused American musicians' call for civil rights for blacks lay behind the East Bloc artists' battle for their own civil rights against much more repressive regimes. And where some rockers could croon—or scream—about love, peace, and brotherhood, it often failed to line up with their personal lives. Pete Townshend of the Who even smacked Yippie leader Abbie Hoffman on the head with his guitar for interrupting the Who's set at Woodstock.[5]

Like jazz and country and western before it (both also 100 percent American music forms), what made rock revolutionary when it arrived on the scene in the 1950s was not its lyrics or political preaching but rather its essential liberating form. All three styles shared a common thread of liberty, in which the band starts together, then after a few verses or choruses, introduces soloists, followed by a reunion at the end. This musical genre symbolized the nation's essence like no other music forms, in that it reflected both the communal and the individualistic nature of American society. But by

1960, American rock had begun to lose its dynamism, having drifted away from the revolutionary sounds and moves of Elvis Presley to sappy love songs and appearances in B-level movies, such as *King Creole* and *Flaming Star*.

The Beatles transformed American rock from nonthreatening, simplistic, feel-good tunes popular in the 1950s into a sophisticated (and rebellious) medium, returning it to its roots. They were aided in that transformation by a radical new instrument, Leo Fender's new electric guitar with its distinct sound tailored perfectly for rock and roll. Soon the Gibson company's Les Paul, with its more "bluesy" sound, joined with Fender's to create a recipe for a cultural explosion: a radical new instrument with a new sound mixed with several streams of music—much of it (country, folk, R&B, and rock) rebellious in nature—together energizing the largest generation of prepubescent Americans in history.

These trends collided with a fourth development: a radical turnover in talent from the original rock and rollers. Already, however, Buddy Holly, Ritchie Valens, and J. P. Richardson (aka the Big Bopper) were dead; Jerry Lee Lewis had become a pariah due to his scandalous marriage to his thirteen-year-old cousin; and Little Richard had been born again, playing only gospel music between 1957 and 1963. Carl Perkins's "Blue Suede Shoes" was already considered an "oldie," and had increasingly come to be identified with a new subvariant of rock called "rockabilly." On top of that, Perkins was three years older than Presley, four years older than Roy Orbison, and almost a decade older than up-and-comers such as Gene Pitney and Ricky Nelson. In teen years, like dog years, that made Perkins ancient. And the King? Elvis's "rock star" was waning. He was increasingly absorbed with making movies, and most of his songs came as tie-ins to his films. Though "Jailhouse Rock" became a classic, more often the material proved second-rate and forgettable.[6] Both Bing Crosby and Frank Sinatra, big crooners of the forties and fifties, had transitioned from music to Hollywood, though Sinatra still occasionally ducked into a studio and emerged with a new "easy listening" hit. Elvis, on the other hand, slipped into an artistic funk for years.

On the eve of the Beatles' arrival in the United States, then, American music featured a top 40 of such forgettable songs as "18 Yellow Roses" (Bobby Darin), "Abilene" (George Hamilton IV), "500 Miles Away from Home" (Bobby Bare), "Baby Workout" (Jackie Wilson), and "The Bounce" (The Olympics). The longest-lasting hits were Peter, Paul, and Mary's cover of "Blowin' in the Wind" by Bob Dylan—a folk song; "Blue Velvet" by Bobby Vinton; and "Be My Baby" by the Ronettes. The number one song of the year was the lightweight "Dominique" by the Singing Nun. In short, by 1964, American "rock" had disintegrated into a bland, non-threatening, marshmallow-gray medium.

Even before they set foot in America, the Beatles had begun to shake up rock and roll. After honing their talents in Hamburg, the Silver Beatles— consisting then of John Lennon, Paul McCartney, George Harrison, Stuart Sutcliffe, and Pete Best—returned to Liverpool where the band had formed. There, Sutcliffe left the band and, while playing a gig at the Cavern, the group replaced Best with Richard Starkey (aka Ringo Starr). The renamed "Beatles" had not only brought in a new drummer, but had incorporated a heavy dose of R&B, particularly Sam Cooke and Ray Charles, into their act—something the American surf groups were slow to do. This would provide the key infusion that had begun in the United States with Presley, Little Richard, Chuck Berry, and Buddy Holly, in which R&B would be given a "white" makeover for mainstream Caucasian audiences. Under the careful guidance of their manager, Brian Epstein, the Beatles donned fashionable suits, submitted to bowl-type haircuts, and, most important, smiled a lot. In England, that look made them conservative and acceptable; in America, it gave them the aura of youthful rebelliousness. Either way, the image (along with the music) sold.

The Beatles also arrived at a critical point in American social history, although the sixties weren't as radical, nor the fifties as dull, as previously thought. Historians have assumed that because little outward evidence of nonconformity and rebellion were on display in the 1950s, American society was somnambulant, even catatonic. According to this interpretation, it took the radical sixties to shake the United States out of its stupor and confront the "real issues" of women's rights, race, sex, and individuality. Pointing to the sameness of new businesses in the 1950s such as McDonald's and Holiday Inn, critics argued that their similarities reflected a dull, cookie-cutter world. Nothing could be further from the truth. The revolution had begun shortly after World War II when, using pent-up savings and constrained desires, Americans unleashed their consumptive fury on retailing, travel, and above all, auto purchases.[7] A car culture transformed the United States into a new nation of transportation liberty; one in which average people were no longer confined geographically for work or play; one in which (unlike the steamboat, railroad, or even stagecoach), *individuals* could control their own time and simultaneously make a statement about themselves through the style and model of auto they chose.

Confronted with a Red menace and an atomic threat abroad, as well as the growing challenge of racial tensions at home, Americans well understood what serious problems they faced. What historians have viewed as sameness and uniformity was superficial—a calm layer concealing turmoil beneath it. With the mobility of the automobile people moved to new surroundings, tried different foods, and mingled with ethnic groups and dialects they had never seen before. This rapid exposure to the new served to make those things that were familiar all the more desirable, even necessary. It was this search for the familiar that inspired Ray Kroc to create what was to become the first true fast-food restaurant chain, McDonald's, in 1955. Kroc made every McDonald's the same in its appearance, food delivery, and approach. For families traveling cross-country, relying on greasy spoon diners, the constancy and reliability of McDonald's was heaven-sent. The same was true for Kemmons Wilson, whose Holiday Inns offered standardized hotel rooms at a reasonable price for travelers previously at the mercy of local roadside inns. Even the most famous theme park in the country, Walt Disney's Disneyland, emphasized these standard, traditional themes with its "Main Street."[8]

Music, too, felt the tensions brought on by a mobile society. With people moving all over the country, the demand for familiar music led to the national market for a "top 40" of songs that Alabamians relocated to California or Iowans vacationing in Florida could recognize. Berry Gordy fit perfectly into this mass national music market. Having started Motown Records in the early 1960s with the intention of reaching the larger white audience, Gordy polished rhythm and blues acts by dressing them in tuxedos and evening gowns, grooming the artists with elocution lessons and interview skills, and introducing what has become classic Motown choreography. By the end of the decade, Motown songs constantly made the top ten hits, and Gordy became one of the wealthiest African Americans in the USA. More important, white kids in Phoenix were just as likely as black kids in Detroit to listen to the Four Tops, and Minnesotans were as likely as Mississippians to sing "Baby, baby, where did our love go?"

Having already brought R&B standards into their act, the Beatles more than any American rock group were superbly poised to reach the largest possible audience. Possessing a new sound and new (and, for Americans, unusual) clothing styles, the group also benefited from the timely introduction of 33 rpm records, known as LPs (for "long play"), which had made up a smaller part of the market until 1963. The Beatles' *Please Please Me* album (later released in the United States as *Introducing the Beatles* on Vee-Jay Records) was among the pioneering LPs introduced. As music historian Jonathan Gould observed, "LPs were the first records to be sold in foot-square cardboard jackets faced with glossy cover art, which served as an alluring advertisement for the music within . . . [allowing the cover to become] a companion piece to the listening experience: a contemplative object that functioned like a fan magazine," putting a face to the voices on the album.[9]

While those forces converged, John Lennon and Paul McCartney, in the summer of 1963, penned what would become the Beatles' signature song, "She Loves You." From the crash of Ringo's tom-tom roll to the harmonic, energetic refrain of "yeah, yeah, yeah," "She Loves You" constituted the apex of the Holland-Dozier-Holland "hook," which allowed people who only heard the song one time to be able to sing along the next time. Eschewing any instrumental intro at all, and bursting straight into the chorus, the song captured all elements of the Fab Four's sound: a unique blend of the Lennon/McCartney/Harrison voices (which have proven difficult to replicate by almost any group) driven with the powerful Starr/McCartney/Lennon rhythm section. This was "it": the Beatles had succeeded in combining the smooth melodies of Elvis, Orbison, Pitney, and Nelson with the hard-charging guitar of Chuck Berry, topped off with the energy of Jerry Lee Lewis and Little Richard. Black, white, soft, cool, suave, rough—the Beatles had it all. Dubbing the phenomenon "Beatlemania," the British press paved the way for the arrival of the Fab Four on American shores.

It didn't hurt that the Beatles had already grafted Motown onto their act: on their second album, *With the Beatles*, Lennon sang Gordy's 1959 song "Money (That's What I Want)" and the Smokey Robinson hit "You Really Got a Hold on Me" as well as the Marvelettes' "Please Mister Postman." This led Black Panther Eldridge Cleaver to boast that they were "injecting Negritude by the ton into the whites. . . . soul by proxy," even as other radical blacks such as LeRoi Jones (Amiri Baraka) complained that the Beatles were "stealing music . . . stealing lives."[10] Either way, when the Beatles were booked on the Ed Sullivan Show on February 9, 1964, it was in many ways a homecoming for a moribund American rock music industry, and in other ways, a revival. More than 70 million viewers tuned in to watch, including Rev. Billy Graham, who broke his rule about never watching television on Sunday to see the moptops. "They've got their own groups," mused McCartney. "What are we going to give them that they don't already have?"[11] In reality the Beatles were giving back rock and roll to the nation that invented it, reminding Americans of who they were.[12]

Britain had another gift for America, though it arrived too late to keep the Beatles touring. In late 1965, Jim Marshall and his son, Terry, were selling Fender amps and other musical equipment from their store in London. Rock legends such as Pete Townshend and Ritchie Blackmore frequented the shop and complained that Marshall needed more guitar equipment, whereupon Jim began modifying the Fender amps in his store by adding larger speakers and more power. Townshend was impressed, but hardly satisfied, with the first iteration of the "Bluesbreaker" amp, named for British blues legend John Mayall and the Bluesbreakers. Mayall's band featured a young guitarist named Eric Clapton, who first used the Marshall sound on the group's *Beano* album. Already, however, Townshend was pushing Marshall for more power. By 1966, further modifications impressed an American guitarist residing in London, Jimi Hendrix, who so loved the Marshall sound that he offered to buy two of the amplifiers immediately. (Someone had already discovered that two of the Marshall speakers could be linked to a single power head, yielding the famous Marshall "stack" that would become a common feature on stage.)

Americans responded immediately to this brave new electrified world. Bob Dylan was booed offstage when he first went electric at the 1965 Newport Folk Festival. "People were horrified," said Peter Yarrow of Peter, Paul, and Mary. "It was as if it was a capitulation to the enemy—as if all of a sudden you saw Martin Luther King, Jr., doing a cigarette ad."[13] "Where's Ringo," some shouted from the audience. Nevertheless, Dylan's 1965 song "Like a Rolling Stone" changed the genre forever, moving radio songs from 2.5-minute cookie-cutter molds to a stunning six minutes of nasally, whiney, angst-ridden depth that once and for all merged folk and rock. With the door opened, English bands swarmed into America by the dozens in the famed "British invasion." The Kinks, the Dave Clark Five, Herman's Hermits, the Rolling Stones, and others arrived either physically or on vinyl. Ray Manzarek of the Doors called the invasion an "irresistible force" and "a juggernaut," adding, "we were all in awe of their success, if not their musical accomplishments."

Immediately American musicians "saw the headlines" about the Beatles and the other groups and "drooled. . . . My mind did a cartwheel at the possibilities," Manzarek wrote.[14] The "invasion" sparked immediate American responses. One of the first was the Byrds covering a Dylan song, "Mr. Tambourine Man," and a soulful New York group, the Young Rascals, turning out hits like "I Ain't Gonna Eat Out My Heart Anymore" and "Good Lovin'." The bubble-gum, feel-good music was ever-present on the *Billboard* top 40 hits of 1965 ("Can't You Hear My Heartbeat" by Herman's Hermits, "Game of Love" by Wayne Fontana and The Mindbenders, and "This Diamond Ring," by Gary Lewis & the Playboys) along with a heavy influence of Motown ("My Girl," by the Temptations, "I Can't Help Myself [Sugar Pie Honey Bunch]," by the Four Tops, and "Stop! In the Name of Love," by the Supremes).

There is no question that the most radical directions of the Beatles' musical careers were still ahead of them with *Revolver*, the White Album, *Sgt. Pepper's Lonely Hearts Club Band*, and *Abbey Road*, or that their musical genius did much to define rock during the ensuing six years. However, they were also drifting into the drug culture that had in many ways already swirled past them. Long before the flower children of San Francisco began toking, before Hunter S. Thompson went "gonzo," and before Timothy Leary urged his disciples to "tune in, turn on, and drop out," English author Aldous Huxley dabbled in psychedelic drugs (in his case, mescaline).[15] Imbibing in only low doses, Huxley tried LSD (lysergic acid diethylamide), also nicknamed "acid." But Huxley had a "good trip," and pronounced such drugs harmless and even useful, in that they could turn anything ordinary into something of universal import—oatmeal became the substance of the cosmos, bird droppings were Hindu death-wheels. As Huxley described acid's power, "Eternity in a flower. Infinity in four chair legs, and the Absolute in the fold of a pair of flannel trousers!"[16] Or, more realistically, madness in a chemical flake the size of a booger—but no one at the time was concerned with the evil effects of mind alteration when saving Western consciousness was at stake.

The Beatles had made drug use acceptable for the middle class, being the first celebrities to make reference to drug use in their lyrics and public comments. Most of them dropped acid in 1966. Four years later, John Lennon spoke of his first trip: "I did some drawings at the time. . . . I've got them somewhere—of four faces saying, 'We all agree with you.'"[17] Lennon and George Harrison, especially, saw the expressive power of drugs, but for different reasons. The mystically attuned Harrison sought nirvana; Lennon sought only himself, seeking to reach a sort of genuine autobiographical plane. "I was suddenly struck by great visions when I first took acid," he recalled, labeling the view he had from the other worlds "real life in cinemascope."[18]

It was also noteworthy that at the very time the Beatles discovered drugs they also began to discover taxes, or the impoverishing effects of them. On the *Revolver* album (1966), George Harrison first discovered "even though we had started earning money, we were actually giving most of it away in taxes. It was and still is typical."[19] His song "Taxman" constituted the group's first real foray into political criticism. Over the next decade, numerous English rockers would relocate to France, Switzerland, or the United States to escape Britain's high tax rates, even while continuing to champion "social justice" and welfare programs they claimed to favor.

"Taxman" wouldn't be the last political statement the Beatles made, with the White Album of 1968 featuring one of the most famous calls to revolution ever, aptly named "Revolution." A John Lennon–written song, "Revolution" was recorded in two versions on the album—one "straight" for top 40 radio, and one psychedelic, indulging every electronic gimmick Lennon and George Martin could throw in. "Revolution" asked, "You say you want a revolution/ Well, you know/ We all want to change the world," then warned "But if you go carrying pictures of Chairman Mao, you ain't going to make it with anyone anyhow." In two lines, Lennon distanced himself from both the "Establishment" and the icons of the counterculture, the Communists.[20]

Every artist now had a new, "invisible" partner in production, the recording studio. Increasingly, albums such as the Beach Boys' *Pet Sounds* and the Beatles' *Sgt. Pepper* demonstrated the production capabilities suddenly available to artists as the technologies spread like wildfire. Jimi Hendrix capitalized on the sounds in his 1967 album *Axis: Bold as Love*, then, less than a year later, followed up with one of the greatest albums of all time, *Electric Ladyland*, which in sheer mastery of the knobs surpassed anything the Beatles had done, only to be matched by Cream's *Disraeli Gears*, which combined psychedelic-fantasy lyrics ("tiny purple fishes run laughing through her fingers," how their "naked ears were tortured by the sirens sweetly singing") with Eric Clapton's innovative guitar wah-wah pedals.

At the same time, the San Francisco sound, led by groups such as Jefferson Airplane, and shortly thereafter, Moby Grape, brought a completely different approach to the psychedelic music scene. *Surrealistic Pillow*, released in 1967 during the "summer of love," featured equally bizarre lyrics ("one pill makes you larger, and one pill makes you small") mixed with a new approach to studio musicianship that called for elevating rawness and energy over precision and accuracy. Guitars were occasionally out of tune, vocalists went flat and sharp, with lead singer Grace Slick trailing off whenever she couldn't sustain a note, but it was all fresh and innovative. Indeed, it was precisely what musicians on drugs would be playing! Like many other rockers, however, the Airplane admitted "we didn't give a shit about politics. . . . We wanted the freedom to make our own choices."[21] In 1968, Bob Dylan stunned an interviewer who had derided him about one of his prowar friends when he said, "People just have their views. . . . Anyway, how do you know I'm not, as you say, *for* the war?"[22] Brian Wilson of the Beach Boys observed, "You can always write about social issues but who gives a damn. I want to write about something these kids feel is their whole world."[23]

Indeed, while somewhat left in their leanings, few of the top musicians allowed themselves to be drawn into the maelstrom of radical politics. Hendrix, in particular, refused to be pigeonholed as an anti-American political voice. After being arrested for riding in stolen cars, he was given a choice of jail or the army, and he enlisted in May 1961, completed boot camp, and was assigned to the 101st Airborne at Fort Campbell, Kentucky. His friends and officers remembered him as a poor soldier, who habitually missed bed checks and thought about little except playing a guitar.[24] He later reminisced about his parachute training ("once you get out there everything is so quiet, all you hear is breezes") and told Dick Cavett only that he had been stationed at Fort Campbell. But on other occasions his comments were mixed. In 1962, he took pride in being in the 101st, saying "I'm in the best division: the 101st Airborne. That's the sharpest outfit in the world."[25] He met Billy Cox, who would be his bass player in Band of Gypsys, at the post recreation center, and the two formed a band called the King Casuals.[26] In interviews with *Melody Maker* magazine, where he mentioned his military experience, he claimed to dislike the army. Yet in 1969, the same year, in his second *Melody Maker* interview, Hendrix was pressed by European reporters to comment on the Vietnam War, and he shocked them by comparing Vietnam to D-Day: "Did you send the Americans away when they landed in Normandy? . . . No, but then that was concerning your own skin. The Americans are fighting in Vietnam for the complete free world. . . ."[27] In 1969, when asked about racial issues in the United States, Hendrix insisted, "Music is stronger than politics. I feel sorry for the minorities, but I don't feel part of one."[28]

Despite conservatives labeling them as such, rockers were not inherently anti-American. In fact, many American musicians framed their protest as a call to return the nation to its "roots," not lurch toward communism. Some were overtly patriotic. Brian Wilson's lyricist on "Heroes and Villains," Van Dyke Parks, had a brother in the State Department who died while on assignment in West Germany. Parks recalled, "I was dead set on centering my life on the patriotic Ideal. I was a son of the American revolution. . . ."[29] In retrospective mythology, rock became the "voice" of a protest generation. But the reality was somewhat different. Rare Earth singer and drummer Peter Rivera recalled, "We didn't get into politics."[30] One of the band's hits, "Hey, Big Brother" (1971), featured lyrics laced with antigovernment paranoia ("Take a closer look at the people . . . and notice the fear in their eye"), but as Rivera noted, the band just took songs that sounded good. "We were criticized for not having political views," he pointed out, "for not leading a crusade. But we were just a good-time band."[31] Leftist writer Peter Doggett complained that although rockers dabbled in revolution, and briefly spouted incendiary rhetoric, in short order they "plunged into rampant egotism, self-enlightenment, drug abuse, religious cults, Hollywood celebrity status, anything that would protect their fame and leave them free of political responsibility."[32] Doggett's leftist perspective led him to conclude that "revolutionary rock . . . and its idealistic ideology . . . was compromised and sold in the very instant it was made" by the villains in the "music business." This allowed rock stars to "pose as radicals, and radicals as rock stars, compromising their idealism but feeding off each other's cultural power."[33] While it's an appealing interpretation, it fails, time and again—as Doggett's own examples show—not because rock was taken over or compromised by the evil music industry, but because rock and roll's own revolutionary impetus toward freedom could never cohabit with the radical leftist inclination toward unlimited state power for very long.

When rock musicians actually interacted with leftist extremists in person, worlds collided and Marxism received a quick body blow. Al Kooper, founder of Blood, Sweat & Tears, had volunteered to form a band for Abbie Hoffman's Chicago protests in 1968. He left a classic Fender guitar in a dressing room and it was stolen, whereupon Kooper confronted Hoffman: "Hey, my f——ing guitar got ripped off. What are you going to do about it?" Hoffman replied, "Nothing. F——k you. So what, if your guitar was ripped off?" Kooper noted, "That was the sum total of my political career. . . . I never did another benefit like that."[34] Similar reality descended on a plethora of rockers who quickly distanced themselves from Hoffmanesque violence and rhetoric. Mick Jagger, no supporter of the Vietnam War, scoffed at the demonstrators in Grosvenor Square. "For what?" he asked. "There is no alternative society. . . . You can have a left-wing revolution . . . but they're just the same."[35] A few, such as protest regulars Country Joe and the Fish, regurgitated the most radical punch-lines ("We're in a revolution right now," he said in Chicago, "a lot of people are going to get hurt"), but Mick Jagger put things in better perspective: "It's stupid to think that you can start a revolution with a record."[36]

Many musicians paid a heavy price among the critics for their lack of enthusiasm for anti-American and anticapitalist movements. *Ramparts* critic Michael Lydon whined that the Jefferson Airplane exuded "Theatricality [with] Harmless words and grand gestures rather than truly radical action," Jagger was derided by the anarchist magazine *Black Dwarf* as a "home counties Tory," poet Adrian Mitchell said of the Beatles, "Many people hope that their courage increases," and *Village Voice* reviewer Robert Christgau lamented that the moptops' lukewarm response to revolution has taken "much of the pleasure out of their music for me."[37]

When it came to the Vietnam War, music in general lagged rather than led as a medium of social protest. One study of antiwar music came to the surprising conclusion that the music industry did not produce any top antiwar songs until mid-1969, when public opinion polls had shifted decidedly against the war. John Lennon's "Give Peace a Chance," recorded in June 1969, and Creedence Clearwater Revival's "Fortunate Son," recorded three months later (about David Eisenhower's status in the Navy Reserve), were among the first true rock criticisms of the Vietnam War.

Rather than leading an antiwar parade, musicians were in the rear. As late as 1965, the number one song in the country was "The Ballad of the Green Berets" by Staff Sergeant Barry Sadler.[38]

Specifically when it came to the subject of the Vietnam War, "rock music and its musicians were noticeably silent."[39] Antiwar songs made up less than 1.5 percent of the one thousand singles on the top 100 chart from 1965 through 1974.[40] Even one of the anthems of the protest movement, Buffalo Springfield front man Stephen Stills's "For What It's Worth," was about a local crackdown on Sunset Boulevard, not the war. Nevertheless, early on, pundits from both Left and Right credited music with shaping public opinion about the war. David Noebel, in *Rhythm, Riots, and Revolution,* claimed that pro-Communist musicians sparked the antiwar movement, and Jerome Rodnitzky, while dismissing the specific impact on the war, nevertheless praised Noebel's perceptions about "the persuasive power of the musical idiom."[41] Another study of teens and the importance of lyrics showed that only a quarter of all listeners liked a song primarily because of its lyrics.[42] Even one of the earliest and most famous antimilitary songs, Barry McGuire's "Eve of Destruction"—which warned that nationalism and religious hatred would soon destroy the world—was misunderstood by over 40 percent of listeners.[43] The oft-misunderstood fact is that rock was *revolutionary* in how it changed emotions and attitudes, but not nearly as *political* as many fondly remembered.[44] Or, as Doggett complained, "pop music, in the revolutionary sense, was a non-starter, a fake revolt."[45]

Barry Friedman, a publicist commenting on the career of Buffalo Springfield, noted the cynicism and materialism behind the protest façade: "I was believing all this peace and love shit. [Unfortunately] they were young guys who wanted immediate success. Promise them a Maserati, they'll follow you anywhere."[46] The name of the game was to be "authentic," and with authenticity as a social critic came the insulation from the critics necessary to have a top-40 hit. Jon Landau, one of Bruce Springsteen's advisers, pushed him to "acquire a more explicitly political and social voice."[47] Put another way, if an artist wasn't inherently Left, sufficiently activist, and socially aware, he could practice the tune until it came naturally. Authenticity cut both ways, though. Lennon once noted "there's a lot of uptight maniacs going around wearing f__king peace symbols."[48]

Whatever their political views, artists did not cotton to activists commandeering their stage. Abbie Hoffman's attempted political diatribe at Woodstock was not the first time radicals attempted to seize the stage from the musicians. At a 1968 Mothers of Invention concert in West Berlin, students tried to harangue Frank Zappa into leading a march on NATO headquarters, only to be told by the iconoclastic rocker, "You have bad mental health." When one student leaped on stage during the concert to deliver an address, Zappa instructed the keyboard player to run the organ through a fuzztone and lean on the keys—"that's an ugly f—ing sound," he noted.[49] Nor did radicals like it when their heroes seemed too comfortable with their capitalist surroundings: the radical MC5 sparked a riot in 1969 when fans saw them getting out of a plush limousine.

The most important point to note is that rock (and country music, too, which proliferated its own brand of revolution) was spontaneously generated, without a whit of government support! Indeed, to the extent that rock is, and has always been, "countercultural," it has been so precisely because it has not been beholden to government in any way. The fact that America's greatest contributions to music—jazz, rock, country and western, blues—were all entirely homegrown, private-sector phenomena should give pause to any liberal who wants to support the arts by soaking taxpayers through government funding.

Supposedly the 1969 Woodstock Music and Art Fair would kick off a new "Age of Aquarius." The event was touted as "a new stage in the psychic evolution of the world, a mass celebration of what the 1960s was all about," wrote one left-wing critic, David Dalton of *Gadfly* magazine.[50] But Woodstsock was much different in reality from the sanitized film version. Moochers and freeloaders broke down the chain-link fences and scrambled inside by the thousands for a free concert, turning the festival into "an undeclared disaster area, beset by the shortages of food, water, shelter, and sanitation commonly associated with floods and earthquakes."[51] Woodstock concluded with Jimi Hendrix playing "The Star-Spangled Banner" as masses of zonked-out kids lay in mud and filth. It was a symbolic scene in so many ways. Only a year after the curtain came down, Hendrix would die from a self-induced drug overdose. (He would be joined by Janis Joplin, who also performed at Woodstock, a month later, and Jim Morrison the following year.)

Even as Hendrix's "truly apocalyptic" rendition of the national anthem blasted over a "battlefield, [with] zombies crawling over a field littered with paper cups, plastic wrappers, and half-eaten food, gnawing on corn husks, slobbering over ketchup- and mustard-smeared half-eaten hot dog rolls, sprinkled with ants," the loose bond of political revolution and rock had already permanently unraveled.[52] Reporter and Hoffman confidante Ellen Sander discovered this when she found herself caught up in the music and ignoring the revolution. She wrote Hoffman a few days later, chiding him for being so "enraptured with the vision of yourself as the latter-day Che . . . that you'll make anything and anyone your enemy. . . . [The] age of politics is over," she advised. "Get it on, dance to the music. . . . Everyone else loved it at Woodstock. The only unhappy people there were the political crazies."[53] None other than Joan Baez, the queen diva of protest songs, delivered a pragmatic assessment of the event: "it wasn't any f__king revolution. It was a three-day period during which people were decent to each other because . . . if they weren't, they'd all go hungry."[54] *Woodstock* (the film) captured a stoned Stephen Stills admiring the tenacity of the crowd: "You people have got to be the strongest people I ever saw. Three days, man, three days." In moments, however, Stills leaped onto a waiting helicopter to hoist him back to a luxury hotel, a detail not overlooked by Hoffman, who sneered, "There's no morality here. . . . The helicopters bring in champagne for Janis Joplin's band, and people are sick in the field. . . ."[55]

Instead of sparking a revolution, Woodstock constituted the petering-out of a movement. Over the next few years, critic Peter Doggett complained, artists "swapped their revolutionary idealism for self-obsession."[56] An election night party in 1972, the year Richard Nixon crushed George McGovern, displayed the utter collapse of the music/revolution nexus when Jerry Rubin, Abbie Hoffman, Allen Ginsberg, and John Lennon alternately wept, screamed at each other, and "sprawled helplessly on the floor," culminating in Lennon's tirade about "middle-class Jews" and drunkenly bellowing "Up the revolution."[57] Having previously been suspected of being a CIA plant himself, Lennon now viewed Rubin as working for the Agency! Dejectedly, Doggett described the guests as slipping away, embarrassed to be around the "midwife of the revolution, [who] had mutated into its decomposing corpse."[58] As if to heap dung onto the ashes, the year's top song was the bland "The First Time Ever I Saw Your Face" by Roberta Flack, and the top ten contained such watered-down wonders as Harry Nilsson's "Without You," "Baby, Don't Get Hooked on Me" by Mac Davis, "Alone Again (Naturally)" by Gilbert O'Sullivan, and entries by two Sinatra-era artists, Sammy Davis, Jr. ("The Candy Man"), and Wayne Newton ("Daddy Don't You Walk So Fast"). American heavy rock remained a powerful influence—one of many—but it was temporarily displaced at the top by a new phenomenon, disco. By 1977, when John Travolta took to the cinematic dance floor in his white suit as the Bee Gees sang in falsetto, the message was clear. Forget protesting: "You Should Be Dancing."

And yet the real revolution was still at the door. The Beatles had done their job by revitalizing an *American* institution, rock and roll, which then ricocheted off into a totally unpredicted direction. At the very time American rock was losing some of its revolutionary bite, dividing into numerous substreams, including punk, soul, metal, pop, and so on, the power of Western music had already shot out of the West like alien transmissions from deep space, and it was headed straight for the Iron Curtain. At the same time the samizdat writers were battling for freedom, prodding with their verbal bayonets, rock and roll was using music as a rallying cry. In the form of 45 or 33 rpm vinyl records, Western rock found its way into the hands of Communist youths. When the original records weren't available, young people listened to Western music secondhand, with records "distributed on discarded X-ray plates—plastic photographs of bones imprinted with record grooves."[59]

Following the student-led Hungarian revolt in 1956 over the quashing of pro-freedom reforms, the new government, led by János Kádár, sought to neutralize the simmering revolution by allowing hundreds of Wurlitzer jukeboxes to enter the country. (As a result, Hungarians would come to refer to all jukeboxes as "Wurlitzers.") Budapest became a hotbed of bloc-rock, as did Sopot, Poland, where an aspiring journalist and club owner, Franciszek Walicki, packed his Non-Stop Club with Polish cover bands playing Jerry Lee Lewis, Carl Perkins, and Elvis. He even created the first true Polish rock act in 1958, ultimately named the Reds and the Blacks. A second band he formed, the Blues and the Blacks, featured a singer named Czesław Niemen, who eventually performed in Paris and sang the first Polish rock and roll hit songs. In Romania, officials decried the music, which they said aroused "animal instincts" and developed the youths' "cruelty, contempt, and destructive urges."[60] NATO strategists took notice, observing in the journal *Revue militaire generale* that the obsession with rock and roll took attention away from Marx and Lenin. Elvis's arrival as a new private in Germany terrified the Communists, who saw him as a new weapon in the Cold War.

East Germany cracked down on rock in 1958, mandating that 60 percent of any music performed had to come from the "people's democracies." But when American folk/protest singer Pete Seeger toured the Iron Curtain countries, the Soviets saw an opportunity to enlist an American artist in the revolutionary cause. Seeger made twenty-eight appearances in the USSR, in addition to concert dates in Poland and Czechoslovakia. Yet at his Moscow concert, when Seeger led the audience in the gospel hymns "Michael, Row the Boat Ashore," and "We Shall Overcome," he demonstrated that by its very nature, revolutionary music was always positioned against "the establishment." What did the Soviet listeners have to overcome but communism?

While in the West, "protest" music criticized the democracies, behind the Iron Curtain, the music condemned the Communist governments as "the Man." A clear example of this contrast can be seen in the German Wolf Biermann, who left Hamburg for East Berlin to build a new Communist world, then proceeded to criticize the German Communist state. Biermann ridiculed Stalin—an act that, only a few years before, would have earned him a bullet from the secret police—and even after he was imprisoned, he continued to record songs that bashed the government. By 1965, Party functionaries denounced his music as "toilet-stall poetry" and "pornography."[61] Within the USSR itself, protest songs were gaining popularity. In the 1950s, Russian singer-songwriter Alexander Galich criticized Stalin, even if he did so somewhat subtly.

Then came the Beatles, whose songs, images, and paraphernalia traveled everywhere from Leipzig to Leningrad. Young people sported moptop haircuts and Beatles buttons sent to them by relatives in the West. Indeed, the Fab Four became counterculture role models—young, funny, and full of energy—in stark contrast to the aging gargoyles of the Communist elites. Riots occurred in Czechoslovakia after local Beatles look-alike bands performed. One reporter, horrified, wrote of the fan behavior, "They wriggled, they fell off the platform and crawled back onto it. . . . I expected them to bite each other at any minute."[62]

Instantly, a host of copycat Iron Curtain bands appeared, including the Illes in Hungary, Bundaratsite in Bulgaria, the Red Guitars in Poland, Olympic in Czechoslovakia, and Time Machine (formed when the father of the guitar player smuggled home a copy of *A Hard Day's Night*) in the USSR. Before the "Prague Spring," Czechoslovakia even had a rock music magazine, *Melodie*. The freest of the Soviet bloc countries, Czechoslovakia produced hundreds of bands with names such as Strangers, Buttons, and Hell's Devils—all, of course, registered with the state. But Beatlemania crossed all borders. When the film *A Hard Day's Night* opened in Poland in 1965, many young people skipped school and rushed to the cinemas as the *bitels* conquered Warsaw.[63] Czech schools responded to the absenteeism by offering a six-part series on modern music, which included studies of Elvis and Bill Haley and the Comets. The first Iron Curtain hippies were likely Czechs known as the "little Marys" (*manicky*), but the phenomenon spread throughout the Soviet bloc. One of East Germany's leading musicians, Horst Krüger, completely abandoned classical and jazz to play rock and roll, and when a popular Leipzig band, the Butlers, was forcibly broken up for "damaging art," troops had to use water cannons to disperse protests at the high schools.

At first, the Soviet hierarchy attempted to ridicule the Beatles, describing Ringo Starr as Tarzan and "a monkey" and claiming the band was "already out of date" in 1964.[64] Copycat bands proliferated, including Falcon, Guys, Little Red Devils, and dozens of others. Alexander Gradsky, later called "The Old Man of Moscow Rock," was just fourteen years old when he went "into a state of shock" after hearing the Liverpudlians for the first time. Gradsky went on to form the Slavs with Mikhail Sholokhov, the grandson of the Nobel Prize–winning novelist, and the band became the top rock act in Moscow. Everywhere, rock caused rebellion. Several Western bands played Czechoslovakia and East Germany in 1966, sparking violent scuffles. Hollies singer Graham Nash saw "all this shooting outside the hotel."[65] Authorities halted further tours, and when they canceled a concert in Riga, protesters held a six-hour demonstration with banners proclaiming "Free the Guitars!" In spring 1967, tours resumed, including a Rolling Stones appearance in Warsaw where some fans experienced ticket problems. Irate kids stormed police barriers and provoked the police to respond with tear gas and dogs. Inside the Palace of Culture, where the show took place, the Stones stopped in mid-song when they noticed that the Communist Party elites were sitting in the first rows. Keith Richards grabbed drummer Charlie Watts and said, "Stop playing, Charlie." Pointing to the Party members in the front, he shouted, "You f——ing lot, get out and let those bastards in the back sit down front."[66] Needless to say, the Stones were not invited back to the Soviet bloc.

Rock bands were at the center of the Prague Spring, particularly the Primitives, one of the earliest Soviet-bloc psychedelic bands. As Alexander Dubček liberalized Czech society, the likelihood of intervention by the Soviets grew, culminating in the Warsaw Pact invasion of August 20, 1968. Of course, oppression just fueled the protest singers' fire. Marta Kubišová, the singer for the Golden Kids, penned the anthem of the Czech resistance with her "Prayer for Marta," which was followed by the shocking self-immolation of Czech student and martyr Jan Palach in January 1969. Another leading Czech protest song, by Moravian singer Karel Kryl, was 1969's "Close the Gate, Little Brother," which became so popular that Kryl toured Czechoslovakia performing three concerts a day and selling 125,000 copies of the song despite the fact that he had no manager and no agent.

Dubcek was replaced by Gustáv Husák in 1969, whereupon the Beach Boys and the Tremeloes were invited to the annual festival in Bratislava. After a spectacular ascent, the Beach Boys had drifted far behind the Beatles in their popularity in America, as critics panned them as shallow and unimaginative. Their onetime leader and songwriter, Brian Wilson, battled mental illness and schizophrenia, exacerbated by drugs, and was unable to travel. His bandmates thus looked at the European tour as a means to regain their momentum, and in turn Czechoslovakia welcomed them as a sign of the return of "Spring." In June, in front of a packed house at Lucerna Hall, after knocking out their hits "Sloop John B" and "Barbara Ann," the Beach Boys dedicated the song "Break Away"—about individuality and freedom—to Dubček, who was in the crowd. The tour reinvigorated the Californians, but even if "Spring" hadn't returned, the Communist states quickly realized that the juggernaut called rock and roll could not be ignored.

East Germany, which couldn't control Western radio signals like Radio in the American Sector and Radio Free Europe's show *Compass*, instituted

DT-64, which played rock, as did Hungary's *Csak Fiataloknak* (*For Youth Only*), or the Hungarian "Amateur Hour" show, *Ki Mit Tud* (*Show What You Know*). Western bands continued to arrive, including the Animals, who played six Baltic cities in Poland in 1966, and the Rolling Stones, who played Warsaw in 1967. An East German reviewer warned that these bands were the voice of a "new Fuhrer."[67] When they arrived at the airport, the Stones were greeted by an army of fans and later, at their concert, they found three thousand ticket holders joined by another eight thousand people who wanted in without paying (an example of socialist principles in action, some would say). A fracas broke out, followed by a mob rampage quelled only by riot police. (In the act, one policeman was killed.) Nevertheless, a high-level official promised that "the trumpets of the Beatles are not the trumpets of Jericho which will cause the walls of socialism to come tumbling down."[68]

Hungary, the first Iron Curtain nation to roll up the fence in 1988, was the vanguard of rock liberalization, most notably due to the band Illes. Following the release of *Sgt. Pepper's Lonely Hearts Club Band*, Illes performed its original tunes in Sgt. Pepper–type uniforms. When interviewed in England, the band criticized the Hungarian government, and when it returned home, found its concerts sharply limited. Illes was banned from television appearances, and its new album was prevented from being released. The band reemerged after a year, apparently contrite, and released a new album dedicated to Angela Davis—but this was a façade for reviving the assault on freedom in Hungary through lyrics that challenged the Communists to look in "their own backyard." A song called "If I Were a Rose," referring to the street that had been crushed beneath tank treads during the 1956 uprising, slipped through the censors long enough to be recorded by a leading female singer, only to have the copies confiscated upon release. Another song critical of the Stalinist era, "Europe Is Silent," was not released until 1983, and was not played on state radio for four years after that.

In the Soviet Union, despite a relentless propaganda campaign against Western dress and music, young people continued to favor pop music and "hippie" attire. Pictures of Jagger and Hendrix were pasted over Communist slogans on walls. Nikita Khrushchev could rant all he wanted about how rock sounded like "static" or the sound of a trolley car, but that did not diminish the burgeoning market for Western music in Lenin's heartland. Following Beatlemania, the USSR tried co-opting the new medium to create "state" rock groups and sponsor-approved "variety shows," a kind of Ed Sullivanski. *Melodya*, the state-run publishing house, released some of the Beatles' sheet music, and by the 1970s, the state allowed hits by some Western artists, including Elvis Presley and Tom Jones, to be disseminated throughout the USSR legally. Soviet youth clubs had been established to contain the conflagration, but they hardly worked as planned. By the late 1960s, hundreds of rock bands had appeared in Moscow, including Hairy Glass, Nasty Dogs, Symbol of Faith, Bald Spot, and the Best Years. Perhaps the greatest limitation to the expansion of rock was not direct state interference, but the dearth of guitars and drum sets, most of which were imported. When the first guitar shop opened in Moscow in 1966, the entire stock sold out in minutes.[69] A massive electric underground developed, run by the *fartsovshchiki* ("hustlers"), who hung out around Western tourist sites and cultivated contacts with smugglers. The authorities tolerated concerts, but even then musicians weren't necessarily safe from intrusions by the police. At a Winds of Change concert in the late 1960s, government thugs routinely came on stage to seize instruments. Censors unplugged acts in mid-performance. Bands from the Baltic states (which would lead the resistance to Moscow in the early 1990s) emerged as the leading rockers, in the process eliciting a massive migration to Latvia as the center of Soviet hippiedom. State-sanctioned beatings were administered and heads shorn, yet nothing seemed to quell the rebellion emerging from the guitars. Slowly, Western visitors began to notice the hundreds of *hippi* on Soviet streets. Massive illegal concerts took place in woods and forests; musicians, required to submit lyrics to censors, shrugged them off and performed in bars, clubs, canteens, even dorm rooms without publicity so as to avoid authorities. Bands struggled, not only with police, but with pathetically obsolete equipment making the amplified sounds that emerged even more grating on Soviet ears, accustomed to decibels one-tenth that put out by even primitive amps.

The Curtain came under constant pressure from inside and out. Blood, Sweat & Tears performed in Romania in 1970, greeted by chants from fans of "U-S-A." After that, authorities watched the group's concerts intensely. At another stop, officials turned dogs on the crowd, and afterward, all remaining Blood, Sweat & Tears shows were canceled. In 1977, Czech rockers sparked a riot when a concert was canceled, leading to a rampage of burning, window-smashing, and bottle-pelting of police that would have brought a smile to Jerry Rubin's face (except the cops were commies!).[70] A similar East Berlin concert, intruded upon by police, erupted in a bloody reaction against the cops when the concertgoers "turned on the security forces, beating them, stripping them, and setting their uniforms on fire."[71] Hungarian and Polish punk rockers openly mocked the "fat, bald idols" of state-sanctioned bands. The state brought the Hungarian Coitus Punk Group to trial for referring to Stalinist extermination camps and Soviet nuclear weapons in its songs, and its members were thrown in the slammer for two years.

Ironically, to the west, American groups met with hostility at their European concerts. Frank Zappa recalled, "When we first started to go to Europe in the sixties, there was some of that . . . with all the student activism and all that crap. We had a bunch of riots then. But then it all died down."[72] By the 1980s, however, the Mothers of Invention found it had returned. With "the anti-American sentiment around, it is hard to go on-stage and do what you do with the emotional freight that is attendant to European attitudes toward American foreign policy."[73] So while American rockers paid a price for merely being from the United States—where artists and audiences alike were free to bash the United States—East bloc rockers yearned for that degree of liberty, which indeed came in fits and starts.

Even Poland, under tighter control than Hungary and Czechoslovakia, nevertheless experienced a "punk explosion" in the early 1980s. When the British metal band Iron Maiden began its tour at the Torwar Sports Hall in Warsaw, the crowd unfurled a "SOLIDARITY" banner. Polish punk proved the most abrasive and courageous in East bloc rock, with bands producing songs such as "The Ape Factory" (the equivalent of Pink Floyd's 1979 attack on education, *The Wall*). A Polish band named Locked Ward had its logo, a giant "O" and "Z," displayed as the "Z" scrawled through the "O," a sign of anarchy, while another band renamed itself SS-20 after a Soviet nuclear missile. At a live concert, the Perfect changed its approved lyrics to "Don't be afraid of [Polish dictator Wojciech] Jaruzelski."[74] That little trick got the band banned. It was no use. Other groups instantly filled the void. When Toilet sang, "I am a tank, I am a tank, my only purpose is to destroy," they were not referring to American machinery. And just like the earlier bloody battles between the "mods" and the "rockers" in Britain, street violence between the "punks" and the "poppers" (those who preferred more mainstream rock) swept through Poland. The

Communist government was incapable of picking sides or of stifling the growing social criticism by either group.

But in a closed society, the dynamics for sustained artistic criticism were vastly different from those in the West. Without sponsorship by the state, a band had to face economic reality (whereas in the West, private patrons and fans could usually keep even the least commercially successful genius alive for a while). Some musicians, including Zbigniew Hołdys, the Perfect's bass player, complained that even as bands ranted against the "establishment," the same government they criticized was raking in the cash from the concert halls where these groups performed. (Nevertheless, it was an ironic turn on the not-unfounded gripes of American musicians that they did all the work while the record companies got all the profits.) Over time, Hołdys himself would apologize for antigovernment sentiments expressed in concerts. This, of course, only lent greater credibility to the "genuine" artists who refused to "sell out."

Within the press, articles expressly discussing rock music were mostly banned. However, just as the written samizdat expressed the language of liberty, so too did the *magnitizdat*, a do-it-yourself recording circulated to eager listeners. Not surprisingly, a rock and roll band, the Plastic People of the Universe—who took their inspiration from none other than Frank Zappa—had been at the forefront of the Czech Charter 77 movement in 1978. But getting to that point for the Plastic People reflected the pitfalls of Iron Curtain rockdom and provided an interesting glimpse of what happens to state-sponsored artists. A "state" band had official sanction and received instruments from the government. Certainly the lure was understandable, since state groups were permitted to play concerts and clubs, and, because of their professional status, receive higher (and regular) pay. It came at great cost. Charged with protecting "the red rose of Marxism," bands had to submit their lyrics to censors months before they could record them. One Czech singer battled the bureaucrats for days about his hair length, which, he argued, was necessary to "sell" good Communist music to the proletariat in the West. Renegades gave up official sponsorship for support from local clubs, and even fire brigades, to pay their bills. The Plastic People of the Universe began as a sanctioned band, whose repertoire of saucy Western material cost them their protected status in the fall of 1970. They dropped out and started their own music festivals, which attracted large crowds and police attention.

During a concert in 1976, Plastic People and other musicians were arrested: the band members were given eight- to twelve-month sentences for disturbing the peace, and the government harassed the band and its fans for the remainder of the decade.[75] A similar fate awaited the German musician Klaus Renft Jentzsch, whose band Renft had touched off the Leipzig riot. Jentzsch was summoned before East German officials in September 1975, and they informed him that his group had been declared "no longer existent." When Jentzsch asked if that meant "banned," the commissars said, "you no longer exist."[76] Within a year, two members were in jail, and one had emigrated to the West, but the East German Ministry of Culture quietly established a *Sektion Rockmusik* to try to put a Communist spin on rock by infusing lyrics with solid Leninist phrases.

Wolf Biermann, who had already been banned, slipped bootlegs of his songs to West Germany. Labeling himself East Germany's "officially recognized state enemy," Biermann holed up in his apartment to write. CBS Records managed to sign him, and, more miraculously, found a way to get sound crews inside East Berlin to record him. Here was a die-hard believer in communism forced to hide out in his flat in Communist Germany, while his supposed class enemy, the capitalists, sent its lackeys to tape his songs. Granted a travel visa to perform in Cologne—under the provision that he not sing "Stasi-Lied," an anti–secret police song—Biermann arrogantly told the audience that East Germany was "the better Germany," provoking catcalls, but then proceeded to play "Stasi-Lied." The "Better Germany" was not amused and revoked his citizenship. As Timothy Ryback observed in his history of rock behind the Iron Curtain, "Biermann, a proclaimed Communist, found himself banished to the capitalist West, forcefully exiled from a county that used machine guns and barbed wire to keep millions of citizens from fleeing."[77] The unfortunate Biermann had to make do with a 350,000-mark villa in Hamburg and another half-million marks in record sales, even as East German police were turning the dogs anew on concertgoers at Alexanderplatz. But his exit sparked an exodus of high-profile entertainers, who demanded to leave. The East German government accommodated them rather than allow them to dissent at home.

Of course, that failed as well. Large-scale rock riots broke out in East Berlin in June 1987, following a concert across the Wall by Phil Collins, David Bowie, and the Eurythmics that featured massive loudspeakers aimed eastward. When security forces tried to disperse the thousands pressed against the Wall on the eastern side to listen, violence erupted. If you can't beat 'em, join 'em, the Communists concluded, and in June 1988 when Pink Floyd and Michael Jackson were scheduled on the western side, the East Berlin government slated Bryan Adams, the Wailers, and Big Country, enlisting figure skater Katarina Witt as the moderator. Pink Floyd's concert was uneventful in East Berlin, but the restrictions evident in the East led *Le Monde* to sum up the dueling concerts with an editorial about liberty called "East Berlin Loses the Rock War."[78]

The surrender documents were all but drawn up when the Communists invited Bruce Springsteen to perform in front of 160,000 people. While the German propagandists had actually read Springsteen's lyrics and knew about his signature antiwar song, "Born in the USA" (he "uncompromisingly points out the inequity and injustices in his country," noted *Neues Deutschland* approvingly), the thousands of young people did not get the memo. Here were the flowers of communism, waving American flags, raising their clenched fists, and singing along, "*Born . . .* in the USA! I was . . . *born* in the USA" as though they really *wished* they had been born in America!

Soviet attempts to control rock by co-opting it through state-approved VIAs ("Vocal Instrumental Ensembles") were hardly any more successful than the Hungarian, German, or Czech variants. Offered generous financial support, the VIAs tugged at the underground, and while they muffled the protest of rock a little bit, they also spread the music into the factories and towns. But for every officially sanctioned VIA, "a thousand amateur rock-and-roll outfits hammered out covers of the latest Western hits," with estimates putting the number of nonsanctioned bands at 100,000.[79] One such group, Tsvety ("Flowers"), managed to conduct national tours without caving in to state VIA requirements. Led by Anastas Mikoyan (who later took the name "Stas Namin"), Tsvety broke the Moscow ice. Then *Mashina vremeni* ("Time Machine") jumped in, blending a Soviet style with Led Zeppelin and Deep Purple sounds. Initially employing lyrics with double entendre, the band soon moved to outright scorching social criticism. "Battle with Fools," for example, proclaimed that if one killed all the fools in Soviet society, no one would remain. The songs immediately spread throughout Soviet youth courtesy of the black market. Unable to defeat Time Machine, Soviet authorities finally made the group a state-authorized band.

Artemy Troitsky, the Soviet equivalent of Cleveland disc jockey Alan Freed, promoted what, by Western standards, would be decidedly unhip concerts in the 1970s, including a flute/cello band called Aquarium, whose influences included Bob Dylan and Jim Morrison. However, it wasn't long before the guitarist at a 1979 Aquarium concert began rubbing his Fender Telecaster guitar against the microphone stand before lying on stage. An official watcher group, a "judging committee," was dumbstruck, and left in protest. "We bear no responsibility for the performance of such hooligans," snorted one of the judges.[80] The lead guitarist, Boris Grebenshikov, later to emerge as the "Soviet Union's premier rock star," spent countless hours reading Tolkien and Western music magazines and was described by Troitsky as "a fairly self-indulgent but democratic guru."[81] He would later disavow much influence from groups such as the Beatles (although most Russian bands borrowed heavily from the Liverpudlians, adding a distinct Russian bard element). Grebenshikov was well familiar with darker bands such as R.E.M., and spoke in religious overtones about music, likening it to "a middle person between God and people . . . a musician should be . . . an intermediary between God and people."[82] Having already made an enemy of the Pope, communism was now aligned against both God and rock and roll.

As if to confirm his prophecy, the most popular musical event of the early 1970s was *Jesus Christ Superstar*, the Tim Rice musical. In 1971, a complete English-language performance of the opera was staged in Vilnius, Lithuania's major municipality—even before it opened in London. Subsequently, virtually every rock event in the USSR began to include some tip of the hat to the musical. By the end of the 1970s, the nightly news program *Vremya* used the theme song as its introduction! God and rock and roll had proved to be the combination that would ultimately destroy communism. But Troitsky and others gave it a push. Troitsky wrote a key 1975 story published for the Soviet youth journal about British rockers Deep Purple, fully aware that "Russian rock . . . was a power tool of subversion and resistance. . . ."[83] Iron Curtain ears were more attuned to British rock, finding American black rhythms, up to that point, unappealing. But where American music had the black-white tension, Soviet rock and roll touched on equally dangerous (and rebellious) themes: betrayal, alienation, drugs, alcohol, and teen loneliness. The government repeatedly promoted Troitsky, whose ideas gained currency.

At the same time—long before Mikhail Gorbachev's celebrated glasnost—British and American country and rock groups were allowed inside the USSR, beginning with Roy Clark and Cliff Richard in 1976, the Nitty Gritty Dirt Band in 1977, and Elton John, who appeared in Leningrad in 1979, although each performer had to clear censors. (Ironically, the avant-garde rocker Frank Zappa refused to perform in the USSR when invited, out of protest against its oppression.)[84] Others, more appropriately perhaps, simply rebelled. Elton John, told he could not play the Beatles' "Back in the USSR," did so anyway during his encore, and a previously polite, even quiet, auditorium erupted. After a series of highly publicized concerts failed to materialize, Soviet authorities returned again into the fog of distrust and suspicion among the youth. John Lennon's death in 1980 produced both respect (Radio Sofia in Bulgaria dedicated two hours to Beatles music and a popular Estonian band wrote a song, "Requiem," in his memory) and the predictable propaganda, with East German papers reminding readers of the thousands of people murdered every year in America.

When Moscow hosted the Olympic Games in 1980, it opened the floodgates for Western sounds and influences, and the first true rock clubs opened in Leningrad and Moscow within a couple of years. Groups found they could tour within the Soviet Union, and the government discovered the commercial potential of allowing them to do so. The phenomenon came full circle in 1986 when a double LP called *Red Wave: 4 Underground Bands from the USSR* was released in the West. Soviet rockers actually went on tour, visiting France and Japan the following two years. The swell of rock and roll that took place in 1987 sparked a sudden and significant antirock music backlash (Bulgaria attempted one last time to shut down its rock clubs, and Czech police interrupted several concerts)—but even that fizzled quietly, and the Communists quickly started sponsoring rock festivals. The Bulgarian band Milena Rock Cooperative (named after the Cyndi Lauper-ish Milena Slavova) led the new heavy metal charge; and by 1988, Bulgarian party newspapers ran ads for concerts featuring the British band Uriah Heep.

Spies such as Vasili Mitrokhin, whose smuggled notes revealed the anti-Soviet influence of rock music, warned that radio broadcasts from the West were producing "unhealthy signs of interest in . . . pop stars" and "almost surreal" levels of subversion in some Russian cities.[85] Spy memos reported that 80 percent of Soviet youth listened to Western music broadcasts, which "gave young people a distorted idea of Soviet reality," and repeatedly noted the "treasonable nature" of such music.[86] No less than Jim Morrison, the iconic Doors revolutionary, summed it up when he said, "I've always been attracted to ideas that were about revolt against authority, like ideas about breaking away or overthrowing the established order. I am interested in anything about revolt, disorder and chaos, especially activity that seems to have no meaning."[87]

Romania sponsored sociologists to study the "youth problem," and officials moaned that the young had embraced materialism and cosmopolitanism.[88] But the real development was, as always, "in the grooves," as *American Bandstand* fixture Dick Clark used to say. By the mid-1980s, Soviet youths were importing less Western music and began making copies of Soviet rockers, who no longer needed to imitate the Americans or the British—in either style or rebellious lyrics. A final crackdown by Konstantin Chernenko proved the last, wheezing gasp of a totalitarian society seeking to control youth and music, a scene straight out of *Footloose* with the overprotective preacher trying to pull the plug on kids "dancin' in the streets."

Gorbachev's glasnost policies did not create anything new, but merely reflected what was already in progress. If anything, as Russian rock critic Artemy Troitsky argued, glasnost conceded rock and roll's victory, while at the same time producing "the biggest anti-rock backlash [in the Soviet Union] of the past couple of years [i.e., 1986–1987]. It was initiated by some Russophile writers, supported by certain officials in the Ministry of Culture . . . under the banner of glasnost."[89] In 1987 piano-rocker Billy Joel became the first American star to tour the Soviet Union with a fully staged show. Joel even recorded a live album in Leningrad, and in 1988, the government sold airtime to Pepsi, which flashed commercials featuring pop superstar Michael Jackson with his metal-studded jacket. When the Berlin Wall came down a year later, rockers like Joel and Springsteen could, metaphorically, point with pride to small sections they helped crack open. Certainly the Iron Curtain rockers tipped their hat to the Americans: "The whole spirit of the 60s [in the USA], the rebellion against the establishment, affected significantly the spiritual life of my generation and of the younger people," recalled Czech writer Václav Havel, "and in a very strange way, transcended into the present."[90] And while rock music may have had limited impact in America and

Britain when it came to fomenting a political revolution, pop music played a central role in ripping apart totalitarianism.

Recently, some academics, realizing that they had been had by the mythology of anticapitalist, anti-American rock, have displayed amusing gymnastics in trying to backpedal their way out of their arguments. One asserted that "rock was not inherently anti-Communist" (and of course many conservative critics wrongly charged it with being overly pro-Communist).[91] In fact, rock by its very nature was antiestablishment. When that same critic claimed the "rock 'revolt' was not *against* the dominant culture, but *within* it," the circular logic approached Hendrix-level lyrical nonsense: all revolutions begin within the dominant culture—but against what? The same Stephen Stills who warned "There's something happening here" would have had the same reaction to the Iron Curtain police (although the Soviets would have jailed him for such observations), and, like Wolf Biermann or the Plastic People of the Universe, would have no doubt written some East Bloc version of Neil Young's "Ohio" to commemorate those killed by German riot police.

Perhaps power chords emanating from stacks of Marshall amplifiers did not literally shatter the Berlin Wall, and perhaps the mythology of the influence of rock music in transforming any culture has seen its share of hyperbole, but even critics don't question the fact that the music of liberation played *some* role in undermining totalitarian states. As Timothy Ryback wrote in *Rock Around the Bloc*, "Western rock culture has debunked Marxist-Leninist assumptions about the state's ability to control citizens."[92] A fitting Stalinist-style monument, Ryback continued, to the heroes of socialist rock would depict a young man in blue jeans, "head thrust defiantly upward. In his hand, where the Stalinist war hero once gripped his Kalashnikov . . . this long-haired warrior would clutch the electric guitar."[93] And perhaps what was always assumed to be just Western rebelliousness in rock was deeper than once thought. John Kay, the vocalist whose version of "Born to Be Wild" became an American anthem of liberty used in the counterculture movie *Easy Rider*, was born Joachim Krauledat in Tilsit before escaping to the West to start Steppenwolf. Jan Hammer, famous for his synthesizer work with the Mahavishnu Orchestra, and later for the music in *Miami Vice*, grew up in Czechoslovakia.

Little difference existed between the 1980s rockers' visits to the Eastern bloc and Louis Armstrong's jazz tours of the 1950s (denigrated as "mud music"), except that Armstrong's were sponsored directly by the U.S. government, while the rockers' were the equivalent of volunteer missions. If, however, the lyrics themselves didn't send the youths to the barricades, the music form introduced them to individuality in a much different way. In both cases—the jazz of the 1950s and the rock of the 1980s—the essential, unique character of Western free societies was on display within the music: the very structure of most rock and jazz features a verse or two played/sung by the entire band, followed by solo breaks, before eventually (sometimes after tortuously long solo interregnums) the entire band reunites to finish the piece together. Western music, then, showed that individuals can and do work well together voluntarily, but unlike in "socialist" music, individuals had freedom to stand out, even if it meant baldly outshining the rest of the band. Or, as Timothy Ryback observed, "the triumph of rock and roll [behind the Iron Curtain] has been the realization of a democratic process."[94]

Rock and roll's contribution to the collapse of communism provides one more piece of evidence that the human soul longs for freedom in all areas. It was a principle the Founders understood when they limited government's ability to intrude on the arts, speech, and business. In later years, they would differ over the wisdom of founding a national university, for example, with George Washington calling for the establishment of such a college in his final address to Congress in 1796.[95] But virtually all support for such a university—as well as for such "big government" projects as the large internal improvements measure that Thomas Jefferson supported (but which Congress failed to pass)—sprang from concerns about maintaining national defense. Alexander Hamilton, likewise, had based much of his advocacy of protective tariffs on the need to ensure the supply of muskets and uniforms for the American military, not as a sop to business.

More than a few expressed misgivings about Congress involving itself in any way in the arts. Many objected to the government's purchase of Thomas Jefferson's personal book collection after the British burned much of Washington, D.C., in 1814; and four years later critics decried the government's paying John Trumbull $32,000 for four paintings about the American Revolution (including his masterpiece, the *Declaration of Independence*).

Overall, though, the Founders were cautious in their support for government aid to any kind of art or entertainment, aware that with money came strings, and with strings, political agendas. With a few exceptions, they favored keeping government out of human affairs whenever possible. They certainly understood that the arts (as well as business or education) could have its seamier side; people were not angels, but rather humans who would abuse liberty from time to time, and government's purpose was to limit their ability to do this. But deciding when art was harming people always bordered on censorship, and with censorship came political control. Thus the Founders would have recoiled at Andres Serrano's *Piss Christ* on several levels, most obviously its disgusting disrespect for Christianity, but also, more significantly, on the grounds that taxpayers were forced to fund such denigration of their fellow Americans' religion.

It is essential to recognize that, just as the Founders never imagined the government would interfere with its citizens' diet, they never imagined it would try to control the arts. As a consequence, they never felt the need to comment on or expressly prohibit what they felt was much too ridiculous to consider. When John Adams wrote to Abigail in 1780, "I must study Politicks and War that my sons may have the liberty to study Mathematicks and Philosophy. My sons ought to study Mathematicks and Philosophy . . . in order to give their Children a right to study Painting, Poetry, Musick, Architecture, Statuary, Tapestry, and Porcelaine," he meant to establish a prioritized list of that which was necessary to enable that which was desirable. He did not intend that government fund "Tapestry and Porcelaine." Washington, likewise, insisted, "The arts and sciences essential to the prosperity of the state and to the ornament and happiness of human life have a primary claim to the encouragement of every lover of his country and mankind," but he meant individuals should "encourage," not the state. Jefferson, who once said, "I am an enthusiast on the subject of the arts," never once attempted to make it the government's job to support them or fund them.[96]

The Founders' vision of keeping speech and the arts free of government control and money has largely been abandoned. If Woodrow Wilson's propaganda campaigns of World War I didn't permanently link the two (though one can argue that, in wartime, propaganda and censorship are necessary), certainly Franklin Roosevelt's public works programs did. During the Great Depression, the federal government paid artists and writers to engage in myriad projects—some admirable, most of them make-work, but none of which were judged by the private sector to be valuable prior to the New Deal. Rock music's rebellion, therefore, in an ironic way, constituted a grand act of defiance against government control over the arts. After all, the BBC refused to even play the Beatles at first, which led them to American shores!

Had the Founders been alive to see the Beatles' arrival in 1964, they most likely would not have joined in singing choruses of "Yeah, yeah, yeah" or screamed in delight. (For that matter, I don't think a record exists of George Washington ever even letting out a "Yahoo!") But the Founders' intuitive appreciation for liberty as a self-regulating force would have led them to smile benignly at Beatlemania and shake their heads at the marvel of youth and the genius of those lads from Britain. George Washington, James Madison, and even Thomas Jefferson likely would have grudgingly signed on to federal funding of Louis Armstrong's Cold War tours as necessary for national defense. They certainly would have approved of Radio Free Europe. And while they would have been horrified by the "devil music" of rockers such as Ronnie James Dio, or the nihilistic death metal of Metallica, one can't imagine them backing legislation—like the kind Tipper Gore championed in the 1980s—to stop it.

Nor can one seriously entertain visions of James Madison or Alexander Hamilton (who always struck me as opera types, anyway) throwing stacks of Led Zeppelin records onto a bonfire. These same Founders danced jigs that originated in rebellious Irish glens, enjoyed Mozart and the Psalms put to music, sang songs of freedom that were handed down by recalcitrant Scots, and solemnly joined in fervent hymns from the English Puritan heritage. (It is worth noting that Mozart, in his day, embodied the term "revolutionary," so here were revolutionaries listening to a revolutionary!)

Washington was entertained by string quartets, when popular songs of the day were "Drink to Me Only with Thine Eyes" and "The President's March" by Philip Phile. Both Jefferson and Washington enjoyed Haydn, but the Squire of Monticello could also be heard humming Scotch songs and Italian hymns, and Jefferson family sheet music included "Draw the Sword, Scotland," "The Jolly British Tar," and "Comin' Thro' the Rye."[97] For the record, Washington could not carry a tune in a bucket, though his household was musical. Later, it's been said, Abraham Lincoln particularly enjoyed the songs of Stephen Foster and, remarkably, his all-time favorite was "Dixie"![98]

It was all the music of revolution, perhaps to a different beat, but revolution nonetheless. When a Christian rock group, the Elms, in 2006 sang "Who Puts Rock and Roll in Your Blood?" they clearly answered, "God." The Founders would answer the question slightly differently. "Who puts rock and roll in your blood?" Not the State!

6.

RONALD REAGAN TRIES TO KEEP THE PEACE . . .
AND MAKES HIS BIGGEST MISTAKE

It is not a field of a few acres of ground, but a cause, that we are
defending, and whether we defeat the enemy in one battle, or by
degrees, the consequences will be the same.

THOMAS PAINE, THE CRISIS, 1777

Even if Ronald Reagan had done nothing but end the Cold War, his place in history still would have been assured. But by simultaneously rescuing the American economy from a decades-long death spiral, and by touching off a boom that spawned 14 million new jobs and almost twenty-five years of prosperity, Reagan ensured his place next to Washington, Lincoln, and the Roosevelts as one of the most influential presidents in America's history. His sunny optimism, unrelenting faith in America's virtues and foundations, and relentless determination to make the American dream a reality for the citizens has elevated him to the highest echelons of our leaders. By liberating millions, Reagan's place in the *world* aligns him with the greatest champions of human freedom who ever lived.

Yet Reagan had shortcomings. His own admitted failing was that he was unable to change the culture in Washington, D.C., in such a way as to reduce the size of government. For that, while he may have been naive—*no* administration, including some of the earliest small-government advocates such as Thomas Jefferson, had successfully controlled the growth of government for long—he nevertheless fell in line with virtually every one of his predecessors, liberal or conservative. Martin Van Buren, Grover Cleveland, and Calvin Coolidge, all of them dedicated to containing the size of the federal government, all watched per capita spending increase during their tenure. The Gipper fully understood the threat posed by an ever-growing federal bureaucracy, in terms of both weights placed on the nation's enterprise and, more important, infringements of the freedoms of its people.

If Reagan's greatest and most timeless triumph was in foreign policy, so was his greatest error, and, in the latter case, it was a two-fold error. First, he deployed the U.S. Marines in Lebanon as part of a "peacekeeping" mission that not only lacked an attainable goal, but also did not employ rules of engagement sufficient to allow the Marines to protect themselves. Such missions, unfortunately, were common during the Cold War in both Republican and Democratic administrations. After a suicide bomber attacked the Marine barracks in Lebanon, however, Reagan—after attempting to stay the course—finally withdrew the forces. By doing so, he indeed took the prudent military action, and, most likely, made the wisest political choice. Had the marines stayed, there is little evidence that they could have made much of a difference. Unfortunately, the withdrawal of the U.S. forces constituted a second edge of that troubled blade, for it displayed a lack of appreciation for the longer-term threat: the growing danger posed by the rise of Islamic fundamentalism.

Certainly Ronald Reagan knew radical Islam existed. In *An American Life*, he wrote:

> I don't think you can overstate the importance that the rise of Islamic fundamentalism will have to the rest of the world in the century ahead—especially if, as seems possible, its most fanatical

elements get their hands on nuclear and chemical weapons and the means to deliver them against their enemies.[1]

He had seen the shah of Iran toppled and Anwar Sadat assassinated by Muslim radicals; he was supremely sensitive to the need to ensure Israel's survival; and he appreciated the crumbling political situation in Lebanon, with the disputes between its Sunni and Shiite Muslims and Maronite Christians. At least four separate crises would emerge from the Middle East in Reagan's first term: the ongoing destruction and chaos in Lebanon; the Iran-Iraq War; Israel's ongoing struggle for security (including the attack on the Iraqi nuclear reactor); and the attempt by Reagan to reach out to Arab "moderates" through such overtures as the sale of Airborne Warning and Control System (AWACS) aircraft to Saudi Arabia in 1981. In his second term, Reagan's compassion and flawed assessment of the Iranian regime as reasonable parties with whom the United States could deal would provide a final ironic reaction from militant Islam in the form of the Iran-Contra affair.

One of Reagan's mistakes in dealing with the Islamic world was that he (and virtually everyone else in government at the time) believed a large number of "moderate Muslims" existed in such hard-core Islamic nations as Saudi Arabia. Operating under this misconception, Reagan approved the AWACS sale, which originated in the Carter administration, to Saudi Arabia. "I was told," he said, "the planes would not materially change the balance of power in the Arab-Israeli conflict [and] I thought the Arab world would regard it as a gesture showing that we desired to be evenhanded in the Middle East."[2] Reagan saw the AWACS sale as a palliative to the Saudis, tied in part to reducing "the threat of a Soviet move in that direction."[3] Invoking the language of Richard Nixon and Jimmy Carter, Reagan argued for "stability" and "peace between Israel & the Arab nations."[4] During a meeting with Israeli prime minister Menachem Begin, Reagan argued again that the sale would "bring the Saudis into the peace making process."[5] Begin was not persuaded, and it "annoyed" Reagan that he lobbied Congress hard against the sale, despite indications to the president that he wouldn't. Reagan signaled his displeasure through the State Department, noting that he "didn't like having representatives of any foreign country . . . trying to interfere with . . . our domestic political process and our setting of foreign policy."[6] The AWACS sale, however, was supported overwhelmingly by former national security staffers, twenty-eight of whom came out on October 5, 1981, to support the deal. Reagan came to consider the sale of the AWACS as "a donnybrook" and a fight "we could not afford to lose. I believed it was a battle that *had* to be won to advance the cause of peace in the Middle East."[7]

Acting on intelligence that an Iraqi nuclear plant was developing fissionable materials, the Israeli air force used F-15As, sold by the United States to Israel on the condition that they not be used for offensive purposes, to destroy the Iraqi Osirak reactor in a raid ("Operation Opera"). The attack only strengthened the Saudi arguments that they needed the AWACS, helping Reagan win the fight. (Later, Reagan wrote that he "spent more time in one-on-one meetings and on the telephone attempting to win on this measure than on any other.")[8] Dealing with Begin over the bombing of the Iraqi nuclear facility, however, was a different matter. The Israelis had not given Reagan advance warning of their attack on the reactor, which irritated him greatly. The prime minister, he wrote in his diary, "should have told us & the French, [and] we could have done something to remove the threat."[9] Of course, Begin had only seen Reagan in action for a few months, and despite his high hopes for the new administration, he had only the Carter record of doing nothing to remove the threat upon which to base his decision.

On Wednesday, June 10, 1981, Reagan held more meetings about the Osirak bombing and resolved to ask Congress to investigate whether or not the condition of sale had been violated. He wrote in his diary, "Frankly, if Cong. should decide [a violation occurred], I'll grant a Presidential waiver. Iraq is technically still at war with Israel & I believe they were preparing to build an atom bomb."[10] Saddam Hussein, in Reagan's view, was a "no good nut," who "was trying to build a nuclear weapon" so he could "be the leader of the Arab world—that's why he invaded Iran."[11]

As Reagan tried to ease tensions created by the Israeli raid, Lebanon continued to fester. Lebanon had had a volatile history since France had promised it independence in 1943, and upon the eviction of the Vichy forces in 1946, the nation achieved fully independent status. After the creation of the state of Israel and the first Arab-Israeli war in 1947–48, refugees from Palestine moved to Lebanon as a long-term tactic by Arab states to create a "Palestinian refugee crisis" that they blamed on Israel (despite the fact that the Arab states themselves never invited refugees to settle in their countries).

During the Suez Crisis of 1956, the pro-Western Lebanese president Camille Chamoun maintained diplomatic relations with the United States, Britain, and France in the face of hostility from Egypt and Syria. At first the militia of the Christian Phalange Party supported Chamoun and Prime Minister Rashid Karami, but after Muslim demonstrators threatened the government in 1958, the Phalangists overthrew the Karami administration and installed their own dictatorship. Meanwhile, Palestinians residing in neighboring Jordan had been evicted, and thousands crossed the border, joining the 400,000 Palestinians already in camps there, to form a "state within a state" inside Lebanon under the loose control of Palestinian Liberation Organization (PLO) strongman Yasir Arafat. The PLO soon gained complete control over western Lebanon, and the Lebanese army, composed of fixed ratios of different religious groups, found itself helpless to control the growing power of the militias. Maronite Christians, Phalangists, Shiites, Sunnis, the Communist-backed Druze, and the PLO all had their own militias.

Arafat's PLO militias began to stage attacks against Israel from inside Lebanon. Between 1969 and 1975, the PLO violated numerous truces, treaties, agreements, and arrangements with the tacit approval of neighboring Muslim states. Violence erupted between Sunnis and Phalangists, followed by Phalangist counterstrikes against PLO fighters, which led to the Black Saturday killings of Christians and the reprisals in which virtually all Muslim travelers attempting to cross Phalangist roadblocks were killed. An assault on a PLO camp in January 1976 was followed by the PLO assault on the nonmilitarized Christian town of Damour, in which one thousand helpless Christians were slaughtered. People of every stripe and religion then fled for their lives. President Suleiman Frangieh, a centrist with support from Muslims and Christians, invited Syria, out of desperation, to enter and restore order. Ultimately, after an Arab League summit gave Syria a mandate to keep the peace, a large Syrian force remained in Lebanon, controlling the Bekaa Valley. The nation was divided into a PLO-controlled southern section and a Christian-controlled section of eastern Beirut. Oddly, Syria supported the Christian militias because of the threat to Syria by PLO-related terror groups, and Syria found itself all but allied with the Christians and Israelis against the Palestinians, Druze, and Muslim militias. When the leader of the antigovernment Druze, Kamal Jumblatt, was assassinated in 1977, the Syrians were blamed, further shuffling the alliances. PLO attacks across the Lebanese border into Israel escalated, leading to a quick Israeli invasion, followed by a withdrawal.

Various free agents were also adding to the chaos, including the Abu Nidal Organization, which attempted to assassinate Israeli ambassador Shlomo Argov in London in 1982. Abu Nidal was protected and supported by Saddam Hussein's Iraq (and continued to be sponsored by Iraq long after critics of George W. Bush claimed there were "no terrorists in Iraq").[12] Nevertheless, in 1982, after further attacks into Israeli territory from Lebanon, Israel invaded southern Lebanon to clear out the PLO rocket bases. Moving to the outskirts of Beirut, the Israeli units crushed the PLO and left Arafat desperate for a negotiated truce to save what was left of his military. The United Nations obliged on June 26 with a Security Council resolution that demanded a withdrawal of the Israeli and PLO forces. At that time, a bipartisan group of U.S. senators had written Reagan urging him to dismantle the PLO in Lebanon and to force all Syrian troops out. Clearly, there was great concern about both the PLO and Syria, less so than about Israel. Reagan dispatched Philip Habib to negotiate a truce and finally, in 1982, he got the various groups to agree to a cease-fire. Meanwhile, throughout the cease-fire, the PLO continued to shell Israel in more than 270 documented attacks.

The claims and counterclaims in the region were astounding and insurmountable. Naturally, the Arab-Israeli struggle for the territory once called Judaea (then renamed "Palestine" by the Romans) was the best known, but at the same time Syria claimed it had an ancestral right to Lebanon, which it deemed a creation of France. Christian minorities, of course, were so small as to be unsafe under the control of almost any Muslim state. Just a few hundred miles to the east, Iraq and Iran engaged in a war of stunning carnage. No Muslim nation—not Jordan, not Syria, not Egypt, and not Saudi Arabia—wanted the "Palestinian refugees," as they would constitute a festering abscess inside the host country, posing not only a drain on all social services (such as they were in Muslim countries), but more important a constant threat of political insurrection. So as the PLO demanded the extermination of Israel, Syria worked to crush the PLO and Christian militias in Lebanon. Saudi Arabia funded Arab violence against Israel, all the while stomping on radicals within its own borders.

Reagan's approach to most issues was direct and simple, focused on cutting through the obfuscation to arrive at an action item. This tactic would produce some of his greatest victories: cutting taxes created jobs and boosted the economy; confronting the Soviets and matching their military buildup brought down the Evil Empire; deploying cruise and Pershing missiles forced Gorbachev into the Intermediate Nuclear Forces Treaty. Thus, when it came to the difficulties in Lebanon, Reagan relied on a surprisingly leftist maxim, namely that if the parties would just "talk it out," they could reach an agreement. Moreover, he had felt the need to reprimand Israel again and again, first over the surprise raid on the Osirak facility, then in December 1981, when the Israelis annexed the Golan Heights (a hilly range of strategic importance to Israel), then again during Begin's meddling in the AWACS debates. After the Golan rebuke, Begin blasted Reagan with an "angry letter" in which he invoked Vietnam and told Reagan the United States had no business telling Israel how to behave. According to Reagan's autobiography, *An American Life*, Begin's response was "Mind your own business."[13]

Unwilling to heed Reagan's calls for restraint, the Israelis advanced to Beirut in an apparent effort to crush the PLO completely. In June, Israeli forces laid siege to Beirut, until finally, after entire neighborhoods were leveled from both sides' shelling, the UN passed a resolution vetoed by the United States because it maintained the PLO as a "viable political force" in Lebanon.[14] Reagan again dispatched Philip Habib, who arranged a truce on August 12 that called for the withdrawal of both Israeli and PLO elements, to be replaced by a multinational force of Marines assisted by French and Italian military units. Reagan's defense secretary, Caspar Weinberger, opposed the involvement of Americans because, as he saw it, there was no clear mission to accomplish. Years later, he told PBS, "there hadn't been an agreement of that kind [supposedly reached on May 17 through Habib]," and while "a buffer force is fine if you insert it between two warring factions that have agreed there should be a buffer force in there," if the two factions had no such agreement, the force "would be in very grave peril."[15] Moreover, he argued, the recommended forces were too lightly armed. He would later note that "Marines that are properly armed and have the rules of engagement that allow them to defend themselves are quite a different thing than Marines who are forced to sit on a Beirut Airport and do nothing effectively."[16] But Weinberger lost the argument. He later blamed himself for his failure to persuade the president on the issue, noting that it resulted in "a force that was almost a sitting duck in one of the most dangerous spots in the Mideast . . . unable to protect itself."[17] The Multinational Force (MNF) arrived on August 20. Ronald Reagan had just made the biggest mistake of his eight-year presidency.

Here, the ghosts of both Harry Truman and Dwight Eisenhower haunted America, shaping Ronald Reagan's response to the threat. Truman had employed the United Nations to thwart the invasion of South Korea in 1950 by the North. That was a clear-cut case of aggression, and if a situation ever demanded "collective action," Korea was an early, and crucial, test. In taking the invasion of South Korea by the North to the UN, Truman wanted to build a broad anti-Communist consensus. By a stroke of luck, the Soviets were boycotting the Security Council when the vote was taken, permitting one of only two uses of the UN for military action between 1947 and 2000.

Yet Truman's broader objective of using the UN as a buffer against communism was patently impossible in the emerging "Bandung Generation" (as Paul Johnson labeled it, referring to the 1955 Bandung Conference) characterized by tin-pot dictators and Communist thugs, most of whom identified with the Soviets' view of "social justice." These were leaders immersed in anti-imperialism, ready to exert retribution on the former capitalist occupiers and extract reparations by nationalizing industries and socializing their economies. Cloaked with a fig leaf of democracy—indeed, often bequeathed an astounding structure of representation by the colonial powers (some possessing more legislators per person than America or England)—the Third World states often collapsed into barbaric dictatorships overnight. Kwame Nkrumah of Ghana had his chief justice arrested in 1963 for acquitting suspected traitors, and the judge died in jail. By that time, Nkrumah was not only encouraging his followers to refer to him as "The Redeemer," but had claimed, "I represent Africa and . . . speak in her name. Therefore, no African can have an opinion that differs from mine."[18] What made Nkrumah's ascension particularly odious was that Ghana had been considered a model state, buttressed by a court system, commissions, and councils; it possessed virtually all the trappings of Western representative government without any of the substance. Nigeria, little more than a collection of tribes, was forced into nation-state status, only to split apart with the Biafran civil war of the mid-1960s. No sooner had Belgium handed over control of the Congo to the locals than former post-office clerk and beer salesman Patrice Lumumba, the new prime minister, issued an edict that raised the pay of all government employees, save those in the army. A mutiny immediately erupted, with soldiers pillaging throughout Léopoldville. They booted the UN staff out of their hotel rooms while the United Nations sat on its hands. Gangs and looters overran the country, Europeans fled in droves, and Katanga province declared its independence under Moise Tshombe.

When Dag Hammarskjöld, the UN secretary-general, finally ordered in "peacekeepers" (drawn largely from the inefficient and exceptionally unprofessional militaries of the "nonaligned" nations rather than from the West), they became part of the problem. To a significant degree, Hammarskjöld himself was "played" by the Congolese rebels. Before long, Col. Joseph Mobutu (later Mobutu Sésé Seko) overthrew Lumumba, who was under house arrest and "protected" by the UN, in a coup. Convinced he had the numbers to defeat Mobutu, Lumumba ordered his supporters to stage a jailbreak and attempted to set up his own state in Stanleyville. There, Mobutu's men captured him and transported him to Katanga, where he was executed. Tshombe soon left the country he helped create to assume the position of prime minister in the Congo, before being dismissed a year later.

Such intrigue and brutal power politics were the norm in postcolonial Africa: Togo experienced a coup in 1963 (its president was murdered); mutinies occurred in Kenya, Uganda, and Tanzania in 1964; the president of Gabon was overthrown that same year before French paratroopers saved his government; Dahomey (now Benin), the Central African Republic, and Upper Volta (now Burkina Faso) all suffered coups in 1965; and by 1968, sub-Saharan Africa had witnessed more than sixty coups, mutinies, military takeovers, or attempted revolts.[19] In less than a decade, Dahomey, Nigeria, Sierra Leone, Ghana, Togo, Upper Volta, Zaire, and Congo-Brazzaville suffered a total of twenty-two coups, and within fifteen years, just under half of the newly independent African states were ruled by dictatorships or military juntas. With this abominable record, the UN should have had abundant "peacekeeping" opportunities, yet was AWOL for most of these events. In the Congo—the one time UN peacekeepers genuinely attempted to enforce a peace—the cost was high. A RAND Corporation report concluded:

U.N. achievements in the Congo came at considerable cost in men lost, money spent, and controversy raised. . . . As a result of these costs and controversies, neither the United Nations' leadership nor its member nations were eager to repeat the experience. For the next 25 years the United Nations restricted its military interventions to interpositional peacekeeping, policing ceasefires, and patrolling disengagement zones in circumstances where all parties invited its presence and armed force was to be used by U.N. troops only in self-defense.[20]

Indeed, UN peacekeeping operations were seldom approved unless, however ironic, peace had already been decided and there was little risk of violence![21] Most of the activities of UN forces have involved monitoring cease-fires, overseeing demilitarized zones, and running fact-finding missions. Virtually all of the rhetoric of the United Nations was directed at a single African state, South Africa, because of its white government and apartheid system.

Despite the striking ineptitude and callousness of the United Nations, both Truman (in Korea), then Eisenhower (in Korea and Suez) had bought into the notion of collective security involving the UN. Based on the pitiful performance of the League of Nations, not to mention the UN's own brief history of incompetence, both presidents should at least have been suspicious of such efforts. Outside of the Security Council, the United States still substantially controlled the UN in the early 1950s, and therefore both presidents still saw the UN as a force for genuine security. That would change in the Suez Crisis of 1956, in which Ike superficially and temporarily seemed to achieve a great victory by shuffling off the matter to the United Nations. In reality, he perpetuated an arrangement that, more than ever, opened the United States to the dictates of "world opinion."

Briefly, the details of the crisis were as follows: Britain, France, and Israel combined to attack Egypt over Gamal Abdel Nasser's nationalization of the Suez Canal. That constituted a serious economic blow to Britain, but direct intervention threatened to bring in the United States and other Arab nations. A scheme was hatched (the Protocol of Sèvres) to have Israel invade the Sinai, then Britain and France would generously step in to maintain a safe zone of sixteen kilometers on either side of the canal, wresting control of the canal back from Egypt. In what proved to be a typical Western-versus-non-Western military conflict, the British-French-Israeli units routed the

Egyptians, but also drew the ire of the world community. Suez was, after all, a military victory displaying British might; but it also exposed Britain's moral and political weakness, as Prime Minister Anthony Eden (whom historian Paul Johnson called a "pathetic sacrificial victim") had no stomach for standing up to world opinion. But Britain's decline also revealed another undesirable trend: that of allowing the United Nations to act as any kind of neutral arbiter.

In keeping with the new internationalist tone, and genuinely concerned about the escalation of a regional conflict into a new, hot theater of the Cold War, Ike threw Suez into the UN's lap, thereby abandoning the British and the French. From then on, all operations involving the United Nations ceased to be about establishing a clear winner or loser (which scholars of so-called peace studies have determined actually shortens wars and reduces casualties).[22] Instead, the focus was on borders, truces, negotiations, conferences, agreements, pieces of paper, disarmament, and above all, cooperation. This was the case in Korea, where there was no winner, nor even a final treaty. There remained only an ongoing cease-fire negotiation, which afflicted the world with a dictatorial state well into the twenty-first century. Despite the UN Charter, which authorizes it to use force, the United Nations' own panel report on peacekeeping operations states that "the United Nations does not wage war," thus making it nearly impossible to determine a winner, and therefore, bring about a true resolution to the dispute.[23] Unlike Korea, however, the Suez affair produced a completely one-sided solution: UN peacekeepers were to be withdrawn at Egypt's request, which meant that, as soon as the Egyptians had rearmed, Nasser would demand the removal of the peacekeepers so he could attack anew.

Eisenhower, despite the praise heaped on him by Johnson, who called him "the most successful of America's twentieth-century presidents" (an astounding comment, given Reagan's record), had ceded significant control over American foreign policy to the UN. A body increasingly made up of the hate-America crowd, governed by a Security Council arrangement that permitted a single member to issue a veto—thereby empowering the USSR to prevent virtually any action that might limit its expansion—the UN had, by the 1950s, become a mechanism that constrained American influence. It certainly was not a neutral arbiter, or even a force for peace. From 1945 to 2000, there were more than three hundred wars resulting in 22 million deaths. In only two cases did the UN approve military action to counter aggression: North Korea in 1950 and Kuwait in 1990. There had been a minimum of fifty-five civil wars between 1945 and 1973 alone, and by the mid-1990s, largely thanks to "peacemaking" efforts by the United Nations, the number had more than doubled since 1945.[24]

While the evidence would mount after Lebanon, it was already becoming clear that "peacekeeping" was not only a failure, but likely produced more deaths and continuing carnage than would otherwise have occurred. One authority on peacekeeping noted, "We may [assume] that only a 'just' settlement will really assure a lasting peace, but the empirical evidence for this proposition is unclear."[25] Civil wars rarely ended in negotiated settlements: the obvious problem of how people lived and worked with those who had recently killed their families and burned their towns was, to say the least, thorny. When the research finally surfaced—years after Ike or Reagan participated in UN missions—the scholarship concluded that civil wars were less likely to end in negotiated settlements than other wars.[26] Moreover, soldiers, whose training and primary purpose is to kill people and break things, became "peacekeepers," human shields set between warring tribes, unable to effect a solution and often prevented from defending the innocent. That is, of course, much clearer in hindsight.

At the time, however, much of the impetus behind taking the Korean and Suez conflicts to the UN was grounded in a genuine optimistic belief that the United States could use the organization to build a broad anti-Communist consensus. Of course, this hope was based on the misconception that UN leaders actually *opposed* communism. Led by the guilt-ridden, stoic, moralistic, Naderesque Swede Dag Hammarskjöld, who once described himself as the vessel of a "thirsty" God, and who, like Jimmy Carter after him, ignored realpolitik in favor of a de-Westernized reordering of the world, the UN refused to condemn the Egyptian seizure of the Suez Canal. Instead, it sided repeatedly with the Muslim powers and upbraided the British and French, whose investment had been stolen. But was there any condemnation of the Soviet invasion of Hungary? Nothing to compare with the contempt for the Western powers that Hammarskjöld exuded.

By 1982, then, Reagan had inherited a presidential tradition of inviting the United Nations to participate in U.S. national security decisions. That tradition had gained moral credibility during the Vietnam War, which, critics sermonized, showed the "limits of American power." Reagan didn't buy that line, of course, and his primary focus from the 1980 campaign onward was to restore America's military presence and pressure the Soviet Union, thereby, perhaps, causing the Communist state to crumble internally. The struggle with the USSR colored everything. It lay behind Reagan's invasion of the Caribbean island of Grenada, just two days after the Marine barracks was truck-bombed, to expel the Cubans. It drove his decision to deploy Pershing and cruise missiles to counter the Soviet SS-20s that had been placed in western Russia to threaten Europe. Nevertheless, there were limits to how much even Reagan could do unilaterally or with only a handful of allies. The situation in Lebanon therefore seemed a proper forum for diplomacy and collective peacekeeping.

Jimmy Carter's one successful foreign policy venture, the Camp David Accords, which led to a peace treaty between Egypt and Israel, had also led Reagan to believe that eventually the arrangements could be expanded to moderate Arab states, leading to a "final resolution of the great problems bedeviling the Middle East. . . ."[27] On September 1, 1982, a few weeks after Philip Habib had secured his truce calling for a multinational force to protect Lebanese civilians, Reagan sent a letter to Menachem Begin, arguing that the "population in the north of Israel is now secure," and that the PLO was "militarily weakened and the Soviet Union shown once again to have minimal impact on the truly significant developments" in the region.[28] Calling for a new comprehensive peace proposal, Reagan forwarded his plans to Jordan and Saudi Arabia, and almost simultaneously Begin's cabinet rejected his overtures. The Israelis indirectly continued to encourage other groups to winnow the PLO's ranks. On September 16, two days after the assassination of Lebanese Phalangist leader Bachir Gemayel, the Israelis allowed some 1,500 Phalange militia to enter the PLO camps and kill more than 1,000 PLO and civilians. (Israeli defense minister Ariel Sharon, who was investigated for allowing the Phalangists into the camps, was forced to resign.)

Following these attacks, "world opinion" erupted against Israel. Throughout Europe, demonstrators staged protests. In Italy, they wore badges with the Star of David and the swastika intertwined; in France, there was a school strike against Israel and bar mitzvahs were canceled. Arab scholar Bernard Lewis noted the convenient double standard:

There is no evidence that the teachers of [the Lycée Voltaire] had ever been moved to such action by events in Poland or Uganda, Central America or Afghanistan, South Africa and Southeast Asia, or for that matter in the Middle East where the massacre of Sabra and Shatila . . . lacked neither precedents nor parallels.[29]

Earlier that year, the Syrian army massacred between seven thousand and ten thousand Muslim residents in the town of Hama, but, judging from the lack of outrage, it seems the international community barely even noticed. Thomas Friedman of *The New York Times* described favorably the ending of the threats of Muslim extremists against supposedly "moderate" Arab governments.[30] According to this logic, Muslim governments are fully justified in massacring civilians if it ensures their security. But as Lewis pointed out, there was a key distinction: "In Hama, [the] possibility [of blaming Israel] did not exist; therefore the mass slaughter of Arabs by Arabs went unremarked, unnoticed, and unprotested."[31]

On Wednesday, September 28, a force of 1,746 United States Marines arrived on the shores of Lebanon along with approximately the same number of French and Italian troops. As the Israelis finally withdrew from the region, Muslim and Druze militias began to battle openly, and the Lebanese army disintegrated. Scarcely two days earlier, two UN observers hit a land mine and were killed, demonstrating just how deadly peacekeeping could be. Despite having opposed the mission from the beginning, Secretary of Defense Caspar Weinberger arranged for the Marines to stay at the Beirut Airport. But they were not the only new visitors to Beirut: Shiite Muslims from Iran had arrived to extend their Islamic revolution into Lebanon.[32] Five months earlier, one of their operatives had detonated a car bomb at the U.S. embassy in Beirut, killing sixteen Americans (including the top CIA Middle East researcher). That act should have tipped off Reagan's usually acute antennae that no conventional peace deal would be possible there. After meeting with the families of the victims at Andrews Air Force Base, Reagan might have reconsidered, if it hadn't been for a crucial substitution of negotiators. Habib, who had been quite successful, informed Reagan he wanted to retire. In his place, Reagan sent George Shultz.

As secretary of state, Shultz had proven reliable, but he was a throwback to Eisenhower-style diplomacy. Reagan biographer Edmund Morris characterized him as having a "face as blank as a slot machine's," and Nixon warned Reagan to "watch out for him. . . . after a while he'll be disloyal."[33] He bought into the notion that the USSR was economically sound. A conciliator by nature, Shultz cringed at Reagan's confrontational tone with the Soviets. He opposed Reagan's economic restrictions on credits for building the Trans-Siberian pipeline as unduly controversial for our allies. Informed only a few days before the Strategic Defense Initiative (SDI) speech in March 1983, Shultz and his State Department aides opposed "not just the way the missile defense was introduced; evidence suggests they believed that the initiative was an ill-thought-out idea."[34] Shultz at the time feared "destabilization," although later he came to admit that SDI struck fear into the hearts of the Soviet leaders, thereby providing extreme leverage in negotiations.

Shultz scoffed at Reagan's vision of a world without nuclear weapons, a view that most of his associates at State shared. "Doesn't he understand the realities?" Shultz's aide Richard Burt asked.[35] At a Monday meeting prior to Reagan's Wednesday SDI speech, Shultz and presidential science adviser George Keyworth discussed "Star Wars" in front of the president. "Shultz called me a lunatic," Keyworth recalled, and said it would destroy NATO and "was the idea of a blooming madman."[36] The Gipper was too polite to tell Shultz the idea for an SDI program was entirely his own. Throughout the SDI announcement, Reagan anticipated that even many of his closest advisers would react the same way as Shultz and would, in Margaret Thatcher's words, "go wobbly." By necessity Shultz had to be involved in the Lebanese mission, but only at the last minute.

Shultz still thought in terms of grand agreements, replete with the signatures of powerful people. He believed no problem was insurmountable if people of goodwill could just talk to each other, and this reasoning certainly rubbed off on Reagan. Shultz and Deputy National Security Advisor Bud McFarlane won Reagan's ear on this issue, and so Reagan continued twisting arms for his earlier Lebanon peace proposal, persuading King Hussein of Jordan "to work on the Syrians."[37] Reagan came to like Hussein a great deal—"His Majesty is a solid citizen," he wrote in his diary.[38] "He is our hope to lead the Arab side and the P.L.O. [Reagan always inserted periods] in negotiating with the Israelis."[39] Not only did Reagan feel he could trust Hussein, but he made important inroads with Egyptian president Hosni Mubarak, who admitted privately that both Israel and Syria "may be playing a game . . . cutting up Lebanon between them."[40] Well into September, the "Lebanon Working Group" continued to place Lebanon strategy in the context of Syrian aggression and warned about a "suicidal attempt to go after a U.S. vessel in the Med."[41] Advising that the Syrian strategy through such a move was to "draw [in] the U.S." and "hurt the IMF," the working group warned that the Syrians would "lay the trap" and "force [the] US to escalate." For that reason, the "US cannot reverse [itself], can not withdraw."[42]

Lost in the stream of analysis was the larger issue, which, at the time, all but the Syrians had ignored. The biggest menace was that of a rising Islamic fundamentalism that threatened some of the most oppressive Muslim dictatorships in the region, not to mention Israel and the United States. Jihad was not "business as usual," not just routine violence in the Middle East. A profound reordering of much of Islamic society had occurred since the Second World War, much of it of course related to the founding of Israel. But that was only an excuse, the rowdy drunk in the bar obscuring a room full of inebriates. At a much deeper level, the stunningly rapid expansion in prosperity in the West and parts of Japan had, literally, left the Muslim states in the dirt. A few nations, such as Saudi Arabia, had vast oil wealth dispersed among a handful of families. Other Islamic countries—Egypt, Yemen, Morocco, Algeria, and Syria, all of which lacked substantial oil reserves—received second-class treatment from their Muslim brothers. Those nations remained pitifully backward. Western prosperity encompassed Israel, which in a matter of years had built resorts and farms on land the Arabs had left barren for centuries.

Israel provided a convenient scapegoat for these states and their virtual dictators. Government schools propagandized against the Jews relentlessly. Nonie Darwish, an Egyptian whose father was killed supervising Gaza, recalled of her education, "The hatred of Israel and our obligation to pursue jihad was somehow worked into every subject we discussed in school. In fact, clearly, the main goal of our education was to instill a commitment to destroy Israel."[43] Jews were "portrayed as devils, pigs, and an evil, occupying force."[44] The foundation of Israel, however, only focused Muslim anger—it didn't create it. Instead, a new brand of fundamentalist Islam had arisen since World War II, lodged primarily in the Wahhabi teachings, but also in the Shiite school of thought. Politically, hatred of the West was funneled into the Muslim Brotherhood, the forerunner of al-Qaeda, founded by Sayyid al-Qutb. Ironically, it was not the founding of Israel that kicked al-Qutb over the railings into radicalism, but his visit to the United States in 1948, specifically, his time as a college student at the Colorado State College of Education (now Northern Colorado University) in Greeley. There, this middle-class former Egyptian bureaucrat (again disproving the maxim that terrorists are pushed into their activities because of privation and lack of education) and lover of Hollywood films confronted sexual liberation such as he had never seen in his native country. The "main enemy of salvation," he later intoned, was sex. Sexual "mixing led inevitably to perversion."[45] By the time he boarded a boat bound for Egypt in 1950, al-Qutb was a full-blown radical and bigot, obsessed with "the white man in Europe or America" who was "our number-one enemy."[46] Nor were Muslims who rejected jihad to be spared. A "Muslim community" did not exist, only an Islamic revival that would sweep the world, beginning with his home country. Promptly, then, he was arrested, tried, and finally executed by the Egyptian government.

Islamic radicalism had already spread, not only through the Muslim Brotherhood, but also through the mosques, where the themes of Jew-hatred and vengeance against the West figured prominently in sermons. Al-Qutb's mantle passed to another Egyptian, Ayman al-Zawahiri, a Cairo surgeon, radicalized since age fifteen, who opposed Anwar Sadat and called for the defeat of the Jewish and American devils. He was, ironically, innocent of charges that he had participated in the assassination of Sadat (he only learned about the plan a few hours before, and took no direct action), but his time in jail turned him into a "hardened radical whose beliefs had been hammered into brilliant resolve."[47] Relocating to the friendlier confines of Saudi Arabia, he met Mohammed bin Laden, whose construction companies did a great deal of kingdom business, and bin Laden's son, Osama, who had himself served jail time for his affiliation with the attackers who struck the Grand Mosque in 1979. Despite the fact that the Saudi government had crushed the siege (and subsequently carried out sixty-seven public beheadings in four Saudi cities), the bubbling radicalism inside the kingdom merely simmered while it looked for other, softer targets. It had not been controlled, and certainly had not been stamped out.

Bin Laden fell under the influence of the "warrior priest" Sheikh Abdullah Azzam, whose view of the world typified that of many Islamic radicals— "Jihad and the rifle alone; no negotiations, no conferences, no dialogues."

Seeing the Soviet invasion of Afghanistan as a struggle against infidels, bin Laden offered to purchase an airline ticket, lodging, and expenses for any Arab (including family members) who joined the mujahideen.[48] When he joined the holy warriors himself in 1986, he was reunited with Zawahiri, and in 1988 the two formed al-Qaeda ("the Base"). At the time, of course, neither of these malevolent misfits had appeared on the radar screen of any major intelligence service, save perhaps those of Egypt and Saudi Arabia. It's doubtful that even Israel knew who they were, nor at the time was it apparent they would become such malignant viruses infecting Middle Eastern politics and religion.

Meanwhile, a radicalized strain of Islam that blamed all Muslim problems on Israel, the West, and apostates *was* metastasizing, and it was far more pervasive than all but a handful of Western analysts were willing to admit; the preoccupation (including Reagan's) with "moderate Muslims" ignored the reality that when it came to Israel, there *were* no moderate Muslims. Bud McFarlane, who at the time supported the Marine mission, later saw clearly how the events in Lebanon tied into radical Islamic views of a "weak" America and noted of the subsequent Iran arms-for-hostages deal that, "there is, in terms of western logic, a very good case that there ought to be moderates in Iran. That is logical. It is not, I think, the reality."[49] Robert B. Oakley, who worked in the State Department's counterterrorism office during the negotiations with Iran, came to the conclusion even before McFarlane that there were no moderates in Tehran. Nonie Darwish, who grew up in Egypt and who, through her job as an editor and translator for the Middle East News Agency, interacted with Westerners, came to appreciate the hatred and anger into which Muslim children were indoctrinated through their school systems. Yet even some of her friends, including those considered well educated by Western standards, had fully internalized the radical jihadist teachings.

To most Americans, including those in the Reagan administration, radical Islamic fundamentalism still hadn't registered. In Karen DeYoung's 640-page biography of Colin Powell, for example, there are only two references to Islamic fundamentalism, and, based on their public comments, it seems that neither Secretary of State George Shultz nor Secretary of Defense Caspar Weinberger thought much about it.[50] Navy Secretary John Lehman came the closest of anyone in the administration to identifying Islamic radicalism as a significant threat, but he focused almost entirely on the PLO.[51] William Clark was attuned to the issue, but he had just resigned as national security advisor. Congressman Newt Gingrich (R-GA), usually noted as a visionary, impressed White House staffer Ken Duberstein with a speech that warned that neither the American people nor the news media were "intellectually prepared" to deal with the world as it was, and that the media was still "covering Viet Nam and Watergate."[52] Yet even Gingrich failed to mention Islamic fundamentalism. In box after box of correspondence, memos of meetings, and policy debate contained in the Reagan Library, one searches in vain for the words "Islamic," "Islam," or "Muslim," and even when discussions turned to topics such as the *Achille Lauro* or Iranian hostages, they were almost universally defined as "illegal acts," not "terrorism."[53] One exception occurred in July 1982 when Reagan referred to terrorism in a speech as a "worldwide threat." But he still did not blame Islamic fundamentalism.[54] To reporters at a press luncheon on October 24, 1983, Reagan reaffirmed the Cold War context by tying together Lebanon, KAL 007 (the Korean airliner shot down by the Soviets), and Grenada.[55]

Why did so many people, including Reagan, misjudge the extent and depth of this Islamic sea change upon them? Why, despite a connect-the-dots history of carnage worthy of a pointillist, did so few of the Western intelligence agencies appreciate its significance? Diplomats downplayed it; traditional Cold Warriors interpreted it as a smaller piece in the global conflict between free and Communist nations; and all but the Israelis treated Islamic terror as a massive case of "Arab boys gone wild." But there was a track record of blood and horror whose starting point varied depending on whom you asked, and while the creation of Israel was a convenient excuse, the descent into jihad was a long process most visible initially in the rash of airline hijackings.

Probably the first example of a terrorist hijacking occurred in 1968 when an El Al flight was hijacked by militant Palestinians. The same group (Popular Front for the Liberation of Palestine) seized other flights, then the group hijacked four airlines simultaneously from different international terminals and landed them at Dawson's Field in Jordan. Hostages were traded for released prisoners, and the incident prompted President Richard Nixon to introduce the air marshal program in 1970. Two years later, Yasir Arafat's Fatah organization sent Black September terrorists to take the Israeli

Olympic team hostage, killing 11 athletes and coaches before their rampage ended. Another hijacking—one of the most dramatic ever—unfolded in 1976 when Palestinians took Air France Flight 139 and flew it to Entebbe Airport in Uganda, where the terrorists found safe haven under Ugandan thug dictator Idi Amin. Israeli commandos flew to Uganda, assaulted the airport buildings where the hijackers kept the captives, and rescued 105 passengers while killing all the hijackers. But the next year, the Palestinians were at it again, hijacking a German flight that was forced down in Somalia before a similar rescue occurred in which 86 passengers were freed (the pilot died in the rescue), and the hijackers were again eliminated. In the first two years of Reagan's presidency, more Islamic-related hijackings occurred, including one of a Pakistani jet and another of a Kuwaiti airplane. The severity of this threat was probably obscured by the fact that, between 1970 and 1982, ten other major hijackings took place, each at the hands of a different non-Muslim group and each perpetrated for its own (sometimes incomprehensible) reasons. These included the Aer Lingus hijacker who demanded that the pope release the "third secret of Fatima," and Garrett Trapnell's 1972 demand that Richard Nixon release Angela Davis from prison.

Another factor clouding the perceptions of a growing Muslim terrorist threat was the overwhelming early focus on Israel. Bombs went off routinely in crowded markets in Jerusalem and Tel Aviv, but the Western press ignored the incidents. In 1976 alone, five separate bombings and a grenade incident produced a crimson flood in Israel. Palestinians seeking to fire a SAM-7 missile at an El Al plane at Nairobi's airport were stopped before they could complete their mission. However, many other terrorist incidents worldwide were misreported as non-Islamic-related attacks. These included two hijackings in 1976 alone by the Moro Liberation Front in the Philippines, the "Red Guerilla" bombing near the Iranian consulate in San Francisco, and the assassination of three Rockwell employees in Iran. Nor did the press consider attacks against the Syrian government (which sided with the Lebanese Christians against the PLO) as essentially "Islamic terrorism," because they happened *to* Muslims.

The murders of Jesuit priests and Dominican nuns in Salisbury, Rhodesia (modern Zimbabwe), by Muslim militia recruiters, and the seizure of the Washington, D.C., city council chambers (a hostage standoff that was finally resolved without bloodshed) raised no red flags among the media.

Bombs detonated near the U.S.-owned Parisian Discount Bank in 1978, as well as the announcement by the Palestinian Arab Revolutionary Army that it had spiked exported oranges from Israel with mercury a month later, failed to persuade anyone of a large-scale movement. Even in Latin America, where terrorists who bombed the Bogotá hotel office of Lufthansa Airlines invoked the name of Andreas Baader (a pro-Palestinian leader of the Baader-Meinhof gang), no one seemed to link the Islamic killers to a larger world-wide movement. Bombs went off virtually every sixty days in Turkey at some American office or installation, and gunfire into the U.S. consulates in Turkey occurred routinely. Moderates, such as Ali Yassin of Kuwait, or Youssef el Sebai, the former Egyptian cultural minister and editor of *Al Ahram*, were assassinated in 1978. The following year saw more hijackings, more bombings in Israel, ambushes of U.S. military personnel in Iran, the bombing of the Cairo Sheraton, the kidnapping and murder of U.S. ambassador Adolph Dubs in Kabul, Afghanistan, multiple bombings in Turkey and France, plus a bombing each in Cyprus and Vienna. Still more incidents were prevented: a grenade attack in Belgium on Israeli passengers was thwarted by Belgian police, and Berlin police stopped seven Lebanese Muslims from blowing up the city's largest fuel depot.

Collectively, this murderous track record—only a tiny sampling of Islamic terrorism in the 1960s and 1970s—was largely dismissed as the work of "a few individuals," of groups that didn't represent mainstream Islamic thinking. Academics and terror experts said most Muslims were not radicalized, and were not violent. To say that most did not take up the AK-47, however, was quite different from understanding the underlying religious culture that justified those who did. And the very moderates whom the West reflexively cited found themselves at the end of smoking gun barrels. Even if *jihad* had at one time only meant "self-struggle," as some Islamic apologists claimed, the definition was juiced between 1960 and 1980 to mean almost exclusively struggle against Israel and her allies. Along with the more militant redefinition of jihad came geopolitical shifts that repeatedly demonstrated the powerlessness of the Muslim states. Israel won war after war; the Saudis, Iranians, Kuwaitis, and Iraqis had their oil, but that seemed to gain them little. If anything, the discovery of oil in the Middle East only confirmed the weakness of the Muslim nations, which relied entirely on the petroleum processing science and technology of the West. Armies of Western workers arrived to do what the Saudis and Iranians could not do, extract the wealth from their own lands. Little had changed from the time the Suez Canal was built—conceived by French engineers, necessitated by Western commerce, funded and protected by British bankers and armies, and driven by the irrepressible Ferdinand de Lesseps.

Hence, at the same time that a new generation of clerics called for "Islamic republics" based on sharia law, the Muslim countries were reminded on a daily basis of their scientific, cultural, and economic inferiority. Much of the blame, of course, lay with the Islamic cultures themselves. As Middle East historian Bernard Lewis pointed out, the decline in agricultural output in the region rested in part on the "low esteem in which the cultivation of the earth and those engaged in it were held by government, the upper classes, and to some extent even religion."[56] As late as 2008, a visitor to Qatar noted that most of the nation's foreign residents were servants who attended to every need of the Qatari citizens:

> There is a clearly defined hierarchy of servitude. At the bottom of the ladder are laborers from Nepal. . . . Next come the Indians. . . . Then there are the Filipinos who, with their English-language skills, work in hotels and restaurants. . . . A Qatari drives up to a store, any store, and honks his horn repeatedly and forcefully. Within a matter of seconds, a Pakistani or Indian or Sri Lankan worker scurries outside into the blazing heat and takes the Qatari's order, then returns a few minutes later with the merchandise.[57]

The writer found that non-Qataris performed *every* "job," from banking and insurance to executive positions—that the citizens did absolutely no real work. Every shop, no matter how expensive the merchandise, was run by expatriates, and citizens paid no taxes. Overtaxed Westerners may see this as nirvana, but in reality no native truly earned anything, and knew it. With work and investment comes pride; without citizens' having a real stake in society, including paying taxes, creativity disappears entirely, as does self-esteem. (A 1978 study of lottery winners discovered that over time they soon reverted to previous levels of satisfaction, deriving less pleasure from everyday events such as buying clothes or talking to friends. "Lucky wealth," obtained without commensurate work or investment, yielded *dis*satisfaction.)[58]

Obviously, the Palestinians were not frustrated because of their wealth, nor, at the time, did that apply to the majority of Iraqis or Iranians, but the results were the same. Lewis summarized Islam's descent as a "development . . . overshadowed by a growing awareness" of the loss of "creativity, energy, and power," and "a passionate desire to restore . . . bygone glories."[59] Instead, military defeats constituted acts of shame in the Arab mind. Virtually none of the reasons given by apologists for Islamic violence—poverty or lack of education—accurately characterized the actual terrorists, hijackers, or suicide bombers. One study of four hundred terrorists concluded that three-quarters were middle class and two-thirds had a college education; and a group of medical doctors were responsible for the failed Glasgow bombing plot of 2007.[60]

Islam saw itself as challenged by only one force: Christianity, and, more specifically, Christianity as personified in Western culture. Over time, the Islamic world had defeated the pagan Eastern cultures, even the Mongols, whose onetime presence in the Middle East is virtually invisible today. While the Mongols accomplished militarily what Christian Europe could never do (i.e., military conquest of the Islamic lands), the dominance of Western militaries was becoming obvious by the Middle Ages, when European knights first bested Muslim armies at Tours and then later at Malta, and even in the defeat in which the Muslims captured Byzantium—but which was achieved only through the acquisition of Western cannons (which themselves could not be mass-produced by the Turks).[61] Bernard Lewis points out that in virtually every area of life, Islam has adopted Western traditions and cultures— its architecture almost exclusively uses Western techniques, its literature has become dominated by newspapers and novels rather than Koranic verse, and even a revolutionary Shiite government such as Iran's finds it necessary to produce . . . a constitution! The West has dominated the infrastructure, amenities, and services of virtually all Muslim cities, and there is "no desire to reverse or even deflect the processes of modernization" except in the rare case of Afghanistan's Taliban.[62] As an Algerian put it, his country "was once the granary of Rome, and now it has to import cereals to make bread. It is a land of flocks and gardens, and it imports meat and fruit. It is rich in oil and gas, and it has a foreign debt of twenty-five billion dollars and two million unemployed."[63]

Nevertheless, the point is not whether the Islamic fundamentalist revolution unfolded because of shame, poverty, military ineptitude, or any other factor; the point is that it was real and overlooked. No event should have shaken the proponents of the "moderate Muslim" view more than the revolution in Iran in 1979, which filled the government with the very radicalized Shiites that Western apologists said did *not* constitute the "average Muslim." Despite the fact that no financial crisis or widespread unemployment existed prior to the revolution, the new theocratic regime was hugely popular, with more than 10 percent of the population involved in the demonstrations. (In contrast, the French Revolution, the Russian Revolution of 1917, and the Romanian Revolution of 1989 all had less than 1 percent of the population involved in the rebellion.) Shah Mohammad Reza Pahlavi, a U.S. ally (who, thanks to both radical Islamic and Soviet propaganda, was depicted as a U.S. "puppet"), had modernized Iran to a level approaching that of Turkey by 1978. The shah's father, Reza Pahlavi, had abolished sharia law in favor of Western jurisprudence, prohibited traditional Islamic clothing, and banned the separation of sexes and the veiling of women. Each of these actions prompted clashes with the Muslim clerics, including a rebellion at a shrine in 1935. A combination of British and Soviet troops installed Mohammad Reza Pahlavi after his father was deposed in 1941, and when a revolution drove him out in 1953, Americans organized a military-led coup that put him back in power. Iran constituted a key southern roadblock to Soviet expansion, and along with Pakistan made up part of the "containment" fence. Seeing an opportunity to foment dissension, the Soviets played on the shah's habit of ignoring his own constitution and counted on popular reaction to the brutality of the SAVAK secret police. Imams had no more use for the pagan Soviet Union than they did for the (in their eyes) apostate shah, but they allied temporarily with the Communists in order to oust Pahlavi.

One particular cleric, the Shia Ayatollah Ruhollah Khomeini, had opposed the 1963 reforms that broke up large landed estates (including those of the mosques and religious foundations), granted women the right to vote, and allowed non-Muslims to hold political offices. Following riots and confrontations with Khomeini's forces, the SAVAK placed him under house arrest, then, in 1964, exiled him. From 1964 to 1979, Khomeini fomented a new ideology of Islamic revolution, based on the principle that the West was a plague to be stamped out.[64] Jihad and martyrdom, he preached, were essential parts of Islam. As for most of his fellow clerics, the martyrdom part never seemed to reach Khomeini. He promulgated the concept of *Velayat-e*

Faqih (guardianship of the [Islamic] jurists) to enforce sharia law. Some Iranians rejected Khomeini, including constitutionalists and leftists, but both groups would ultimately be crushed under revolutionary Islam.

When the oil boom brought large numbers of rural, uneducated, and traditionalist Muslims to the cities, they drifted into the revolutionary circles. Inflation ate away their wages. Rumors of SAVAK killing or kidnapping political opponents took on a life of their own. With every new demonstration or protest, the shah's government seemed to violate still more religious traditions, adding to the ranks of the dissenters. At the same time, actions by the shah to crack down and restore order resulted in a new scolding by Jimmy Carter, which emboldened the revolutionaries even further. At any rate, the shah was finished after Black Friday (September 8), when security forces (many of them ethnic Kurds) shot into crowds, killing dozens whom the clerics insisted were "massacred by Zionist troops."[65] The remaining government, suffering from strikes, sought to negotiate with Khomeini, who quickly returned to the country, arriving to chants of "Islam, Islam, Khomeini We Will Follow You!" After naming a competing prime minister and benefiting from the defection of large numbers of soldiers, Khomeini took over permanently when rebels won the streets. By April 1979, the first "Islamic Republic"—formed with a theocratic constitution—came into being.

Without question, the Carter administration was caught unaware, and had "no clear policy" on Iran.[66] Only six months before the shah fled, the CIA assured Carter that it "is not in a revolutionary or even a pre-revolutionary situation."[67] The CIA's association with the shah's regime made matters even worse. Yet Carter's national security advisor, Zbigniew Brzezinski, assured the shah that he had the full support of the United States. A year later, the ailing shah was admitted to an American hospital for cancer treatments, causing a new wave of protests in Iran. Khomeini demanded that the shah be shipped back home to face execution, and Carter refused. On November 4, 1979, mobs labeling themselves the "Muslim Student Followers of the Imam's Line" crashed into the compound of the U.S. embassy in Tehran and took fifty-two of the diplomats and staff as prisoners. A half-dozen diplomats escaped and held out at the Canadian and Swiss embassies. Carter dallied, both unsure as to how to proceed and temperamentally unsuited to dramatic military action; his inaction only convinced the fundamentalists of his weakness and lack of resolve. Underscoring Carter's seeming ineptitude, he later launched a complicated rescue mission that failed abysmally, and Americans were subjected to film of Iranians picking over the charred bodies of American soldiers and airmen.

Iran, naturally, played a part in Carter's defeat in the 1980 election. Later, leftists would assert that Reagan had planned an "October surprise" that would allow a successful resolution of the hostage crisis in time to benefit himself. In fact, a congressional task force found no evidence whatsoever to support such nonsense, but there was discussion among some of Reagan's advisers of working with the republicans inside Iran, where Sadegh Ghotbzadeh urged a deal with Reagan, should he win. Abolhassan Banisadr, Ghotbzadeh's rival, also claimed that he'd had discussions in Spain with representatives sent from Reagan (and later disavowed those comments).[68] Banisadr went so far as to warn the ayatollah that Reagan's election "would signify a change in the American mentality [to] a shift to the concept of intervention in the affairs of others."[69] Khomeini snorted, "So what if Reagan wins? . . . He and Carter are both enemies of Islam."[70]

Indeed, negotiations that had moved along briskly suddenly stalled at Iran's end, mostly out of a hatred for Carter. But privately even Khomeini feared Reagan's "cowboy" reputation.[71] In the October 27 debates, Reagan reiterated his "no-negotiations-with-terrorists" mantra, termed the whole episode a national humiliation, and called for a congressional investigation into Carter's handling of it. (Ironically, the hostages were released and arrived on U.S. soil only minutes after Reagan was sworn in as president on January 20, 1981.)

Certainly with the Iranian revolution there was little doubt that Islamic radicalism had changed dramatically from the actions of a few to the voice of an entire nation. Jihadism had also now revealed itself to be a religious, not a political, movement with certain core influences which the West had yet to grasp. Central to those influences was the Islamic emphasis on honor and shame. Similar in many ways to World War II–era Japanese Bushido culture, many Muslim societies (though certainly not all) suffered from a heightened sense of shame. Japanese military culture demanded nothing less than *gyokusai* ("glorious self-annihilation"). Kamikaze attacks relied entirely on fanatical "honor deaths."[72] In the Middle East, these were not new concepts. T. E. Lawrence described the importance of *sharraf*, or honor, in his *Seven Pillars*

of Wisdom. A modern authority on Arab psychology notes that Islamic society "worships strength and has no compassion for weakness"; John Laffin's *The Arab Mind Considered: A Need for Understanding* (1975) recounted
the Arab's "sexual frustrations and obsessions, his paralysing [sic] sense of
shame."[73] Similarly, Nonie Darwish related the experience of women in such
shame-based cultures, where the slightest misstep would bring dishonor to
an entire family, and the careful hiding of possessions, so that envious people
would not give them the "evil eye."[74]

Ronald Reagan, stepping into the Middle East vipers' nest, was therefore still guided by a worldview that reflected two basic interpretations of
the region. First, he and his advisers blamed Soviet mischief in the region
for some of the turmoil, which they determined could therefore be offset by
U.S. power. This overlaid the tendency of Washington to view everything
within the prism of traditional Western-style government boundaries.[75] But
the pot was boiling with or without the Soviets' help. Second, the Reagan
administration perpetuated the view that Islamic radicalism remained a
minor, but growing, influence, and that more traditional motivations, such
as territory, prosperity, and above all, peace, would be valued in reaching a
long-term agreement between the Muslims and Jews.

The last in a long line of events to challenge such a worldview occurred in
April 1983, when Hezbollah, one of the newest terror groups, sent a suicide
bomber driving a delivery van laden with two thousand pounds of explosives
into the compound of the U.S. embassy in Beirut. Driving the stolen van
through an outbuilding, the jihadist plowed the truck-bomb into the lobby
and killed 63 troops and wounded another 120. Yet Reagan's reaction—to
send Habib to discuss both Israeli and Syrian troop withdrawals—indicated
he hadn't yet fully grasped the motivations of Hezbollah (occasionally operating under the name "Islamic Jihad"), which was funded and supported
by Iran. Congress, as was typical, voted economic aid for Lebanon. The embassy itself was moved to a more secure location, but a week before the U.S.
Marines arrived, another car bomb killed 20 Lebanese and two American
soldiers at an embassy annex. (After the Marine barracks was bombed, there
would be more car attacks on the U.S. and French embassies in Kuwait in
December 1983.)

Throughout September, Reagan made personal phone calls to the family
of every American serviceman killed in Lebanon—"difficult, terrible calls,"

as he described them.[76] He consoled himself with the thought that "our efforts seemed to be working, giving time to the Lebanese, the Syrians, and the Israelis to work out a solution to their problems."[77] In fact, any "solution" that did not deal directly with the nature, funding, and operation of Islamic jihad in the region had no hope. And then, at a critical point, Reagan's most trusted aide, Californian William Clark, who had served as the national security advisor, asked to be relieved of his duties. Clark was worn out, and wanted a slower-paced job at Interior, to which he was transferred. Clark's departure may not have changed any of Reagan's policies in the Middle East, but of all Reagan's advisers, Clark seemed particularly attuned to the necessity for reasoned, hard-line measures.

One other Reagan adviser, Jeane Kirkpatrick, the ambassador to the United Nations, seemed to have a prickly, no-holds-barred attitude. She also had, according to Reagan, "bad chemistry" with Shultz. Kirkpatrick had a deep sense of Israel's isolation, and made the case for fairness at the UN forcefully. Because of her tensions with Shultz, however, Reagan hesitated to name her as Clark's replacement, instead turning to Bud McFarlane. The only other truly outspoken "hawk" among Reagan's closest advisers, Secretary of Defense Caspar Weinberger, was outspoken in his reluctance to displease the Muslim states on the grounds that the United States needed oil.

As Reagan noted in his autobiography, Lebanon was still on his mind when he went to Georgia on October 21 for a golf outing. Overnight, his focus shifted from the Middle East to a tiny island in the Caribbean when the Organization of Eastern Caribbean States appealed for help. Grenada, an island about ninety miles north of Venezuela, had undergone a bloody coup led by the Marxist Castro wannabe Maurice Bishop, who invited Cubans in to build a massive airfield. Neighboring islands, including Jamaica, Bermuda, and Barbados, were concerned about Bishop even before the Cubans arrived. Now, certain that they would be the next targets, they pleaded with Reagan to intervene. The United States did have a direct interest in protecting the eight hundred Americans at the medical school on the island, and Reagan had already ordered the U.S. Navy to station a flotilla close by to keep tabs on Bishop. That night in Georgia, after consulting with the Joint Chiefs of Staff, he decided to move quickly before the Cubans could bring in reinforcements or take the students hostage. A little-reported event took place the next day while Reagan was on the golf course, when a gunman took over the pro shop and held seven hostages. He wanted to speak to the president, face to face. Quickly he was captured and the hostages were unharmed (he actually let one go to buy a six-pack of beer!).[78]

At 2:30 that morning, just hours after Reagan had escaped personal danger, the phone rang. Bud McFarlane, the new national security advisor, had stunning news. A Mercedes-Benz truck, loaded with explosives equivalent to twelve thousand pounds of TNT, had plowed through a barbed wire fence at the parking lot of the Beirut International Airport, where elements of the Second Marine Division were headquartered. It accelerated past two sentry posts—the sentries, constricted by rules of engagement, were slow to fire—and slammed into the building. Instantly, the four-story structure was lifted up by the force of the explosion, shattering its concrete supports, then it collapsed, crushing those inside, and killing 241 Marines. It was the bloodiest day in Marine history since Iwo Jima in 1945. Two minutes later, a similar truck bomb detonated at the barracks of the French First Parachute Regiment in the Ramlet al Baida area of West Beirut. There, the bomber took the truck down a ramp into the underground parking garage, killing 58 French soldiers, making it the worst military loss for France since Algeria.[79] Sniper fire hindered the rescue attempts at both sites.

Having spent the previous night in the living room of his Georgia hotel monitoring the situation in Grenada, Reagan's staff spent a second night listening to the reports roll in from Lebanon. As Reagan put it, "the news from Beirut became grimmer and grimmer."[80] It was, Reagan said, a "despicable act." Weinberger, who opposed the deployment, still blamed himself. "The fact that I had been warning against this very thing didn't give me any slight satisfaction," he recalled eighteen years later. "It was terrible to be proven right under such horrible circumstances."[81] Reagan returned to Washington, where he was briefed further, and shortly afterward the CIA confirmed that the attack emanated from the Hezbollah training camp in the Bekaa Valley, although Weinberger later stated, "we still do not have the actual knowledge of who did the bombing of the Marine barracks . . . and we certainly didn't then."[82] Beirut, he said, was "an absolutely inevitable outcome of doing what we did, of putting troops in with no mission that could be carried out." The United States, he continued, had put a referee in the middle of a "furious prize fight . . . in range of both fighters. . . ."[83] The Joint Chiefs of Staff had grave concerns, but Weinberger admitted he never fully voiced their views:

"none of us marched in and told the president that the U.S. is going to face disaster if the Marines didn't withdraw."[84] Reagan never once attempted to shift blame. Referring to the deployment, he grimly admitted, "Part of it was my idea—a good part of it."[85]

Weinberger's reluctance to get further involved came when the Gipper approved a joint French-American air assault on a staging camp, but at the last minute, Weinberger aborted the mission.[86] In fact, the Muslim radicals expected an attack. Hamza al Hamieh, the Shiite military leader in the Beirut area, blustered to CNN, "None of us is afraid. God is with us . . . We want to see our God. We welcome the bombs of Reagan."[87] Few in the White House fully grasped the religious and apocalyptic overtones in the enemy's boasts: cables from the U.S. embassy revealed that the *Iranians* expected to be attacked as a response to the bombing, and quoted Iranian radio as saying they desired the attack: "This is our hope because we seek *martyrdom* [emphasis added]."[88] Comments such as those underscored the *Islamic* context of the battle, and it was noteworthy that the government-run radio in Beirut referred to the dead American and French troops as "martyrs"—the first time a multinational force casualty had been so categorized.[89] By January of 1984, the CIA's director of intelligence conducted a briefing called "The Terrorist Threat to US Personnel" in which he warned that "Shia extremists are increasingly willing to sacrifice their lives in attacks on the MNF. They are confident they are serving the will of Allah."[90]

While not yet perceiving the struggle as one against a shame-honor culture, Reagan nevertheless applied (with some precision) a Cold War response to terrorism: if Americans "cut and run . . . we'll be sending one signal to terrorists everywhere. They can gain by waging war against innocent people."[91] Internal memos confirm that many in the administration shared this view. Cable files record "the stakes in Lebanon, if we are driven out . . . the radicals, the rejectionists . . . will have won." Yet this was still interpreted within the U.S.-Soviet conflict: "The message will be sent that relying on the Soviet Union pays off."[92] Historian Paul Kengor noted that Reagan was troubled and concerned by the possibility of Islamic terror attacks inside the United States—it was one reason he quit attending church, especially after the assassination attempt by John Hinckley, Jr., as he was afraid an entire congregation would become a target.[93] Repeatedly he cited the actions of a "Middle East madman" in his defense of the Strategic Defense Initiative, and argued that even if the Soviets had no nuclear missiles, such a shield was necessary.

In the wake of the bombing, Congress launched an investigation, and concluded there were "inadequate security measures" at the compound, and that the commander made "serious errors in judgement [and] bears principle responsibility." Worse, Congress claimed, information provided by the Marines afterward was "often inaccurate, erroneous, and misleading."[94] No one was fired, although ultimately Navy Secretary Lehman issued nonpunitive "letters of instruction" to the two commanding officers, a step Defense Secretary Caspar Weinberger found sufficient.[95]

Reagan paid a high political price for Lebanon. While at first, Grenada and Lebanon were linked in the public mind—and indeed Reagan's speechwriters tied them together as part of the anti-Soviet effort—in reality the high public approval of Grenada made Reagan's much lower numbers on Lebanon, noted by White House pollsters, even out.[96] And after the bombing, Reagan benefited from strong public sympathy. Support came from such groups as Al-Mojaddedi of the Islamic Unity for Afghan Freedom Fighters and the Federation of [the] Islamic Association of U.S. and Canada, as well as the National Federation of Syrian-Lebanese American Clubs, and even the National Council of Churches, which supported both Grenada and Lebanon.[97] The National Association of Arab Americans had originally opposed the deployment, but after the Sabra and Shatila massacres reluctantly fell in behind Reagan.

Over time, though, opposition coalesced, and not just from the Left. Conservatives such as Richard Viguerie urged the president to pull the troops out. Democrats in Congress, seeing an opportunity to weaken Reagan, began to revisit the War Powers Act (Congressman Mickey Edwards of Oklahoma called the vote to authorize the Lebanon action "misleading"). And while never close to a majority, a growing minority of letters to the White House expressed concerns about whether the United States was "involved in another no win situation where our troops . . . are not allowed to exert . . . enough force to be victorious."[98] One state senator reasoned, "I am sure that a 16-inch salvo from the [battleship USS] *New Jersey* assures the peace more than a Marine contingent. . . . Strategically they are sitting ducks."[99] A handful of writers favored Grenada, but not Lebanon. Overwhelmingly, those opposed to the Lebanon mission did not disapprove because of the use of military force, but rather because they feared the American troops would not be able to use *sufficient* force. "Americans are tired of losing," said one telegram.[100]

Lebanon slowly moved Reagan away from the notion that the Middle East was just like any other region in terms of its geopolitics' susceptibility to reasoned diplomacy. In December 1983, the administration developed the term "state-sponsored terrorism" to describe, specifically, Iranian-supported terrorist activities. This was a step short towards identifying an entire wing of a religion as dangerous. Shortly after the bombing, Reagan wrote. "I still believed that it was essential to continue working with moderate Arabs to find a solution to the Middle East's problems, and that we should make selective sales of American weapons to the moderate Arabs as proof of our friendship." But "at the same time, I was beginning to have doubts whether the Arab world, with its ancient tribal rivalries, centuries of internecine strife, and almost pathological hatred of Israel, was as serious about supporting our peace efforts in the Middle East as King Fahd of Saudi Arabia and King Hussein of Jordan said they were."[101] Another step was taken early in 1984, when the administration issued NSDD-138, which approved preemptive attacks on persons involved in, or planning, terrorist attacks.[102]

These all constituted significant movement toward a more realistic understanding of what was unfolding in the world, and certainly were light years away from the perceptions of Jimmy Carter. Yet Reagan still believed he could work with individual Muslim regimes to effect larger policy outcomes, most notably through his support of the mujahideen to evict the Soviets from Afghanistan. In 1986, the president sent Clark to Baghdad to meet with Saddam Hussein to persuade him to cease supporting the terrorist training cells inside Iraq. Reagan continued to see Hosni Mubarak of Egypt, King Hussein of Jordan, and the Saudi leaders as reasonable men, and he shaped much of his strategy around them. The reality that, often, even those leaders were not in control of their own countries, or that there was a powerful new radical jihadist view gaining ground across the Islamic world, had not yet become clear anywhere in Washington.

Another factor blurring the perceptions of a militant Islam was "Charlie Wilson's War"—the effort to arm the mujahideen with antiaircraft weapons to aid them in their battle against the Soviets.[103] At the time, as Wilson himself pointed out, the Afghans were the only ones killing Russians. But by separating the anti-Soviet aspects of the mujahideen aid from the prospects that those same "freedom fighters" might soon be governed by the Taliban, the administration once again demonstrated that it did not yet have a fully developed view of the Islamic militant threat. Little evidence has surfaced that the United States ever faced any of its own weapons (directly or indirectly supplied), either in Afghanistan or, subsequently, Iraq. Far more important than the materials of war that the enemy received during this time was the message of weakness that began to emanate from Washington under Carter and continued under Reagan—a message really only perceived by the Muslim radicals, for certainly the Soviets saw no such weakness.

During his second term, Reagan's compassion for American hostages led him to approve an arms-for-hostages deal with the ayatollahs in Tehran. Both George Washington and John Adams had exchanged money and/or weapons for captives in the late 1700s (it was, in part, the demand of a fully outfitted U.S. frigate that finally drove Thomas Jefferson to launch a war on the Tripolitan states). John F. Kennedy authorized the delivery of $53 million in material and another $2.9 million in cash to Fidel Castro to secure the release of the Bay of Pigs prisoners in December 1962. So while the rule of American policy was "don't negotiate with terrorists," leaders had broken it for generations. Under the Reagan plan, Israel would sell TOW (for *t*ube-launched, *o*ptically tracked, *w*ire-guided) antitank missiles to Iran for the war against Iraq in return for Iran's role in securing the release of seven American hostages. What Reagan did not know was that Col. Oliver North (and perhaps his superior, Adm. John Poindexter) had gotten more money for the TOWs than was reported and diverted it into a secret fund to arm the Contra rebels in Nicaragua in violation of legislation of the U.S. Congress. Defenders of Reagan have cited the congressional hearings that followed as evidence that Reagan was unaware of these exchanges, and North, having received immunity, stunned Congress and the media by shouldering the entire blame himself. Reagan emerged tarred by the scandal, but could not be connected officially in any way. Iran-Contra proved a blemish on his second term, and was virtually the only foreign policy stain in the eyes of the public, which had not blamed him for Beirut.

They were, ultimately, two sides of the same coin. On the one hand, Reagan had acquiesced in the deployment of American military troops without the possibility of victory—something he swore not to do after Vietnam.

Reagan later cited the Beirut bombing as the cause of the Weinberger Doctrine, later renamed the Powell Doctrine or the Reagan Doctrine, depending on who wished credit for it. The principles, as Reagan outlined them in *An American Life*, were as follows:

1. The United States should not commit its forces to military action overseas unless the cause is vital to our national interest.

2. If the decision is made to commit our forces to combat abroad, it must be done with the clear intent and support needed to *win*. It should not be a halfway or tentative commitment, and there must be clearly defined and realistic objectives.

3. Before we commit our troops to combat, there must be reasonable assurance that the cause we are fighting for and the actions we take will have the support of the American people and Congress. . . .

4. Even after all these other tests are met, our troops should be committed to combat abroad *only* as a last resort, when no other choice is available.[104]

George H. W. Bush would follow these maxims during Operations Desert Shield and Desert Storm in 1990–91, with Colin Powell's approval. Yet buried within even these guidelines were several pitfalls that would entrap future presidents. President Bill Clinton would stretch to make the Bosnia and Kosovo regions "vital to our national interest." In neither case was a true victory possible, or even desired. Bush himself had ordered an end to combat in Iraq when the collapse of Saddam Hussein's regime seemed imminent and the troops only, in Gen. Norman Schwarzkopf's words, "150 miles from Baghdad." Victory was abandoned in favor of adherence to the United Nations resolutions, violating Reagan's second requirement.

After 9/11, President George W. Bush likewise struggled with clarifying the definition of victory, which, after all, is often simply a matter of the other side giving up (even if informally). When resistance ends, victory occurs. Without any specific leader or organization to force to a treaty table, a conflict can appear endless. It certainly must have seemed so to the Romans in their struggle against Carthage, or to the English in their century-long fight with the French. Yet in both cases, there was an end. Nor is it always possible to protect national security and still maintain the full support of Congress and/or the public, especially in an age when the media is predisposed to hate the application of American power. (During the Iraq conflict from 2003 to 2006, virtually *no* major media outlets routinely discussed American *victory*: virtually all were obsessed with American defeat, typically invoking the terms "Vietnam" or "quagmire" to describe the U.S. effort in the Middle East.)[105] Hence, the demands of keeping America secure and maintaining public or congressional support for a war may be antithetical at times: there is evidence that after Germany was defeated, American opinion was slowly but steadily turning against forcing unconditional surrender in Japan, despite the fact that Japan, not Germany, had started the war!

The Founders were absolutely unanimous in their view that the security of the United States was paramount. Thomas Jefferson, called by one author a "half-way-pacifist" and routinely hailed by modern libertarians as a "small-government" leader, in fact dispatched America's first overseas military force to subdue the Barbary pirates.[106] In doing so, did he violate his own (and George Washington's) dictum to avoid "entangling alliances"? After all, his first action was to seek precisely such an alliance with Britain, France, Spain, and other European countries, only to be turned down. (It is ironic that George W. Bush succeeded in putting together a coalition of more than twenty nations in Iraq whereas Jefferson, lauded by liberals, could not construct a coalition with so much as a single foreign power.) Washington himself did not reject alliances, but rather was concerned that the young United States would enter an alliance before its population and military could keep it from being a pawn. During his tenure as commander of the Continental Army, then as president, Washington had in fact engaged in a number of "entangling alliances," most of them nonaggression pacts with Indian tribes. American leaders all desperately sought an "entangling alliance" with France during the Revolution.

As president, Jefferson was not reluctant to fight Britain: he was certainly a Francophile, but he understood that the American navy was not yet a match for the British, and that any declaration of war would invite an invasion . . . which it did. To a man, the Founders would have applauded Reagan's 1986 air strike on Libya (in retaliation for Libya's role in the bombing of a German disco that killed two Americans, and which was only the latest in a string of terror strikes launched from Libya). At the same time, the Founders would have winced at Reagan's willingness to participate in the Lebanon "peacekeeping" effort—just as they would have been dismayed by the similar actions of Truman, Eisenhower, Kennedy, Johnson, Nixon, Ford, and Carter.

What would George Washington, John Adams, and Thomas Jefferson make of militant Islam, however? It's difficult to say: the closest proxy we have for such a radical movement in their era is the French Revolution, which is to say, a poor proxy indeed. Although ideologically driven, the French Revolution was secular. It would be two hundred years before the fruits of such a secular influence in political life were felt. Nothing in the French Revolution came close to the jihadist dogma of forcing submission to Islam at gunpoint; nor had anyone in America or France witnessed anything close to "suicide bombers" who randomly targeted civilians. Even for the French, who seldom paled at the sight of bloodshed, this would have constituted an outrage against the "rights of man and the citizen." In the case of the Barbary pirates, however, whose actions did constitute the terrorism of the day, Jefferson's response was quick, substantial, and sharp. He sent the entire U.S. Navy to crush all the Barbary States, not just Tripoli (the only one to declare war on the United States).

In terms of employing military force, Reagan learned the lessons of Beirut. But in terms of appreciating the symbolism of the subsequent withdrawal of the troops on the jihadist mindset, Reagan committed an even greater mistake than when he sent in the Marines in the first place. Bud McFarlane, once a supporter of the deployment, admitted in a *New York Times* editorial in 2008 that "the most telling [conclusion about the withdrawal] was the one reached by Middle Eastern terrorists, that the United States had neither the will nor the means to respond effectively to a terrorist attack. . . ."[107] McFarlane's revelation was hardly new in light of Islamic thinking. One only had to look at a Middle Eastern paper, *An-Nahar* in April 1982, which predicted that America's failure to respond to the April embassy bombing would lead to new attacks.[108] That radical Islam was fundamentally antithetical to Western concepts of life and liberty—and thus also to incentives based on those values—was still not evident in the 1980s. Thus pulling the Marines out sent yet another message in an all-too-common string of signals that Americans "won't stick."

Our commitment to the value of life became a weakness in the eyes of jihadists, not a strength, as made evident in Osama bin Laden's 1996 comment: "We have seen in the last decade the decline of American power and the weakness of the American soldier who is ready to wage Cold Wars, but unprepared to fight long wars. This was proven in Beirut in 1983 when the Marines fled after two explosions."[109] Over time, the "two explosions" in Beirut would become a recurring theme for bin Laden: in 1998, he sat down for an interview with reporter John Miller for an article in *Esquire,* in which he called America a "paper tiger" that after "a few blows would run in defeat."[110] Reagan's biggest mistake lay not only in committing the Marines to Lebanon under conditions in which they could scarcely defend themselves, but also in confirming in the minds of the Islamic radicals that the United States lacked resolve by withdrawing them. For a man whose own steadfastness and insight into the Soviet mind ended the ever-present threat of nuclear holocaust, it was an uncharacteristic misjudgment. And, even though he began to correct it almost immediately, America is still fighting the same brand of terrorism today.

7.

BARRY MAKES A SPEECH . . . AND
THE MEDIA GETS CHILLS UP ITS LEG

*No government ought to be without censors, and, where the press is
free, no one ever will.*

THOMAS JEFFERSON TO GEORGE WASHINGTON, 1792

At one time or another, any American over the age of forty thought, or
was told, that the news media was "objective," "fair," and "balanced" in
its reportage of the news. Older Americans remember a time—dominated by
the Big Three (ABC, CBS, NBC) broadcast television networks—when one
actually could not discern the political persuasion of nightly news anchors, or
even most of the reporters. Occasionally, a star like Edward R. Murrow would
take on a controversial story—his most famous being the antics of Senator Joe
McCarthy—and thereby reveal his political bent. Most of the time, however,
the news was, well, "news," which covered the major events of the day, beginning with those that occurred in or affected the United States, followed by, if
time allowed, those that affected other parts of the world.

Fast forward to the 2008 presidential campaign and the media's fawning coverage of Illinois senator Barack Obama. That coverage could have been called a number of things, but not, by any stretch, could it be called "fair," "objective," "balanced," or even "news." Perhaps the grossest perversion of a "news" show was commentator Chris Matthews's statement that he got a "chill" up his leg when he heard Obama give a speech. At the same time, the character assassination of the Republican vice presidential nominee, Alaska governor Sarah Palin, by the media was unmatched in modern history, including the coverage of Richard Nixon.[1] How did American news organizations go from vigilantly scouring out *any* hint of bias to the point that, except for Fox News (which, because it insists on airing both sides in its "fair and balanced" reporting, is viewed by all the other media as "conservative"), *all* the so-called news organizations were, as Rush Limbaugh put it, "in the tank" for Obama? In order to answer this question, we must first examine the early history of American news.

As noted in the chapter on Martin Van Buren, newspapers were certainly not born "fair and balanced" or free of bias. Early broadsides, as newspapers were called, of the Revolutionary era briefly championed or opposed the cause of separation from England (one study found that of the seven papers in Boston, four were "loyalist," two were "patriot" papers, and one, Thomas Fleet's *Boston Evening Post,* attempted to remain neutral during the crisis).[2] After independence, these broadsides gave way to a localized, and rather dull, set of neighborhood gossip rags dedicated to community events and occasional police blotters in which the criminal activities of locals were exposed. New York only had one copy of a daily paper for every thirty-two residents, and as one historian observed, "If *all* the newspapers published in 1790 had been evenly distributed, each American would have received just one issue that year."[3] Van Buren's creation of the Democratic Party, complete with its imperative to "get out the vote," changed the local papers full of "clipped news" into full-time propaganda organs whose editors were paid party hacks who unwaveringly expressed only the views of the party that was footing the bill. As one scholar drily noted, the "press was not particularly responsive to its audience during the 1820–1860 years."[4]

While not universal by any means, cracks in the wall of partisanship had begun to appear as early as 1836, when James Gordon Bennett's *New York Herald* introduced a new "commercial and objective" journalism, proclaiming, "We shall support no party—be the organ of no faction. . . ."[5] Bennett announced that his paper would "record facts on every public and proper subject, stripped of verbiage and coloring."[6] A plethora of "penny presses" interested in circulations, not elections, popped up. They operated on new business models under which they tried to appeal to all subscribers.

But it was the American Civil War that brought about a "revolution in journalism."[7] Suddenly, Americans from both the North and South wanted accurate information, not platitudes or propaganda. They needed to know if Billy Yank or Johnny Reb had been killed, who won the battles, and where the enemy armies were at any given time. (In this, the newspapers often proved far more accurate with their information than the scouts or the intelligence units of either army: as the Battle of Gettysburg loomed, Gen. Robert E. Lee learned the identity of the new commander of the Army of the Potomac from a scout who read it in northern papers.) The "home front . . . wanted unvarnished facts," wrote one scholar, although not everyone submitted to the new demands for accuracy: publisher Wilbur Storey told his reporters, "Telegraph fully all the news you can get and when there is no news send rumors."[8] Nor did it mean that battlefield commanders would willingly cooperate with journalists. Gen. George Meade, the Union commander at Gettysburg, grew so disgusted with the dispatches of one reporter that he tied him up and sent him riding backward on his horse out of his camp with a sign around his neck reading "Libeller of the Press."[9]

Both the demands of obtaining rapid, accurate reports and the difficulty of sending long-winded messages by telegraph, with its maddeningly slow Morse code transmissions, imposed a new discipline of syntax and vocabulary on the news and enhanced the value of the new Associated Press, which could distill a variety of reports in one location and forward them to all newspapers. The AP adapted its reporting to the technology of the telegraph, which "was superimposed on a news-gathering system that *already* placed a premium on the apparent factual accuracy."[10] The telegraph, in particular, was a blessing and a curse, replacing verbose writers with "stringers" who economically submitted bare facts.[11] Wire service reporting required an abbreviated journalistic style. AP, United Press, and other wires each served dozens of newspapers of every political slant, thus requiring the wire service itself to remain as "value-free" as possible.[12] The demands of brevity meant that "wire service journalists focused on crafting stories without overt bias or a strong political point of view."[13]

John Thrasher, the superintendent of the Press Association of the Confederate States of America, instructed his association's reporters to submit clear and concise telegraphic stories, free of opinion or comment.[14] Thrasher insisted that correspondents eliminate extraneous words and instructed them to "see where you can use one word to express what you have put in two or three."[15] He provided an example in which he italicized the words to be omitted:

> OKALONA, April 25—Our cavalry engaged *the* enemy yesterday at birmingham. *The* fight lasted 2½ hours. *The* enemy *were* completely routed, *with* 15 killed *and a* large number wounded. Col. Hatch *of the* 2d Iowa cavalry was seen *to* fall from his horse, which ran into *our* lines and was captured. Our loss *was* one killed and twenty wounded. *The* destruction of *the* bridge prevented pursuit.[16]

This transmission process gave birth to the "inverted pyramid" of reporting, in which the most important facts were stated at the beginning, followed by less important ones, and so on throughout the story.[17] The "lead," or the main point of the story, always went in the headline, and from there, "it was not a long distance to reserving the first paragraph of [the] stories . . . for the most newsworthy facts and then organizing supporting material in descending order of newsworthiness."[18]

The impact of the war and the influence of the wire services transformed journalistic styles and introduced a powerful emphasis on fact over commentary.[19] By 1866, Lawrence Gobright, the AP's Washington agent, concluded, "My business is merely to communicate facts. My instructions do not allow me to make any comments upon the facts which I communicate. . . . My dispatches are merely dry matters of facts and detail."[20] In the decade after the Civil War, "objective" stories still only made up about 40 percent of all news articles, but that share rose to more than 66 percent by 1900, and according to journalism researchers, stories described as "biased" declined sharply after 1872.[21]

After the Civil War, journalists themselves called for standards to purge the profession's excesses. This was nothing new: as early as 1843, editors called for a national convention to establish standards, "enter[ing] into mutual pledges . . . [and] form[ing] a virtuous resolution, that they will hereafter control their passions, moderate their language," in order to "pursue truth."[22] Horace Greeley, editor of the *New York Tribune*, established rules for contributors to his paper, assuring that "all sides" to an argument received attention.[23] In 1889, an article criticizing the press used the word *ethics* in the title for the first time, and a year later the first code of conduct for journalists appeared.[24] Adolph Ochs, who bought the struggling *New York Times*, symbolized the ascent of "objectivity" over partisanship when he arrived in New York in 1896 and instructed the staff "to give the news impartially, without fear or favor, regardless of party, sect or interests involved."[25] Oswald Garrison Villard, publisher of *The Nation* and the *New York Evening Post*, reiterated the concept of "fairness," emphasizing that the objective journalist had to report "both sides of every issue."[26] Other subjects besides politics were increasingly covered, and whatever interested "any one hundred people" merited reporting, but the centrality of fact was established.[27] Even many Progressive-era muckrakers believed that consumers were competent to judge for themselves a product's worth if given reliable information.[28]

Of course, a certain number of elitists, who thought "the people" could not be trusted with the news, remained, with one of their most outspoken members, Edwin Godkin of *The Nation*, maintaining that the columns of newspapers should be "gentlemen writing for gentlemen."[29] Journalists "entered the thriving ranks of professional elites by subscribing to the prevailing tenet that political decision-making required insulation from 'mobbish' and 'irrational' voters."[30] Casper S. Yost, for example, the first president of the American Society of Newspaper Editors (ASNE), wrote that "no people have ever progressed morally who did not have conceptions of right impressed upon them by moral leadership."[31] By "moral leadership," Yost meant himself and his colleagues.

But even allowing for political bias, publisher Richard White in 1869 explained that a journalist should make the "strongest argument" he could for his political party, but was not "at liberty to make intentionally a single erroneous assertion, or to warp a single fact."[32] (Hailing Keith Olbermann!) And it's equally true that some crusading journalists, or muckrakers, pompously saw themselves as the moral voices of society, allowing their activism to bury any traits of basic reporting ethics they may have had. Journalists, *Collier's* blared, needed to cast their beam of light "forward up on the way that must be followed."[33] This is the same *Collier's* that insisted, "Truth is the very kernel of the reporter's art," leaving it unclear as to what happened when the kernel of truth suggested the forward beam was aimed in the wrong direction.[34]

Partly in response to the muckrakers, the Society of Professional Journalists was founded in 1909, followed by a more serious response in 1922 when Malcolm Bingay, of the *Detroit Free Press*, organized the American Society of Newspaper Editors (ASNE) to unite editors "on the common ground of high purpose."[35] Bingay and Casper Yost of the *St. Louis Globe-Democrat* feared that "general attacks upon the integrity of journalism as a whole reflect upon every newspaper and every newspaperman."[36] Editors responded, initially, with ASNE's membership swelling to 100,000 (including editors and editorial page writers) before the numbers started to shrink because of internal disagreements over policy.

A code of ethics or conduct, which ASNE established as the "Canons of Journalism," played a key role in establishing the news business as a profession. The "Canons" embraced the objective position by stating that the "primary purpose of gathering and distributing news and opinion is to serve the general welfare by informing the people and enabling them to make judgements on the issues." Article IV said that "every effort must be made to assure that the news content is accurate, free from bias and in context, and that all sides are presented fairly." *Editor & Publisher* magazine (launched in 1901 and merged with *The Journalist* in 1907) predicted the new standards would eliminate the "Typhoid Marys of Journalism."[37] A reporters' counterpart to ASNE, the Society of Professional Journalists, was also established, stating that "public enlightenment is the forerunner of justice and the foundation of democracy" and that journalists should further those ends by "seeking truth and providing a fair and comprehensive account of events and issues."[38] As if to underscore the point about seeking truth, the Society insisted journalists be "honest, fair, and courageous in gathering, reporting and interpreting information," and test the accuracy of their information to avoid inadvertent error. "Deliberate distortion," the Code of Ethics added, "is never permissible."[39]

The Associated Press also had a managing code of ethics, which any modern reader of AP reports would have difficulty recognizing:

- The good newspaper is fair, accurate, honest, responsible, independent, and decent.
- Truth is its guiding principle.
- It avoids practices that would conflict with the ability to report and present news in fair, accurate, and unbiased manner.[40]

Already, however, reporters and editors were experiencing a tension between what they viewed as their call to be a "constructive critic" of society and still tell the truth and be fair. For example, what if accurate and honest news did *not* criticize society? Cracks in the ethics of journalism began to appear in 1947, with the Hutchins Commission on Freedom of the Press (formed out of concern that wartime coverage was too patriotic).[41] The Hutchins Commission claimed in its publication, *A Free and Responsible Press*, "it is no longer enough to report *the fact* truthfully. It is now necessary to report *the truth about the fact*."[42] Merely allowing facts to establish the truth wasn't sufficient: journalists had to establish the truth before they could present the facts![43] Of course, this raised the question "whose truth?" and earned the answer, "the journalists' truth."[44]

Still, to many journalists of the World War II era, these were radical ideas. Consider the comments of beat reporter Lou Guzzo, who worked for the Cleveland *Plain Dealer* from 1937 to 1942, then again after the war, and recalled the near-dogmatic commitment to objective reporting at his paper: "When a reporter on any beat dared fracture the barrier of objective reporting, his copy was tossed back to him for immediate revision.[45] Neither of his city editors, Guzzo recalled, "tolerated even the slightest hint of bias in news reporting." Further, "the newspaper itself espoused so subtle an editorial stance that virtually no one could state with authority that the *Plain Dealer* editorial board or the staff was conservative, liberal, or whatever. . . ."[46] "Balance in reporting," he later said, "was not simply a textbook venture for the entire *Plain Dealer* staff; it was a badge of honor."[47] Guzzo recalled "the devotion there to balanced and truthful reporting, regardless of the issues or persons involved," an expectation made clear in the "Journalist's Creed."[48] It is important, though, to recognize that the majority of journalists in the

1950s saw themselves as professionals who dealt in facts, not the "framing" of news events.

But some exceptions had already started to appear—Murrow, on television, was the most famous. In print journalism, James B. Reston, the Washington bureau chief for *The New York Times*, started to write "news" columns in 1953 that "clearly reflected his own judgments."[49] Soon, other *Times* reporters began to write similar articles reflecting their own interpretation of the facts. And there was an even more troubling trend: the large journalism schools, such as Columbia, were gaining an inordinate degree of influence over those aspiring to careers in the news, just as New York and Washington had attained unparalleled levels of opinion-making power in the United States. One cannot underestimate how swimming in this self-selecting gene pool affected the media. Sociological studies confirmed that "political choices . . . were dominated more by active personal influence and face-to-face communications than by the mass media."[50] When those influencing others' political choices were members of the media, a significant in-breeding started to develop. Contrary to the notion that the elites were always "conservative," in journalism the predominance of the peer group ensured that primarily liberal views would triumph.

Reporting itself was transformed, giving rise to the notion that journalists should not only serve as messengers but also provide a source of authority, credibility, and power. Journalism's homogeneity went beyond a commonly shared view among reporters about gaining, and extending, the authority of the news media. Rather than diversifying, media elites homogenized even further. From 1964 to 1976, the percentage voting for the Democratic candidate in national elections *never fell below 81 percent*. ABC reporter Frank Reynolds, in an attempt to refute the notion that the network news reflected the attitudes of a group of eastern elites, wound up confirming the fact: "Sure, I suppose there is an Eastern Establishment, left-wing bias. But that just happens to be because the people who are in [the media tend to] feel that way."[51] Theodore H. White commented on the exclusionary social milieu in which the eastern journalists operated: "These people drink together, talk together, read the same esoteric and mad reviews . . . [and] they control the cultural heights. . . . [O]ne who does not agree with them has enormous difficulty in breaking through."[52] Such a bias could prove critical in

1969, when 90 percent of the population watched a television news show regularly.

One cannot overstate the similarity among the editors and publishers of the nation's top papers. In a study of the leadership at four major papers— *The New York Times* (seven subjects), *The Washington Post* (two), *The Boston Globe* (six), and the *Los Angeles Times* (five)—since the 1960s, the biographies reveal that there "is not a single graduate degree among them outside of journalism, and only a handful of years spent doing anything other than reporting and editing."[53] They had, in the process, been "thoroughly inculcated in the creed of newspapermen. They are important. They are privileged."[54] Virtually none have had military experience, and aside from running a magazine or two, none have ever had to meet a real payroll where profits counted. (Increasingly, they all came from the same narrow strip, the New York–Washington corridor, which accounted for some 40 percent of Columbia Journalism School students.)[55] When Hugh Hewitt surveyed a Columbia Journalism School class of sixteen students, he found that none owned a gun, all supported same-sex marriage, and only three had been in a house of worship within the previous week. Only one of twelve eligible to vote had voted for George Bush in 2004, eleven for John Kerry.

In the early 1960s, some vestiges of fairness and objectivity still remained, but John Kennedy's election, administration, and assassination seemed to sweep those away. If anything, the assassination boosted television reporting, even though virtually none of the reporters covering the assassination had witnessed the event. In fact, few reporters on the scene—or anywhere close to the assassination area—saw anything. They failed to follow traditional, reliable news reporting techniques when it came to interviewing eyewitnesses, gathering evidence, and transmitting information from the spot. Many, if not most, of the fifty journalists covering the president never personally saw the attack or heard the shots at Dealey Plaza. Most of the television reporters were "huddled outside Parkland Hospital . . . clutching notepads and pencils, listening to radio journalists paraphrase intermittent wire-service accounts of what had happened."[56] That did not stop them, particularly CBS's Dan Rather, from promoting themselves as "eyewitnesses" and making themselves "central players in the record of Kennedy's assassination."[57] The media also immediately labeled Lee Harvey Oswald as the "assassin" before the evidence had proven his guilt. After Jack Ruby shot and killed Oswald, the *New York Times* headline read "President's Assassin Shot to Death." Oswald had not even stood trial, much less been convicted.[58] *Newsweek*, reacting to Oswald's statement that he had not killed anyone, termed Oswald's denial "a lie."[59]

The failures associated with poor assassination coverage (never tracking down the witnesses who saw "other shooters," or explaining the discrepancies in various stories of multiple ambulances and caskets at the Bethesda Naval Hospital) took its toll on reporting as a profession.[60] In 1968, pollster George Gallup told an audience, "Never in my time has journalism of all types—book publishing, television, radio, newspapers, magazines, movies—been held in such low esteem."[61] Rather than returning to objective, fair, and balanced reporting, the news media began to sharply drift in the direction of "gotcha" journalism, as epitomized by the CBS show *60 Minutes*. As David Frum noted, "nothing on television worked harder to spread mistrust" than *60 Minutes*.[62] As the press sought to reclaim its credibility, it scoured the landscape to expose scandals. *The Charlotte Observer* even subjected squeaky-clean evangelist Billy Graham to a hit piece (which proved to be completely without merit).[63]

Vietnam played a role, too, though not the one people generally think of in which brave reporters led the opposition to an "immoral" war. Rather, much of the change came as a result of the news industry feeling that the Kennedy administration, followed by the Johnson administration, was not providing honest and accurate information. Certainly the media did little to cover the troops. As one historian of *The Washington Post* put it, "especially after LBJ's 1964 landslide, the . . . Great Society programs were highly exciting to *Post* editors, reporters, and editorial writers. The war . . . was an annoying distraction."[64] Television news had a more significant impact than the major news magazines, which according to one study dedicated only about 7 percent of their coverage to the war.[65] Whatever the press's role in achieving a defeat in Vietnam, James Reston, of *The New York Times*, claimed the media was responsible: the "reporters and cameras were decisive in the end. They brought the issue of the war to the people . . . and forced the withdrawal of American power from Vietnam."[66] The Tet Offensive provided a shocking transition during which reporters began to be more sympathetic toward the North Vietnamese. Comments in the media about the North Vietnamese plummeted from 100 percent negative prior to the event to only 29 percent negative afterward. On the other hand, negative comments about both the Johnson policy and the South Vietnamese rose by 70 percent and 600 percent, respectively.[67] The failure of journalists to follow even basic rules of objectivity during the Vietnam War should have been obvious to even the most casual observers. Reporters *never* relied on documents or statements from "official" sources in the North, or from any of the Communist participants, because they knew them to be false, controlled, or contrived. Yet it never dawned on these journalists that there was a disconnect in their criticism of the administration—the same system that allowed reporters to criticize government openly by creating and maintaining a free press was deemed less credible than the totalitarian governments that repressed such freedom.

Until the arrival of George W. Bush, no president was more hated by the media than Richard Nixon, who won election in 1968, then reprised that with a massive 1972 victory. In the later campaign, Nixon realized what the Democrats had handed him with the nomination of George McGovern, telling his staff, "Here is a situation where the Eastern Establishment media finally has a candidate who almost totally shares their views."[68] The president noted that the nation would "find out whether what the media has been standing for during these last five years really represents majority thinking."[69] Nixon won a crushing landslide over McGovern, who carried only the District of Columbia and Massachusetts. The magnitude of Nixon's victory stunned and terrified elite journalists. McGovern's popular vote total—29.1 percent—was the lowest ever by a major party's candidate. The reaction was predictable and chilling: one powerful editor responded to Nixon's election, "There's got to be a bloodletting. We've got to make sure that nobody ever thinks of doing anything like this again."[70] When he referred to "anything like this," he meant *winning an election.* Historian Paul Johnson said the aim of the powerful editors and publishers was "to use the power of the press and TV to reverse the electoral verdict of 1972 which was felt to be, in some metaphorical sense, illegitimate."[71] Watergate handed them their issue—their means—to force Nixon out.

With coverage of the scandal reaching "saturation levels . . . on the front page and on the evening news day after day," Nixon's popularity finally fell.[72] As Nicholas von Hoffman wrote, "It wasn't journalism; it was lynching. Not only were the pretentious canons of the trade chucked overboard; so were fairness and common sense."[73] Moreover, the journalists never came close to investigating the *key* allegation, namely whether the order for the break-in actually came from Nixon, or, as G. Gordon Liddy has argued, from Nixon's White House counsel, John Dean.[74]

Nixon never forgot, or forgave, his treatment by the press. In 1989, when advising the newly elected president, George H. W. Bush, Nixon warned him that reporters were "inherently adversarial":

> TV reporters always claim to be "speaking for the people," but they are really speaking primarily for themselves. In many ways, they are political actors, just like the President, mindful of their ratings, careful of preserving and building. A President must respect them for that power, but he can never entirely trust them.[75]

Ripping the façade off objective journalism, Nixon told Bush, through a "memo" published in *TV Guide*, that the "media don't have to be convinced. They have to be outfoxed, outflanked and outperformed . . . [and] will use his failures to pursue [their own agendas]."[76]

If reporters expected applause for their destruction of Nixon, they were in for a surprise (although they certainly applauded each other). By 1966, the media was already held in low regard, with a 29 percent approval rating, falling still further to 18 percent by 1971. A slightly different survey about press "leaders" in ten institutions showed that they had indeed gained a little ground in public levels of confidence, but by 1980 their "respect levels" had plummeted to 16 percent.[77] A similar Gallup poll revealed that journalists and reporters ranked below pollsters and funeral directors as having honest and ethical standards, although reporters came in ahead of lawyers and insurance salesmen! Yet it was hardly a joking matter: overall, the composite surveys used by Harris to examine overall institutional leadership showed a complete collapse of public confidence after the Kennedy assassination.[78]

Journalists' assault on Nixon had come at a great cost—the integrity of journalism itself. Rather than reestablishing its credibility, the mainstream press had lost the trust of the public. In the process, journalism fought back by attacking the public itself and moving further left. In a 2001 study of business and media elites, nine out of ten business leaders said that "people can be trusted," while only seven of ten of the top editors, reporters, and publishers in the study thought people were trustworthy.[79]

Peter Brown, an editor at the *Orlando Sentinel*, conducted a survey in which he sent a professional pollster to reporters in five midsize U.S. cities, as well as the large metro area of Dallas–Fort Worth. Brown and pollster Bill Hamilton devised two separate surveys. One polled 500 residents and 478 journalists in five cities: Dayton, Ohio; Tulsa, Oklahoma; Syracuse, New York; Roanoke, Virginia; and Chico/Redding, California; while the other survey used a massive (by polling standards) database of 3,400 home addresses of journalists in thirteen news organizations—including the Minneapolis *Star Tribune*, *The Washington Post*, Denver's *Rocky Mountain News*, and many other large- to midsize city papers. In the first survey, the pollster phoned residents in those areas at random and asked the same questions posed to the reporters.

They found that journalists were more likely "to live in upscale neighborhoods, have maids, own Mercedes and trade stocks, and less likely to go to church, do volunteer work or put down roots in a community."[80] Taken together, the profile revealed a class of people far removed from the lifestyles of "average" Americans. Journalists were "twice as likely as others to rent foreign movies, drink Chablis, own an espresso maker and read magazines such as *Architectural Digest* and *Food & Wine*."[81] They did not have many children, lived in expensive urban neighborhoods, avoided rural areas, bowling, auto races, yard sales, coupons, or pickups. With this patchwork of shared elite values, "advocacy of elite interests comes so easily that it scarcely seems like bias at all," said one media observer.[82]

Michael Kelly, the late writer and editor for *The Atlantic* and other publications, confirmed the cultural uniformity of journalists, especially those in Washington:

> They are parts of a product-based cultural whole, just like the citizens of Beverly Hills. . . . They go to the same parties, send their children to the same schools, live in the same neighborhoods. They interview each other, argue with each other, sleep with each other, marry each other, live and die by each other's judgment. . . . Not surprisingly, they tend to believe the same things at the same time. . . . They believe that nothing a politician does in public can

be taken at face value, but that everything he does is a metaphor for something he is hiding. . . . Above all, they believe in the power of what they have created, in the subjectivity of reality and the reality of perceptions, in image.[83]

Joel Kotkin and David Friedman, two researchers who specialize in studying high-tech businesses, said "the news media have come to resemble a modern-day caste, largely dominated by a relative handful of individuals sharing a common background and, in most cases, common real estate."[84] Despite hiring more minorities and women, "in their class and education . . . the media have become ever more rarified."[85] Journalists appeared to prove Bernard Goldberg's assertions that there was, indeed, leftward media bias: a 1981 Brookings survey of journalists found that 51 percent said the Washington press corps had a political bias, and 96 percent of them perceived it as a liberal bias.[86]

Journalists are paid substantially more than the average American (42 percent of journalists earn $50,000 or more, compared to 18 percent of the general public); are almost twice as likely to support abortion (82 percent to 49 percent, according to a separate *Los Angeles Times* survey); and are far less likely to support prayer in schools or attend church. Most important, while the media elites live more like the rich than they did "average Americans," they held a deep-seated hostility to capitalism and conservatism. A subsequent study by Indiana University scholars found that median income among journalists has continued to increase, rising nearly 40 percent since 1992.[87]

Eron Shosteck, in his April 27, 2000, column, "Pencil Necks," for the *National Journal*, conducted an extensive Nexis database search to find out how balanced the political terminology in journalism really was.[88] The term "partisan Republican" appeared 85 times in a ninety-day period, whereas "partisan Democrat" only appeared 58 times in the same three-month span. Use of the term "hard right" (683 times) and "far right" (267) appeared more than twice as often as "hard left" (312) or "far left" (130). Worse, when searching for references to "extreme right," the database search collapsed because it exceeded 1,000 citations, whereas a search for "extreme left" only produced 58 hits. It was perfectly acceptable for a journalist to label a Republican as "far-right" or "ultra-conservative," but sometime in the

1980s, major news organizations ceased calling Communist dictators (such as Mikhail Gorbachev) "dictators" and instead referred to them as "leaders." A more detailed study of the use of language by "the elite press of the nation" (*New York Times, Wall Street Journal, Washington Post, Christian Science Monitor*, and the *Los Angeles Times*), covering an astounding 1,500 articles from January 1, 1990, to July 15, 1998, contrasted coverage of the National Rifle Association with Handgun Control, Inc., the NAACP, the ACLU, and the American Association of Retired Persons (AARP).[89] Researchers also identified subtle uses of pejorative labels for the NRA, such as "rich and paranoid," loaded verbs of attribution ("claims" or "contends" rather than "said"), and adjectives to discredit sources.

What was the reading or viewing public's response to such blatant bias? People stopped reading newspapers and watching television news. The declines in audiences were so titanic that by 2009, more people tuned in to Rush Limbaugh's show than to all of the top three broadcast news shows combined. Media elites rationalized that the decline was caused by the fact that the "appetite for news is slipping—from 53 percent in 1994 who closely followed the news to 45 percent."[90] Fox News, the only nonliberal news organization in existence, eclipsed the more established and better-funded CNN in June 2000 across the board in what Matt Drudge called a "cable quake."[91] CNN's ratings had crashed, dropping 28 percent in daily viewership and 16 percent in prime time during the first three quarters of 2000, when Fox News witnessed a 42 percent prime-time increase.[92] After the 2000 presidential election, Fox News trounced its cable competition for inauguration coverage, averaging a 2.5 rating to CNN's 2.0 and MSNBC's 1.6.[93] CNN barely beat Fox in total households—by fewer than 2 million homes, despite being available to 23 million more homes. But it was across the board. One quarter of all California television viewers hated the local news so much that they avoided the news altogether.[94]

And yet, the response of mainstream television news people like Jim Lehrer was predictable: the *audience* was nuts. When asked about bias, Lehrer informed "news" guru Stephen Colbert, "If you think we're biased this proves you're the one who's really biased."[95] This astounding comment was little more than a reformulation of the justification given for dismissing anything said by a patient at a mental ward: "If you don't agree with me, you have to be crazy!" Worse, this was the same underlying philosophy that enabled the Soviet Union to put any dissenters in loony bins on the basis that no one in their right mind can dislike communism. Bernard Goldberg provided an apt metaphor: "How would fish know they're wet? Fish have no frame of reference. *They only know wet.*"[96]

A useful exercise to understand media bias is merely to look at the covers of *Time* and *Newsweek*—at one time the top two "news magazines" in America—with an eye toward how they treat liberals and conservatives in the images and the captions. Ron Robinson, of Young America's Foundation, has prepared a stunning PowerPoint slide show of the covers.[97] Among the images, we find:

- Liberal actor Paul Newman celebrated in 1994 as "One of a Kind" with a very flattering photo when he turned seventy years old.
- Liberal CNN founder Ted Turner celebrated in 1997 for his $1 billion gift to the UN.
- Liberal actor Christopher Reeve celebrated for his "heroic battle to rebuild his life" with a photo captioned "Super Man."
- Democrat ex-governor from Vermont Howard Dean, well known for his angry rants, depicted in August 2003 as a smiling, "feisty . . . renegade."
- Liberal musician Bruce Springsteen depicted in 2002 as "Reborn in the USA" with a flattering picture.
- Liberal singing group Dixie Chicks portrayed as the "Radical Chicks," who were victims of a right-wing assault to label them "unpatriotic."

The list goes on, and until Barack Obama, no one got more favorable coverage than Bill Clinton, who, on various (usually smiling) covers, "explains himself," was ready for "show time," and was ready to "stand and deliver." During his impeachment, however, *Time* presented the entire Lewinsky scandal as "a stinking mess" (September 28, 1998), without identifying *Clinton himself* as the cause of it. Covers proclaimed "Amnesty Makes Sense," there is a "case for national service," we are in a "Post-American World," there is a "Religious Case for Gay Marriage," and on no fewer than seven covers (eight, if you include Al Gore's "Last Temptation"), "global warming" is real. *Time* dedicated two different covers to the "Haditha Massacre," but never had a *single* cover admitting that no such "massacre" ever occurred and that it had libeled the U.S. Marines. Seven separate covers in one sense or another offered images and captions critical of the Iraq war.

Both Al Gore and his wife Tipper ("Team Gore") were featured in flattering pictures in *Newsweek* in 1999 when Gore was the Democratic candidate. The following year *Newsweek* described Gore's "Leap of Faith" while *Time* lauded Gore and his running mate, Joe Lieberman, for their "Chutzpah!" Four years later, *Time* called Democratic running mates John Kerry and John Edwards "The Contenders," while *Newsweek* called them "The Sunshine Boys," who "bet . . . on . . . the Politics of Optimism"—as if the Bush/Dick Cheney ticket was pessimistic. Edwards was later heralded as "The Sleeper." Hillary Clinton was posed in a beaming head shot on *Time* ("Hillary: In Her Own Words"), and named by *Newsweek* as one of the "Women of the Year." Later, she was posed in a serious, contemplative shot with "What Hillary Believes," and yet again with *Newsweek*'s "I Found My Own Voice" cover, followed by *Newsweek*'s "Hear Her Roar." By 2004, when she was a declared candidate, *Time* celebrated her as "The Fighter," and she was still smiling when posed opposite Barack Obama with "The Race Is On."

No one, not even Bill Clinton, came close to the adulatory coverage that Barack Obama received on the covers. In 2005, heralded as "A Rising Star," a smiling Obama wanted to "get beyond Blue vs. Red," when in fact he was the most radical candidate to run for president since George McGovern. *Time* chimed in with another complimentary cover, "The Next President," followed by yet another fawning cover, "Black and White" by *Newsweek*. Between 2005 and 2009, Obama would appear on no fewer than forty-one *Time*/*Newsweek* covers, which likened him to FDR and Abraham Lincoln, explained how he would "Fix the World" and "talk us out of a depression," proclaimed him part of the "New Global Elite" and, of course, "Person of the Year." Again, these were the covers of *only* two of the more prominent magazines. Finally, the logical end point was reached with a *Newsweek* cover that heralded, "Obama on Obama," almost a reformulation of "I AM THAT I AM."

Over the same period of years, how did *Time* and *Newsweek* treat conservatives? Pat Buchanan was portrayed on one cover with an unsmiling, suspicious face and the caption "Hell Raiser." In 1996, a serious-looking

Buchanan, hands clasped like a televangelist, was "Preaching Fear," and *Newsweek* characterized him as a "Bully Boy." A picture of House Speaker Newt Gingrich, mouth open and apparently angry, carried the caption "Mad as Hell." On another occasion, a cartoonish version of Newt in an Uncle Sam suit depicted him as "Uncle Scrooge." In a fight with Clinton over high spending, Gingrich and the Republicans shut down the government. The media hated it, just as they had a year earlier when Gingrich cut the number of congressional staffers and *Newsweek* labeled him "the Gingrich Who Stole Christmas." Even when naming Newt "Man of the Year" in 1996, *Time* chose an unsmiling photo with an eerie green background. Robinson presented his findings to the editorial board at *Time*, and was told by the person who designed the cover that they had given the background a greenish tinge to "make Gingrich look more sinister."[98] In 1998, when Gingrich resigned as speaker after relentless attacks by the Democrats, *Newsweek* gleefully portrayed him as "The Loser," while *Time*, depicting him on only half a cover as if he were sinking, intoned, "The Fall of Newt."

Conservative talk show host and the voice of conservatism, Rush Limbaugh was portrayed as breathing fire into a microphone with a banner that read, "Voice of America?" He got another cover, "Rush's World of Pain," when he announced his addiction to OxyContin, accompanied by a tense-looking Rush apparently addressing a press conference. Probably the most famous Rush Limbaugh cover was *Time's* 1995 depiction of a cigar-smoking Rush with Photoshopped smoke curling from his mouth and the caption, "Is Rush Limbaugh Good for America?" The notion that *Time, Newsweek*, or any publication would run a headline, "Is Barack Obama Good for America?" was simply a nonstarter. Yet another Limbaugh cover featured Rush with a blackened "gag" across his mouth reading "ENOUGH," and a supposed "conservative" making a "case against Limbaugh."

Ronald Reagan drew moderately favorable covers, but *Time* still managed to show a photo of Reagan crying with the caption, "How the Right Went Wrong." Of course, every one of *Time's* solutions as to how the Right should correct itself involved moving further left . . . something that indeed would make Reagan cry! Other Republicans who received unflattering covers or captions questioning or challenging their relevance or competence included Chief Justice John Roberts, Tom DeLay, and Karl Rove. Bush's attorney general nominee, John Ashcroft, was presented as wanting a "Holy War," with a second cover asking, "Should This Man Be Attorney General?" No such question, framed in such a way, was *ever* posed of *any* Democratic nominee, no matter how incompetent or dangerous. Quite the contrary, one of the worst attorney generals ever, Janet Reno, was benignly portrayed as "Reno: The Real Thing." Oliver North, when he ran for the Senate in 1994, had his cover captioned "Down & Dirty."

No one came in for more ridicule on the major magazine covers than President George W. Bush. He was portrayed as in a bubble ("Bush's World: The Isolated President . . ."), out of his league in diplomacy (little feet under a giant cowboy hat), loved or hated (shown with a black eye on one side and a lipstick kiss on the other), part of the "Bush Dynasty," "Bushwacked," part of the "Avengers" with Dick Cheney, and "The Lone Ranger," where once again *Time* claimed on its cover he was "increasingly isolated." He was not only depicted, but indicted, in cover shots of the World Trade Center explosion with the headline, "What Bush Knew." After Hurricane Katrina, amid claims by the left that the Iraq war and the cost of the hurricane would bust the budget, he was shown in New Orleans with the caption "No Big Easy." In a commentary on his tax-cut/stimulus plan, he was shown as a goofy game-show host giving away tax dollars in a "$1.6 Trillion Gamble" (which, by the way, worked).

Meanwhile, *Time* and *Newsweek* also managed to run—sandwiched in between the half-dozen negative articles about Iraq, the two articles about the nonexistent "Haditha Massacre," and a bevy of articles on Republican (but only Republican) scandals—at least *four* covers heralding a "new recession" when unemployment was a stunning 4.5 percent! Yet when Obama dramatically deepened the depression in 2009, the major magazine covers couldn't find space for a single message critical of the president's economic policies. Quite the contrary, *Newsweek*, showing a blue and red handshake, ran the headline "We Are All Socialists Now." Suddenly, it was not the president who was responsible for the downturn, but the "rich." *Time* (right under a small box called "Anger Management: Why Obama Is Keeping Cool") explained "How Wall Street Sold Out America."

John McCain, a media favorite so long as he criticized Republicans, found the adulatory press retreating from his side as soon as he decided to run against a Democrat, much less Barack Obama. *Newsweek* juxtaposed the blue Obama as "Mr. Cool" versus the red-faced McCain as "Mr. Hot," playing on rumors that McCain could easily lose his temper. In a clever positioning on a cover called, "Does Temperament Matter?" (to which the answer was "yes" only if it was positive for Obama), *Time* placed Obama next to Lincoln, with McCain in the lower left, looking up at the two of them (for guidance, one supposes).

During the campaign of 2008, the media had a "slobbering love affair," as Bernard Goldberg called it, with Obama. In his book of the same title, Goldberg asserted that it was not the "same old liberal bias we have witnessed for years. In 2008, the mainstream media crossed the line."[99] MSNBC, according to the Project for Excellence in Journalism, came close to nearly totally lopsided coverage, with 73 percent of its stories about John McCain assessed as negative, as opposed to only 14 percent of its stories about Obama being labeled negative.[100] In a single ten-day period, *The New York Times* ran a stunning eleven news stories and three op-eds about Republican vice presidential candidate Sarah Palin's wardrobe, yet in the two months prior, the *Times* had only managed to run two stories examining Obama's close relationship with former and unrepentant terrorist Bill Ayers. Political analyst Stuart Rothenberg said it all when he said journalists "preferred Obama. They liked Obama. They're Democrats."[101]

Not only was coverage biased when it came out of the media machine, but reporters dutifully and obediently refrained from asking Obama potentially embarrassing questions during the campaign. In May 2008, during an interview with Obama, CNN's John Roberts referred to the brewing firestorm over Obama's radical preacher, Rev. Jeremiah Wright, who had, among other comments, stated that the United States had deserved to be struck on 9/11 and called America the "U.S. of KKK A." Yet Roberts astoundingly declared a "Reverend Wright free zone today. So, no questions about Reverend Wright. . . . Is that okay with you?"[102] Can anyone imagine George W. Bush being told by an interviewer during Operation Iraqi Freedom that he had entered a "WMD free zone today, so, no questions about WMDs"?

Obama made the cover of the national newspaper insert magazine *Pa-*

rade twice in five months. The second time, Father's Day, 2009, the White House contacted the magazine and asked for space so that Obama could write an essay on fatherhood. When told it would have to be ready in two days, Obama agreed and it was. This occurred when events in Iran were exploding, and the president had yet to find time to make a statement supporting the protesters trying to overthrow the radical Islamic government there. It led liberal Fox News analyst Juan Williams to explode, "We are going towards a weekend of high tide for kowtowing to the Obama administration," and Howard Kurtz referred to a "giddy sense of boosterism" among the reporters.[103] A few voices on the Left began to question the media's obsession with Obama. Phil Bronstein, writing on sfgate.com, lectured: "Love or lust, Obama and the fawning press need to get a room." Powerful people like Obama always tried to "play" the press, he argued, but "you can blame the press, already suffocating under a massive pile of blame, guilt, heavy debt and sinking fortunes, for being played."[104] Radical feminist Camille Paglia, often a maverick on the Left, derided Obama's frequent avoidance of tough questions, and limits on press-conference topics.

It was inevitable that the research organizations would study the election, and their conclusions were predictable. According to a Pew Research Center Poll, Obama enjoyed almost twice as much favorable press as George W. Bush over the first hundred days, and about 30 percent more than Bill Clinton.[105] Pew described the coverage as "favorable," but that failed to do justice to the utter homage reporters paid to the new president. During the entire campaign, the *only* challenging questions Obama got were from Fox News's Bill O'Reilly. Even foreign press were awed by Obama.

In Germany, when the press attempted to ask about tensions with German chancellor Angela Merkel, Obama cut them off, saying, "So, stop it all of you!"—and they did. Robert Samuelson (no Leftie) in *The Washington Post* likewise warned of the "Obama infatuation," calling it the "great unreported story of our time."[106] Obama, Samuelson noted, "has inspired a collective fawning." Unfortunately, he pointed out, the system only works when the press acts as a brake, or a check, on presidential power. A study by the Center for the Media and Public Affairs, with the highly misleading headline, "Media Boost Obama, Bash His Policies," confirmed Pew's research: the media gave Obama more coverage (and far more favorable coverage) than Bush and Clinton combined. Evening news shows devoted 1021 stories lasting 27 hours 44 minutes to Barack Obama's presidency, with 58 percent of all evaluations of the president and his policies favorable, contrasted with coverage of George W. Bush, who received only 33 percent positive evaluations. Clinton was favorably covered 44 percent of the time. Among the "big three" broadcast news networks, Obama earned 57 percent positive comments on ABC, 58 percent positive on CBS, and 61 percent positive on NBC. But he fared far better in *The New York Times*, where 73 percent of the references were favorable. In contrast, once again Bush had only about one-third favorable comments from those same outlets.[107]

As Bernard Goldberg noted, the press's coverage amounted to the admission that "we need the black guy to win *because he's black.*" Why? Because "helping elect our first African-American president would make liberal journalists feel better about the most important people in their lives—*themselves.*"[108] With such gushing, uncritical coverage, journalists "squandered what little credibility they had left."[109] Credibility? *The New York Times Magazine* blatantly cheered a "new generation," "Generation O," and *New York* magazine celebrated "OBAMAISM . . . a new kind of religion."[110] Perhaps the most amazing journalistic story of the presidential campaign was that the first major penetrating story to delve into Rev. Jeremiah Wright's racially charged hate did not come from any one of the major news outlets, but from rock and roll magazine *Rolling Stone.*[111]

Increasingly, all "news" credibility disappeared. Major newspapers and especially television "news" programs had become entirely propagandistic—reverting very closely to the situation in the 1830s, without the direct connections to, and funding from, the political parties. Nor did the news organizations seem concerned about losing their audience and readers, because, as Rush Limbaugh told Bernard Goldberg, "the mainstream media's audience is the mainstream media."[112] Reporters wrote for each other, to impress each other, to generate prestige points at cocktail parties and social affairs, and, of course, for access to the levers of government when that government was in Democratic hands.

The Founders were adamant that, to paraphrase Jefferson, it was better to have a press without a government than a government without a press.

But the press Jefferson and the other Founders championed was meant to act as a healthy, robust, and fair Fourth Estate that countered the government, investigated its abuses, and challenged its claims. Neither George Washington nor Thomas Jefferson enjoyed complete support from the newspapers of the day, some of which were murderously vindictive (one flatly called for Washington's death). For all their vision, they never foresaw a time when the overwhelming number of free journalists would willingly abandon all criticism of the government. While outlets such as Fox News, the Drudge Report, *The Washington Times*, and Rush Limbaugh's radio show provide some measure of balance, the trend is depressingly negative.

In the short term, we are much more likely to come full circle back to the Jacksonian era of competing partisan presses, where there is virtually *no* "news," but all politics—funded, supported, and editorially controlled by the major parties. Yet while those papers originally collapsed under the weight of their own unprofitability, combined with the Civil War's demand for "hard news," the Brave New World might not offer such hope of righting the ship. The protections the Founders put in the Constitution for freedom of speech were meant to specifically ensure freedom of political dissent by the press—but what happens if the press, for its own purposes, refuses to serve as a check on government? In their well-deserved focus on protecting political speech, the Founders never addressed the possibility that the Fourth Estate would find itself in bed with government itself.

The free market has provided a solution in the form of the Internet, talk radio, and even a few "old-fashioned" media sources in television and newspapers, such as Fox News and *The Washington Times*. New media's power was first demonstrated when Matt Drudge nearly single-handedly forced an investigation into Bill Clinton's affair with an intern, arguably playing a key role in Clinton's impeachment. More recently—while the battle has yet to be decided—it is clear that talk radio, the Internet, and "alternative" sources have at the very least badly stalled, and potentially killed, the Obama administration's health care bill, possibly with a serious impact on Democrats in the 2010 elections. That is the value of a free press. But there already were forces working inside the Obama administration to destroy alternative sources of information: there were plans to impose new regulations on radio stations cloaked under "diversity" requirements that would force owners to abandon all political talk formats under threat of federal lawsuits; and under the guise of "Internet security," the administration announced plans to enact an "emergency shutdown" of Internet servers and Web sites. One does not need to read Jefferson, Madison, Hamilton, or any of the Founders to know what their reaction to such measures would be. One just needs to read the First Amendment to the Constitution.

CONCLUSION

We often forget that the Founders were living, breathing people—that they listened to music, ate and drank, suffered from physical pain and sickness, and paid bills. The genius of the Constitution they wrote, based and grounded on the Declaration of Independence, is in the framework of general order and broad principles it provides. The Founders did not want to dictate every move of the American people, and they trusted that later generations would interpret it based on common sense and, above all, religious direction guiding human virtue. Political scientists have long explained to students that the specifics within the Constitution are limited by intent, with the assumption that people did not need to be told how to conduct every aspect of their daily lives.

Yet running a government, no less than running a country, demands flexibility. Too often, mischief has arisen based on outlandish interpretations of the Founders' desire to protect the federal government so that it could provide for the common defense or address the failings of the Articles of Confederation. There have been three chief sources of the pernicious expansion of government, all of which are loosely defined and open to future interpretation. First, the preamble itself includes the phrase "promote the general Welfare, and secure the Blessings of Liberty to ourselves and our Posterity." What did the Founders mean by promoting the general welfare?

Did they mean the government should regulate what people could wear? What they could eat? What kinds of interior illumination they had in their homes? How they traveled? Certainly not. It is absurd to assert that the Founders in any way, shape, or form *ever* intended government to become involved in the personal affairs of individuals. They had plenty of examples from which to choose if they wanted to include such nonsense: some of the colonies had sumptuary laws that restricted what clothing people could wear (for example, rich people could not wear anything that flaunted their wealth). These, however, were mostly the dying (and pernicious) elements of Puritanism, and none of the Founders sought to incorporate such classism into the Constitution.

Many of the Founders, based as they were in the traditions of the English government, thought it proper to establish a national university or to allow the government to build and maintain roads. Although I would disagree, there is a case to be made for either or both as an element of national security, which is certainly the approach the Founders took. If building freeways and establishing a government-run university were all we had to fear from the government in Washington, D.C., most people would gladly accept these and move on. But if the government had ever tried to meddle in the private affairs of individuals, the Founders would have fought against it. At any rate, as some constitutional historians have observed, the preamble to *anything* does not constitute a binding law—it is merely a statement of goals and objectives, and therefore for anyone to cite the "general welfare" as a proper function of government, then manipulate that into a defense of Social Security or food stamps or housing subsidies, would demand that we establish the intentions of the Founders beyond a reasonable doubt. In such a case, the Founders would clearly have rejected federal "disaster aid," a National Endowment for the Arts, and federal dietary guidelines.

A second way in which the Constitution opened the door for government growth came through the "necessary and proper" clause (Article I, Section 8):

> The Congress shall have Power—To make all Laws which shall be necessary and proper for carrying into Execution the foregoing Powers, and all other Powers vested by this Constitution in the

Government of the United States, or in any Department or Officer thereof.

This, also, has been abused beyond imagination. Note that the clause refers to the "foregoing Powers, and all other Powers vested by this Constitution." Therefore, the so-called elastic clause cannot apply to any powers exercised *outside* the narrow definitions of the Constitution. It was never meant as carte blanche for government to do what it wished. Unless the actions themselves are delineated in the Constitution, they are illegal. Chief Justice John Marshall and his Court, in the famous *McCulloch v. Maryland* case in 1819, validated the Bank of the United States (BUS) under this broad interpretation, and a reasonable argument can be made that while the BUS was neither necessary nor prudent, it was completely constitutional and, as an arm of the U.S. Treasury, helped execute the nation's financial business. Subsequently, however, the "elastic clause" has been stretched further than the truth in Bill Clinton's Lewinsky defense.

It is *not* "necessary and proper" for the United States government to involve itself in local schools; or to dictate a national energy policy in times of peace; or to mount a space program for any purpose *other* than national security (where, in fact, a good case can be made for one). There is no "necessary and proper" intrusion of Uncle Sam into developing property in your own backyard, (even if rare birds do land there once in a while), and there is certainly nothing that can be construed as "necessary and proper" that would allow the federal government to dictate what cars we drive or how they are made. Only a serious judicial reevaluation of the constitutional meaning of this phrase will redress the imbalance.

But that leads to the last area in which the looseness of the United States Constitution has allowed liberals to expand federal power beyond anything the Founders could have conceived: the federal judiciary. As Mark Levin, Andrew Napolitano, and Stephen Powers and Stanley Rothman have explained in detail, the majority of unconstitutional programs and policies have come into existence not through power-hungry presidents or runaway legislatures, but through activist judges employing judicial positivism (i.e., the view that whatever you *want* to use the law for should be permitted—that the law is an instrument of present morality, not permanent principles).[1] The purpose of this book is not to restate these authors' excellent works, but to note that the ambivalence of the Founders toward a federal court system proved a titanic weakness in the Constitution, one created by the experience of the Founders themselves who, throughout their lives, had only dealt with tyrannical parliaments and kings, but never courts. Indeed, to them the courts provided safe havens from the oppression of elected and unelected bodies. Thus we have, over two hundred years later, arrived at the point where in the name of the preamble (when liberals choose to quote the Constitution at all!), by employing the rationale of the "elastic clause" and utilizing judicial activism to circumvent elections, modern liberals have empowered the United States government with the ability not only to open the bedroom door, but literally to peek inside one's stomach or dictate what music one listens to by forcing a contribution to "approved" arts.

When writing this book, all too often I searched for specific comments by the Founders on funding of the arts, or the government's role in advising citizens about diet, or responding to natural disasters, yet I found very few such comments. The obvious conclusion is that such interventions into the private affairs of individuals—even if for "their own good"—were considered so foreign and antithetical to their principles as to scream out by their silence. Many of the events in our history that have led to the expansion of government power have indeed been threats to our survival, including secession by half the nation in 1860–61 and direct attacks on our population in 1941 and 2001. The Founders expected such difficulties to arise and provided remarkable emergency powers within the Constitution, but always trusted that when the threat had subsided, not only would virtuous leaders give power back, but a populace jealous of its own rights would demand it.

We have arrived, however, at the bottom of a ravine courtesy of the "slippery slope." Liberty, lost an inch at a time, is very difficult to reclaim. The argument that "we've already done that" can be accurate, yet irrelevant. If you've already swallowed poison once, it's a good idea not to try it a second time.

The fact that as of 2009, the United States government weighs in on something as fundamental—and utterly out of human control—as climate, or that there are large bureaucracies to provide music, art, and television programs that, if left to the free market, would never see the light of day, testifies to just how deep that ravine is. Moreover, when such issues as the constitutionality of these kinds of activities are raised, the standard sneering dismissal by the mainstream media itself has become a clarion that liberty is eroding. One cannot imagine any politician of any stripe impinging on the freedoms of early Americans without most of the citizenry and at least half of the presses shouting out in response.

Lincoln said reverence for the Law should be spoken at every opportunity. Perhaps a second truism needs to be reiterated unceasingly—that government grows. It always grows, like a living creature it seeks to expand, and like a living creature it will not relinquish what it already has without a struggle. The task for modern Americans, who have grown troublingly comfortable with accepting favors, support, and advice from Washington, D.C., as well as their state governments, is to once again strive to view government as the problem, not the solution. And to paraphrase Lincoln: preach it, brother!

ACKNOWLEDGMENTS

As will be apparent, some of these chapters have proven much more fun to write than others, most notably the chapter on rock and roll. As a former rock drummer (my bands opened for such "Golden Age" rock acts as Steppenwolf, Savoy Brown, the James Gang, and Mother's Finest), it was a particular privilege to interview a number of the top musicians of the era for this research, including Mark Stein and Vinny Martell of Vanilla Fudge, Felix Cavaliere of the Rascals, David Paich of Toto, Robby Krieger of the Doors, Jimmy Haslip, Dave Mason, and Alice Cooper. I thank all of them for their time and thoughts, and for their energy: at times I half-believed I could pick up my sticks and pound out the Fudge's version of "You Keep Me Hangin' On" (but those impulses usually disappeared after a timely nap!).

I would also like to express my gratitude to the Ronald Reagan Presidential Library, particularly Steve Branch and Mike Duggan with the National Archives and Records Administration. At the University of Dayton, I received research assistance from a former student, Peter Cajka, whose work on the Dayton Flood is heavily cited here, and Matthew Kniess. Cynthia King proofread much of the manuscript, and as always, I received generous support from the university in general and the history department in particular. Everywhere I go, I'm asked, "How does a conservative survive in a university setting?" I always reply that I can't answer for others at other institutions, but at UD I have received nothing but support.

Christopher Castelitz also provided valuable research assistance. To Gary Taubes, whose book *Good Calories, Bad Calories*, not only changed my mind but my life, I am deeply indebted. In each case, none of the opinions or conclusions—and certainly none of the errors—that appear here are anyone's but my own.

As always, the crew at Sentinel has been wonderful. Adrian Zackheim helped develop the concept of this book; Brooke Carey, my editor, helped refine it; and my publicist at Sentinel, Amanda Pritzker, has ensured that no stone is unturned in bringing my work to the attention of the media. Writing is a lonely sport, so it's always refreshing to have so many individuals that I can talk to, rely on, and argue with during the process of fashioning a book.

NOTES

PREFACE

1. 1. Samuel P. Huntington, *The Clash of Civilizations and the Remaking of the World Order* (New York: Simon & Schuster, 1996), 58.
1. 2. Mort Zuckerman, "America's Love Affair with Obama Is Over," *U.S. News & World Report*, November 5, 2010, http://politics.usnews.com/opinion/mzuckerman/articles/2010/11/05/mort-zuckerman-americas-love-affair-with-obama-is-over.html.

CHAPTER 1

1. Thomas Jefferson to John Holmes, Thomas Jefferson Library of Congress Exhibition, U.S. Library of Congress, www.loc.gov/exhibits/jefferson/159.html.
2. Donald B. Cole, *Martin Van Buren and the American Political System* (Princeton, NJ: Princeton University Press, 1984), 59.
3. Harold W. Stanley and Richard G. Niemi, *Vital Statistics in American Politics, 1997–1998* (Washington, DC: CQ Press, 1998), 193–95; Donald L. Robinson, *Slavery in the Structure of American Politics* (New York: Harcourt Brace Jovanovich, 1971), 23, 39, 180, 404.
4. George Washington's Farewell Address, http://avalon.law.yale.edu/18th_century/washing.asp.
5. "Federalist #10," in Clinton Rossiter, ed., *The Federalist Papers: Alexander Hamilton, James Madison, John Jay* (New York: New American Library, 1961), 78.
6. John C. Fitzpatrick, ed., *The Autobiography of Martin Van Buren,* in *Annual Report of the American Historical Association for the Year 1918*, II (Washington, DC: American Historical Association, 1920), 125; Cole, *Martin Van Buren and the American Political System*, 96; Mike Wallace, "Changing Concepts of Party in the United States: New York 1815–1828," *American Historical Review* 74 (1968): 453–91.

7. *Albany Argus*, January 29, 1822, and October 8, 1824.

8. Robert V. Remini, *Martin Van Buren and the Making of the Democratic Party* (New York: Columbia University Press, 1959), 41.

9. "United States Federal State and Local Government Spending," 1800, http://www.usgovernmentspending.com/year1800_0.html.

10. Robert Pierce Forbes, *The Missouri Compromise and Its Aftermath* (Chapel Hill: University of North Carolina Press, 2007), 33.

11. Tiarr Martin, "The Growth of Government During the 'Age of Jefferson and Jackson,'" 1989, unpublished paper in author's possession.

12. John Quincy Adams, "Inaugural Address," 1825, in James D. Richardson, *A Compilation of the Messages and Papers of the Presidents, 1789–1897* (New York: Bureau of National Literature, 1897), 294–99.

13. Larry Schweikart, *The Entrepreneurial Adventure: A History of Business in the United States* (Ft. Worth, TX: Harcourt, 2000), ch. 4, passim; Larry Schweikart and Lynne Pierson Doti, *American Entrepreneur* (New York: Amacom Press, 2009), ch. 4, passim.

14. John Steele Gordon, *Hamilton's Blessing: The Extraordinary Life and Times of Our National Debt* (New York: Penguin, 1998).

15. A short, but insightful, analysis of Hamilton appears in Charles Calomiris, "Alexander Hamilton," in Larry Schweikart, ed., *The Encyclopedia of American Business History and Biography: Banking and Finance to 1913* (New York: Facts on File, 1990), 239–48. The best recent work on Hamilton is Ron Chernow, *Alexander Hamilton* (New York: Penguin, 2006).

16. Ron Chernow, *Alexander Hamilton* (New York: Penguin, 2004), 300.

17. See Richard P. McCormick, "New Perspectives on Jacksonian Politics," *American Historical Review* 65 (1960): 288–301, and his "Political Development and the Second Party System," in William Nesbit Chambers and Walter Dean Burnham, eds., *The American Party Systems: Stages of Political Development* (London: Oxford University Press, 1967), 90–116 (quotation "curious exceptions" on 107 fn. 14).

18. McCormick, "Political Development," 107.

19. Richard McCormick, "Suffrage Classes and Party Alignments: A Study in Voter Behavior," *Mississippi Valley Historical Review* 46 (1959): 397–410 (quotations on 402 and 409).

20. Paul Goodman, "The First American Party System," in Chambers and Burnham, *American Party Systems*, 56–89.

21. In our 2004 book, *A Patriot's History of the United States*, Michael Allen and I refer to this as the most important election in American history, for it set the stage for nonviolent transitions of power between groups representing often radically different interpretations of America's character (Larry Schweikart and Michael Allen, *A Patriot's History of the United States from Columbus's Great Discovery to the War on Terror* [New York: Sentinel, 2004]).

22. *Nixon v. Shrink Missouri Government PAC,* 528 U.S. 377, 424 (2000).

23. Chernow, *Alexander Hamilton,* 252.

24. Garry Wills, *Explaining America* (New York: Penguin Books, 1982), 195.

25. *California Democratic Party v. Jones,* 530 U.S. 567, 592 (2000), Stevens's dissent, 19.

26. McCormick, "New Perspectives on Jacksonian Politics," passim.

27. McCormick, "Political Development," 100.

28. Charles and Mary Beard, *The Rise of American Civilization* (New York: Macmillan, 1994), 550.

29. James Stanton Chase, "Jacksonian Democracy and the Rise of the Nominating Convention," *Mid-America* 45 (1963): 229–49.

30. Lynn Marshall, "The Strange Stillbirth of the Whig Party," *American Historical Review* 72 (January 1967): 445–69.

31. McCormick, "Political Development," 107.

32. Richard H. Brown, "The Missouri Crisis, Slavery, and the Politics of Jacksonianism," in Stanley N. Kurtz and Stanley I. Kutler, eds., *New Perspectives on the American Past, vol. 1, 1607–1877* (Boston: Little, Brown, 1969), 241–255 (quotation on 242).

33. Ibid., 242.

34. Ibid., 243.

35. Adams quoted in ibid., 243.

36. Jefferson to Holmes.

37. Ibid.

38. George Dangerfield, *The Era of Good Feelings* (New York: Harcourt, 1952).

39. Brown, "Missouri Crisis," 244.

40. Ibid., 245.

41. Ibid., 245.

42. Van Buren's reputation as opposing slavery is near-universal. As president, however, his actions in the *Amistad* case raise questions about his commitment to ending slavery: he lent every support of the executive branch that he could to the Cubans to reenslave the rebels and return them to Cuba; he had the State Department and federal attorneys working on the side of the Cubans, and had the U.S. Navy standing by to return the captives if and when the court found against them. U.S. Attorney Felix Grundy, without being requested to do so, submitted an opinion supporting the Cuban position and stating that American courts had no right to try the case. See William M. Wiecek, "Slavery and Abolition Before the United States Supreme Court, 1820–1860," *Journal of American History* 65 (June 1978): 34–59, and Samuel Flagg Bemis, *John Quincy Adams and the Union* (New York: Alfred A. Knopf, 1956).

43. Chase, "Jacksonian Democracy and the Rise of the Nominating Convention," 239, and his *Emergence of the Presidential Nominating Convention, 1789–1832* (Urbana: University of Illinois Press, 1973); Van Buren, *Autobiography*, 514; Cole, *Martin Van Buren and the American Political System*, 151.

44. Cole, *Martin Van Buren and the American Political System*, 151.

45. Ibid., 151.

46. Ibid.

47. Remini, *Martin Van Buren and the Making of the Democratic Party*, 120.

48. Cole, *Martin Van Buren and the American Political System*, 177.

49. Richard B. Kielbowicz, "Newsgathering by Printers' Exchanges Before the Telegraph," *Journalism History* 9 (Summer 1982): 42–48.

50. Thomas C. Leonard, *News for All: America's Coming of Age with the Press* (New York: Oxford University Press, 1995), 13, 43.

51. Ibid., 15.

52. Allan R. Pred, *Urban Growth and the Circulation of Information* (Cambridge: Harvard University Press, 1973), 32–34.

53. Robert V. Remini, *The Election of Andrew Jackson* (Philadelphia: J. B. Lippincott, 1963), 77.

54. Ibid., 49.

55. Gretchen Garst Eweing, "Duff Green, Independent Editor of a Party Press," *Journalism Quarterly* 54 (Winter 1977): 733–39 (quotation on 736).

56. Erik McKinley Eriksson, "President Jackson's Propaganda Agencies," *Pacific Historical Review* 7 (January 1937): 47–57.

57. Green in the *United States Telegraph*, February 7, 1826, quoted in Culver H. Smith, "Propaganda Technique in the Jackson Campaign of 1828," *East Tennessee Historical Society Publications* 6 (1934): 53. See also Fletcher M. Green, "Duff Green, Militant Journalist of the Old School," *American Historical Review* 52 (January 1947): 247–64.

58. Thomas Ritchie to Martin Van Buren, March 27, 1829, quoted in John Spencer Bassett, ed., *The Correspondence of Andrew Jackson*, 7 vols. (Washington, DC: Carnegie Institution, 1929), 4:17.

59. Culver H. Smith, *The Press, Politics, and Patronage: The American Government's Use of Newspapers, 1789–1875* (Athens: University of Georgia Press, 1977), 131.

60. Richard B. Kielbowicz, *News in the Mail: The Press, Post Office, and Public Information* (New York: Greenwood Press, 1989).

61. Gerald J. Baldasty, *The Commercialization of News in the Nineteenth Century* (Madison: University of Wisconsin Press, 1992), 7. Also see Hazel Dicken-Garcia, *Journalistic Standards in Nineteenth-Century America* (Madison: University of Wisconsin Press, 1989); Thomas C. Leonard, *The Power of the Press: The Birth of American Political Reporting* (New York: Oxford University Press, 1996), and his *News for All*, previously cited; Charles E. Clark, *The Public Prints: The Newspaper in Anglo-American Culture, 1665–1740* (New York: Oxford, 1994); and Michael Warner, *The Letters of the Republic: Publication and the Public Sphere in Eighteenth-Century America* (Cambridge, MA: Harvard University Press, 1990).

62. See Gerald J. Baldasty's dissertation, for example: "The Political Press in the Second American Party System: The 1832 Election," Ph.D. dissertation, University of Washington, 1978, 140–70. He performed a content analysis of five metropolitan newspapers and four nonmetropolitan newspapers, in which he found that in the city papers, political topics made up more than one-half of all stories, and in the nonmetropolitan publications, nearly 70 percent (Baldasty, *Commercialization of News*, Table 1.1, 23).

63. Richard D. Brown, *Knowledge Is Power: The Diffusion of Information in Early America, 1700–1865* (New York: Oxford University Press, 1989), 280.

64. Smith, *Press, Politics and Patronage*, 131.

65. Washington, D.C., *U.S. Telegraph*, October 7, 1828.

66. *Louisville Public Advertiser*, July 9, 1828.

67. New York *Lyons Western Argus*, August 1, 1832.

68. Carolyn Steward Dyer, "Political Patronage of the Wisconsin Press, 1849–1861: New Perspectives on the Economics of Patronage," *Journalism Monographs* 109 (February 1989): 1–40; Milton Hamilton, *The Country Printer: New York State, 1785–1830* (New York: Columbia University Press, 1936),120; and Baldasty, *Commercialization of News*, 20.

69. Carl E. Prince, "The Federalist Party and the Creation of a Court Press, 1789–1801," *Journalism Quarterly* 53 (Summer 1976): 238–41; Michael Emery and Edwin Emery, *The Press and America: An Interpretive History of the Mass Media*, 6th ed. (Englewood Cliffs, NJ: Prentice Hall, 1988); and Frank Luther Mott, *American Journalism: A History of Newspapers in the United States Through 260 Years: 1690-1950*, rev. ed. (New York: Macmillan, 1950).

70. David Waldstreicher, "Reading the Runaways: Self-Fashioning, Print Culture, and Confidence in Slavery in the Eighteenth-Century Mid-Atlantic," *William and Mary Quarterly*, April 1999, 243–72.

71. Ibid., 247.

72. As Shane White pointed out, print remained an effective means of enforcing the slave system (*Somewhat More Independent: The End of Slavery in New York City, 1770–1810* [Athens: University of Georgia Press, 1991], 114–49).

73. Waldstreicher, "Reading the Runaways," 269.

74. Donald Lewis Shaw, "At the Crossroads: Change and Continuity in American Press News, 1820–1860," *Journalism History* 8 (Summer 1981): 38–50, quotation on 41.

75. Ibid., 41.

76. See table 3 in ibid., 41–42.

77. Jeffrey A. Jenkins and Charles Stewart III, "The Gag Rule, Congressional Politics, and the Growth of Anti-Slavery Popular Politics," unpublished paper, 2003, http://th.myweb.uga.edu/gagrule.pdf.

78. William Lee Miller, *Arguing About Slavery: John Quincy Adams and the Great Battle in the United States Congress* (New York: Vintage Books, 1995); Stephen Holmes, "Gag Rules, or the Politics of Omission," in Jon Elster and Rune Slagstad, eds., *Constitutionalism and Democracy* (Cambridge: Cambridge University Press, 1985), 15–70.

79. See, for example, Larry Schweikart, *Banking in the American South from the Age of Jackson to Reconstruction* (Baton Rouge: Louisiana State University Press, 1987), ch. 4 and passim, and my article "Jacksonian Ideology, Currency Control, and 'Central Banking': A Reappraisal," *The Historian* 51 (November 1988): 78–102.

80. Richard Bensel, *Yankee Leviathan: The Origins of Central State Authority in America, 1859–1877* (Cambridge: Cambridge University Press, 1990).

81. Ibid., x.

82   Alexander B. Callow, *The Tweed Ring* (London: Oxford University Press, 1966).

83. Burton T. Doyle and Homer H. Swaney, *Lives of James A. Garfield and Chester A. Arthur* (Washington: R. H. Darby, 1881), 61.

84. Ari Hoogenboom, *Outlawing the Spoils: A History of the Civil Service Reform Movement, 1865–1883* (Urbana: University of Illinois Press, 1961).

CHAPTER 2

Epigraph: Mark R. Levin, *Men in Black: How the Supreme Court Is Destroying America* (Washington, DC: Regnery, 2005), 33.

1. Don E. Fehrenbacher, *Slavery, Law, and Politics: The Dred Scott Case in Historical Perspective* (New York: Oxford University Press, 1981) remains a classic. David M. Potter, *The Impending Crisis 1848–1861* (New York: HarperPerennial, 1977).

2. Andrew C. Napolitano, *Dred Scott's Revenge: A Legal History of Race and Freedom in America* (Nashville, TN: Thomas Nelson, 2009).

3. A graduate student at Duke, Kelly Marie Kennington, has traced these laws in her dissertation, "River of Injustice: St. Louis's Freedom Suits and the Changing Nature of Legal Slavery in Antebellum America," Ph.D. dissertation, Duke University, 2009.

4. St. Louis Circuit Court Historical Records Project, "Freedom Suits Case Files, 1814–1860," http://stlcourtrecords.wustl.edu/about-freedom-suits-series.php.

5. Napolitano, *Dred Scott's Revenge*, 59.

6. *Strader v. Graham*, 51 U.S. 82 (1850).

7. Napolitano, *Dred Scott's Revenge*, 69.

8. Donald E. Fehrenbacher, *The Dred Scott Case* (New York: Oxford University Press, 1978).

9. Harry V. Jaffa, *Crisis of the House Divided: An Interpretation of the Issues in the Lincoln-Douglas Debates* (Chicago: University of Chicago Press, 1982).

10. James L. Huston, *Calculating the Value of the Union: Slavery, Property Rights, and the Economic Origins of the Civil War* (Chapel Hill: University of North Carolina Press, 2002) explains this dynamic better than anyone.

11. Allen C. Guelzo, *Abraham Lincoln, Redeemer President* (Grand Rapids, MI: William B. Eerdmans, 1999), 210.

12. Fehrenbacher, *Slavery, Law, and Politics*, 230; Jeffrey R. Hummel, *Emancipating Slaves, Enslaving Free Men* (Chicago: Open Court, 1997), 113.

13. David M. Potter, *The Impending Crisis, 1848–1861*, ed. and completed by Don E. Fehrenbacher (New York: Harper Torchbooks, 1976), 284.

14. Guelzo, *Abraham Lincoln, Redeemer President*, 211.

15. Fehrenbacher, *Slavery, Law, and Politics*, 230.

16. "House Divided Speech," in Roy P. Basler, Marion Dolores Pratt, and Lloyd A. Dunlap, eds., *The Collected Works of Abraham Lincoln*, 9 vols. (New Brunswick, NJ: Rutgers University Press, 1953–55), 2:461–69 (henceforth cited as *Collected Works*).

17. Robert W. Johannsen, ed., *The Lincoln-Douglas Debates of 1858* (New York: Oxford University Press, 1965), 19.

18. Abraham Lincoln, "Speech at Peoria," October 16, 1854, in Basler, *Collected Works*, 2:263–64.

19. John C. Calhoun to Percy Walker, October 23, 1847, in Robert L. Meriwether, et al., *The Papers of John C. Calhoun*, 25 vols. (Columbia: University of South Carolina Press, 1959–), 24:617.

20. Huston, *Calculating the Value of the Union*, 146.

21. Jefferson Davis, Speech in the Senate, February 13–14, 1850, in Dunbar Rowland, ed., *Jefferson Davis: Constitutionalist: His Letters, Papers, and Speeches*, 10 vols. (Jackson: Mississippi Department of Archives and History, 1923), 1:279, 283.

22. *Lemmon v. People*, 7 NY Super 681.

23. 20 New York, 562 (Court of Appeals, 1860).

24. Fehrenbacher, *Slavery, Law, and Politics*, 5.

25. Larry Schweikart, *48 Liberal Lies About American History* (New York: Sentinel, 2008), 119.

26. Lerone Bennett, *Forced into Glory: Abraham Lincoln's White Dream* (Chicago: Johnson Publishing, 2007), 147.

27. Jaffa, *Crisis of the House Divided*, 36.

28. Stephen B. Oates, *With Malice Toward None: The Life of Abraham Lincoln* (New York: Mentor, 1977), 138.

29. Jaffa, *Crisis of the House Divided*.

30. Potter, *Impending Crisis*, 301.

31. Fehrenbacher, *Slavery, Law, and Politics*, 246.

32. Ibid., 57.

33. David Grimstead, *American Mobbing, 1828–1861: Toward Civil War* (New York: Oxford, 1998), in a more detailed version of the classic argument that the Civil War was a collapse of the principles of "law and order," notes that the rise in mob violence in the antebellum period was substantially related to slavery and anti-slavery. See also Phillip S. Paludan, "The American Civil War Considered as a Crisis in Law and Order," *American Historical Review* 77 (1972), 1013–34.

34. Fehrenbacher, *Slavery, Law, and Politics*, 99.

35. Grimstead, *American Mobbing*, 248.

36. Ibid., 249.

37. Oates, *With Malice Toward None*, 146.

38. Charles W. Calomiris and Gary Gorton, "The Origins of Banking Panics: Models, Facts, and Bank Regulation," in R. Glenn Hubbard, ed., *Financial Markets and Financial Crises* (Chicago: University of Chicago Press, 1991), 109–74.

39. Albert Fishlow, *American Railroads and the Transformation of the Ante-Bellum Economy* (Cambridge, MA: Harvard University Press, 1965).

40. Charles W. Calomiris and Larry Schweikart, "The Panic of 1857: Origins, Transmission, and Containment," *Journal of Economic History* 51 (December 1991): 807–34 (quotation on 810).

41. Jenny Wahl, "*Dred*, Panic, War: How a Slave Case Triggered Financial Crisis and Civil Disunion," *Carleton College Economics Department Working Paper no. 2009-1*, located at http://apps.carleton.edu/curricular/econ/workingpapers/, 8.

42. Ibid., 13.

43. Ibid., 19.

44. *Cincinnati Enquirer*, April 16, 1857.

45. Allan Nevins, *The Ordeal of the Union: The Emergence of Lincoln, Douglas, Buchanan, and Party Chaos, 1857–1859* (New York: Charles Scribner's Sons, 1950), 156.

46. Ibid.

47. Ibid., 158.

48. Calomiris and Schweikart, "Panic of 1857," 813 and Table 1, 814.

49. Paul W. Gates, "Land and Credit Problems in Undeveloped Kansas," *Kansas Historical Quarterly* 31 (Spring 1965): 41–61.

50. Gates, "Land and Credit Problems in Undeveloped Kansas," 54.

51. Fishlow, *American Railroads*, 202–3.

52. Stephen Salisbury, *The State, the Investor, and the Railroad: The Boston & Albany, 1825–1867* (Cambridge, MA: Harvard University Press, 1967), 308.

53. Huston, "Western Grains and the Panic of 1857," passim, and his *The Panic of 1857 and the Coming of the Civil War* (Baton Rouge: Louisiana State University Press, 1987).

54. Potter, *Impending Crisis*, 145–297.

55. Ibid., 306.

56. *Cincinnati Enquirer*, August 28, 1857.

57. Calomiris and Schweikart, "Panic of 1857," 818.

58. Harry Miller, "Earlier Theories of Crisis and Cycles in the United States," *Quarterly Journal of Economics* 38 (February 1924): 294–329 (quotation on 328), quoting Edmund Dwight, "The Financial Revulsion and the New York Banking System," in *Hunt's Merchant Magazine* 38 (February 1858).

59. Calomiris and Schweikart, "Panic of 1857," 819–20.

60. Cook, "Annual Report," in Calomiris and Schweikart, "Panic of 1857," 822.

61. Melvin Ecke, "Fiscal Aspects of the Panic of 1857," Ph.D. Dissertation, Princeton University, 1951, 80–85, 92–94, 118–20.

62. Huston, *The Panic of 1857*, 20.

63. Allan Nevins and Milton Halsey Thomas, eds., *The Diary of George Templeton Strong* (New York: Macmillan, 1952), 359; Providence *Daily Tribune*, September 18, 1857; Newark *Daily Advertiser*, October 6, 9, 10, 1857.

64. Louisville *Daily Courier*, October 17, 1857.

65. Huston, *The Panic of 1857*, 25.

66. Ibid., 29.

67. William W. Fowler, *Inside Life in Wall Street, or, How Great Fortunes are Lost and Won* . . . (New York: Benjamin Blom, 1971), 133.

68. *Hunt's Merchants' Magazine* 37 (1857); James S. Gibbons, *The Banks of New York, Their Dealers, the Clearing House, and the Panic of 1857* (New York: D. Appleton, 1859), 2–10.

69. James Cook, "Annual Report of the Superintendent of the Banking Department of the State of New York," in U.S. House of Representatives, *Executive Document No. 77* and *Executive Document 107*, 35th Congress, 1st Session (Washington, DC: Government Printing Office, 1858).

70. Fowler, *Inside Life in Wall Street*, 110–13.

71. George W. Van Vleck, *The Panic of 1857: An Analytic Study* (New York: Columbia University Press, 1942); Fishlow, *American Railroads.*

72. James L. Huston, "Western Grains and the Panic of 1857," *Agricultural History* 57 (1983), 14–22, and his *The Panic of 1857 and the Coming of the Civil War* (Baton Rouge: Louisiana State University Press, 1987).

73. *Hunt's Merchants' Magazine* 37 (November 1857); Francis W. Gregory, *Nathan Appleton: Merchant and Entrepreneur, 1779–1861* (Charlottesville: University of Virginia Press, 1975), 212.

74. Huston, *The Panic of 1857*, passim.

75. Larry Schweikart, *Banking in the American South from the Age of Jackson to Reconstruction* (Baton Rouge: Louisiana State University Press, 1987).

76. Huston, *Calculating the Value of the Union*, xiv.

77. Ibid.

78. Nevins quoted in Jaffa, *Crisis of the House Divided*, 57.

79. Douglas quoted in Jaffa, *Crisis of the House Divided*, 58.

80. Robert W. Fogel and Stanley L. Engerman, *Time on the Cross* (Boston: Little, Brown, 1974), got carried away with these efficiencies, claiming essentially that slaves worked harder and were more productive than free labor, and only under subsequent refinement was it clarified that this was due in large part to longer hours and to the "gang system" that only applied to physical field work. See Paul David, et al., *Reckoning with Slavery: A Critical Study in the Quantitative History of the American Negro* (New York: Oxford, 1976).

81. Douglas quoted in Jaffa, *Crisis of the House Divided*, 115.

82. Ibid.

83. Huston, *Calculating the Value of the Union*, 24.

84. Ibid., 27.

85. Ibid., table 2.4, 30.

86. Jeremy Atack and Peter Passell, *A New Economic View of American History from Colonial Times to 1940*, 2nd ed. (New York: W. W. Norton, 1994), ch. 11 and 12, passim; Fogel and Engerman, *Time on the Cross*; Claudia Goldin, *Urban Slavery in the American South* (Chicago: University of Chicago Press, 1976).

87. Huston, *Calculating the Value of the Union*, 80.

88. Larry Schweikart and Lynne Pierson Doti, *American Entrepreneur* (New York: Amacom Press, 2009).

89. See Fred Bateman, James Foust, and Thomas Weiss, "Profitability in Southern Manufacturing: Estimates for 1860," *Explorations in Economic History* 12 (1975): 211–31; and their "Large-Scale Manufacturing in the South and West, 1850–1860," *Business History Review* 15 (Spring 1971): 1–17; Robert W. Fogel, *Without Consent or Contract: The Rise and Fall of American Slavery* (New York: W. W. Norton, 1989).

90. Oates, *With Malice Toward None*, 140.

91. George Fitzhugh, *Cannibals All! Or, Slaves Without Masters*, ed. C. Vann Woodward (Cambridge, MA: Belknap Press, 1966).

92. George Bittlingmayer, "Antitrust and Business Activity: The First Quarter Century," *Business History Review* 70 (Autumn 1996): 363–401.

93. George Bittlingmayer and Thomas W. Hazlett, "DOS *Kapital*: Has Antitrust Action Against Microsoft Created Value in the Computer Industry?" *Journal of Financial Economics* 55 (2000): 329–59.

94. Ron Chernow, *Alexander Hamilton* (New York: Penguin, 2004), 255.

95. Larry Schweikart and Michael Allen, *A Patriot's History of the United States from Columbus's Great Discovery to the War on Terror* (New York: Sentinel, 2006), 90–92.

96. The Constitution of the Commonwealth of Virginia, Section 7, June 12, 1776, http://legis.state.va.us/Laws/Search/ConstitutionTOC.htm.

97. Articles of Confederation, *Documents Illustrative of the Formation of the Union of the American States* (Washington, DC: Government Printing Office, 1927), 27.

98. Mark R. Levin, *Men in Black* (Washington, DC: Regnery, 2005), 25.

99. Ibid., 27.

100. Thomas Jefferson to William C. Jarvis, 1820, quoted in ibid.

CHAPTER 3

1. Larry Schweikart, *America's Victories: Why the U.S. Wins Wars and Will Win the War on Terror* (New York: Sentinel, 2006).

2. Janet Sharp Hermann, "Disaster Relief Then and Now," *The Freeman* 50 (May 2000), http://www.thefreemanonline.org/featured/disaster-relief-then-and-now/.

3. Ibid.

4. David McCullough, *The Johnstown Flood* (New York: Simon & Schuster, 1968), 188.

5. Ibid., 188–89.

6. Ibid., 198.

7. Ibid., 199.

8. Ibid.

9. Larry Schweikart, "William R. Jones," in Paul F. Pascoff, ed., *Encyclopedia of American Business History and Biography: Iron and Steel in the Nineteenth Century* (New York: Facts on File, 1989); Joseph Wall, *Andrew Carnegie* (New York: Oxford University Press, 1970).

10. McCullough, *The Johnstown Flood*, 227.

11. Ibid., 209.

12. Ibid., 226.

13. Ibid., 230.

14. Gary Kleppner, *Ohio and Its People* (Kent, OH: Kent State University Press, 1989). Again, much of this material is from Peter Cajka's unpublished paper, "The National Cash Register Company and the Neighborhoods: New Perspectives on Relief in the Dayton Flood of 1913," 2009.

15. Judith Sealander, *Grand Plans: Business Progressivism and Social Change in Ohio's Miami Valley, 1890–1929* (Lexington: University Press of Kentucky, 1988), 44–45.

16. Curt Dalton, *Through Flood, Through Fire: Personal Stories from Survivors of the Dayton Flood of 1913* (Dayton, OH: Mazer Corporation, 2001), 93–94.

17. Sealander, *Grand Plans*, 45.

18. Ibid., 47.

19. Arthur E. Morgan, *The Miami Conservancy District* (New York: McGraw-Hill Book Company, 1951), 31.

20. "Heroes of the Flood," *Dayton Daily News*, April 12, 1913.

21. Sealander, *Grand Plans*, 48.

22. "Restoration at Dayton Begins," *Massachusetts Globe*, March 31, 1913, in Wright State University (WSU), Special Collections and Archives.

23. "The Disaster in Dayton," *Outlook* 103 (April 12, 1913).

24. *St. Louis Star*, April 21, 1913.

25. *The Dayton Journal*, April 20, 1913.

26. *Dayton Daily News*, April 15, 1913.

27. Peter Cajka, "National Cash Register Company and the Neighborhoods: New Perspectives on Relief in the Dayton Flood of 1913," July 1, 2009, unpublished paper in author's possession, 32.

28. "Disaster in Dayton."

29. Sealander, *Grand Plans*, 49.

30. "Villages Quick to Aid Stricken Dayton," *The Dayton Journal*, April 4, 1913.

31. Henry M. Leland to John H. Patterson, March 31, 1913, National Cash Register Company, Dayton, OH (NCR).

32. Joseph Cauffiel to John H. Patterson, March 28, 1913, NCR.

33. Sealander, *Grand Plans*, 49–50.

34. "Disaster in Dayton."

35. Sealander, *Grand Plans*, 50.

36. Ibid., 81.

37. Ibid., 50.

38. Ibid., 58.

39. Morgan, *Miami Conservancy District*, 31.

40. Sealander, *Grand Plans*, 84.

41. John Edward Weems, *A Weekend in September: The Galveston Hurricane of 1900, the Nation's Deadliest Natural Disaster* (College Station: Texas A&M University Press, 1993); Mary G. Ramos, "After the Great Storm: Galveston's Response to the Hurricane of Sept. 8, 1900," *The Texas Almanac*, 1989, http://www.texasalmanac.com/history/highlights/storm/.

42. Harold Evans, with Gail Buckland and David Lefer, *They Made America: From the Steam Engine to the Search Engine; Two Centuries of Innovators* (New York: Little, Brown, 2004), 264.

43. Ibid., 265.

44. Ibid.

45. "Did Mayor Schmitz Lose His Head?" http://www.sfmuseum.org/1906.2/architects.html.

46. Robin Lampson, "Man at His Best," *The Freeman* 38 (March 1988), http://www.thefreemanonline.org/columns/man-at-his-best/.

47. Ibid.

48. Ibid.

49. Andrew S. Mener, " Disaster Response in the United States of America: An Analysis of the Bureaucratic and Political History of a Failing System," *College Undergraduate Research Electronic Journal*, University of Pennsylvania, 2007, http://repository.upenn.edu/curej/63, 5.

50. Ibid., 7.

51. 18 U.S.C. § 1385. "Whoever, except in cases and under circumstances expressly authorized by the Constitution or Act of Congress, willfully uses any part of the Army or the Air Force as a posse comitatus or otherwise to execute the laws shall be fined under this title or imprisoned not more than two years, or both."

52. Amity Shlaes, *The Forgotten Man: A New History of the Great Depression* (New York: HarperCollins, 2007), 150.

53. Ibid.

54. Burton Folsom, Jr., *New Deal or Raw Deal: How FDR's Economic Legacy Has Damaged America* (New York: Simon & Schuster, 2008).

55. Shlaes, *The Forgotten Man*, 332.

56. U.S. Code Congress and Administration Legislative History for PL 81-875 (1950), 4024; Rutherford H. Platt, *Disasters and Democracy: The Politics of Extreme Natural Disasters* (Washington, DC: Island Press, 1999).

57. Mener, "Disaster Response," 8.

58. Ibid.

59. Platt, *Disasters and Democracy*, 15.

60. Mener, "Disaster Response," 8.

61. *Report of the President's Commission on the Accident at Three Mile Island*, 1979, http://www.pddoc.com/tmi2/kemeny/.

62. Oran K. Henderson, *Commonwealth of Pennsylvania Emergency Preparedness and Response: The Three Mile Island Incident*, in Thomas H. Moss and David L. Sills, *Three Mile Island Nuclear Accident: Lessons and Implication* (New York: National Academy of Science, 1981).

63. See David M. Rubin, "What the President's Commission Learned About the Media," in Moss and Sills, *Three Mile Island*, 98–99.

64. Ibid.

65. Mener, "Disaster Response," 18.

66. James F. Miskel, *Disaster Response and Homeland Security: What Works, What Doesn't* (Westport, CT: Praeger Security International, 2006), 78–79.

67. Saundra K. Schneider, *Flirting with Disaster: Public Management in Crisis Situations* (New York: M. E. Sharpe, 1995), 93.

68. Donald F. Kettl, *The Department of Homeland Security's First Year: A Report Card* (New York: The Century Foundation Press, 2004), 20–21.

69. Ibid.

70. Dennis Keegan and David West, *Reality Check: The Unreported Good News About America* (Washington, DC: Regnery, 2008), 146.

71. "New Orleans Ignored Its Own Plan," *Washington Times*, September 9, 2005.

72. Douglas Brinkley, *The Great Deluge: Hurricane Katrina, New Orleans, and the Mississippi Gulf Coast* (New York: William Morrow, 2006), 23.

73. Ibid., 34.

74. National Oceanic and Atmospheric Administration Web site, http://www.srh.noaa.gov/data/warn_archieve?LIX/NPW/0828_155101.txt.

75. Keegan and West, *Reality Check*, 153.

76. Brinkley, *The Great Deluge*, 39.

77. Ibid., 56.

78. Ibid., 92.

79. Ibid., 64, 93.

80. Keegan and West, *Reality Check*, 147.

81. Brinkley, *The Great Deluge*, 233.

82. Ibid., 233.

83. Ibid., 239.

84. Ibid., 239.

85. Ibid., 214.

86. Ibid., 116.

87. Stephen Brill, *After: How America Confronted the September 12 Era* (New York: Simon & Schuster, 2003).

88. Ivor Van Heerden and Mike Bryan, *The Storm: What Went Wrong and Why During Hurricane Katrina* (New York: Penguin, 2007).

89. Ibid., 129.

90. Keegan and West, *Reality Check*, 156.

91. Brinkley, *The Great Deluge*, 192; Keegan and West, *Reality Check*, 156.

92. Brinkley, *The Great Deluge*, 77.

93. Ibid., 49.

94. Ibid., 199.

95. "Government Can Take a Lesson From Wal-Mart," *Pittsburgh Tribune-Review*, October 14, 2005.

96. Brinkley, *The Great Deluge*, 362.

97. Ibid., 288.

98. Alexander Hamilton, "The Hurricane Letter," September 6, 1772, at Alexander Hamilton Patriot, http://ahpatriot.blogspot.com/2007/06/hurricane-letter-hamilton-to-his-father.html.

99. *Congressional Record*, 49 Cong., 2d Sess., vol. XVIII, Pt. II, 1887, p. 1875.

100. Ibid.

101. *Congressional Record*, 49 Cong., 2d Sess., vol. XVIII, Pt. II, 1887, p. 1875.

102. Quoted in Ron Chernow, *Alexander Hamilton* (New York: Penguin, 2004), 252.

103. Ibid., 379.

104. Michael Greenberger, "Did the Founding Fathers Do 'A Heckuva Job?' Constitutional Authorization for the Use of Federal Troops to Prevent the Loss of a Major American City," http://www.umaryland.edu/healthsecurity/docs/Greenberger%20 Did%20the%20Founding%20Fathers%20Do%20a%20Heckuva%20Job.pdf.

CHAPTER 4

1. A. Kucharski, "Medical Management of Political Patients: The Case of Dwight D. Eisenhower," *Perspectives in Physiology and Medicine* 22 (1978): 115–26. Clarence G. Lasby, *Eisenhower's Heart Attack: How Ike Beat Heart Disease and Held On to the Presidency* (Lawrence: University Press of Kansas, 1997). Cardiologist Mattingly in 1987 claimed that Ike had heart trouble all his life and that Snyder had misdiagnosed Eisenhower's first heart attack in the 1940s, then covered up the record for years after that. Lasby sides with Dr. Snyder, concluding Ike indeed likely had stomach trouble, and the cautionary electrocardiogram that Snyder ordered in 1948 after one of the attacks proved normal (45).

2. Gary Taubes, *Good Calories, Bad Calories: Challenging the Conventional Wisdom on Diet, Weight Control, and Disease* (New York: Knopf, 2007), 4.

3. "The Fat of the Land," *Time*, January 13, 1961, 48–52.

4. Taubes, *Good Calories, Bad Calories*, 5.

5. Paul Dudley White, *My Life and Medicine: An Autobiographical Memoir* (Boston: Gambit, 1945), 220; Jean Mayer, *Diet for Living* (New York: David McKay, 1975), 138.

6. T. Cooper, "Arteriosclerosis, Policy, Polity, and Parity," *Circulation* 2 (February 1972): 433–40.

7. "Why Executives Drop Dead," *Fortune* 41 (1950): 88–91, 144–45.

8. Pedoe H. Tunstall, "Epidemiology of Coronary Heart Disease," in R. Duncan and M. Weston-Smith, *The Encyclopaedia of Medical Ignorance* (Oxford: Pergamon Press, 1984), 95–106.

9. I. H. Page, F. J. Stare, A. C. Corcoran, H. Pollack, and C. F. Wilkinson, Jr., "Atherosclerosis and the Fat Content of the Diet," *Circulation* 16 (August 1957): 163–78.

10. R. Lozano, C. J. Murray, A. D. Lopez, and T. Sato, "Miscoding and Misclassification of Iscaemic Heart Disease Mortality," World Health Organization, 2001, http://www.who.int/entity/healthinfo/paper12.pdf.

11. Taubes, *Good Calories, Bad Calories*, 10.

12. Jane Brody, *Jane Brody's Good Food Book: Living the High-Carbohydrate Way* (New York: W. W. Norton, 1985), 2.

13. J. H. Young, "The Long Struggle for the 1906 Law: Food and Drug Administration," *FDA Consumer*, June 1981, http://vm.cfsan.fda.gov/~rrd/history2.html; W. Root and R. De Rochemont, *Eating in America: A History* (Hopewell, NJ: Ecco Press, 1995), 211.

14. D. L. Call and A. M. Sanchez, "Trends in Fat Disappearance in the United States, 1909–65," *Journal of Nutrition* 93 (October 1967) (2 supplemental): 1–28; Taubes, *Good Calories, Bad Calories*, 11; United States Department of Agriculture, *Consumption of Food in the United States, 1909–1932*, Agriculture Handbook No. 62 (Washington, DC: United States Department of Agriculture Bureau of Agricultural Economics, 1953).

15. H. Schwartz, *Never Satisfied: A Cultural History of Diets, Fantasies, and Fat* (New York: Doubleday, 1986), 46; R. O. Cummings, *The American and His Food: A History of Food Habits in the United States* (Chicago: University of Chicago Press, 1940), 10–24.

16. Tom Standage, *An Edible History of Humanity* (New York: Walker and Company, 2009), 18.

17. John C. Burhan, *How Superstition Won and Science Lost: Popularizing Science and Health in the United States* (New Brunswick, NJ: Rutgers University Press, 1987), 7.

18. Ibid., 188.

19. Ibid., 211–226.

20. Ibid., 239.

21. Ancel Keys, "The Inception and Pilot Surveys," in D. Kromhout, et al., eds., *The Seven Countries Study: A Scientific Adventure in Cardiovascular Disease Epidemiology* (Utrecht: Brouwer, 1994), 15–26.

22. Ancel Keys, "Human Atherosclerosis and the Diet," *Circulation* 5 (January 1952): 115–18.

23. Jacob Yerushalmy and Herman E. Hilleboe, "Fat in the Diet and Mortality from Heart Disease: A Methodologic Note," *New York State Journal of Medicine* 57 (July 15, 1957): 2243–54.

24. Page, et al., "Athero-sclerosis and the Fat Content of the Diet," passim.

25. H. Blackburn, "Contrasting Professional Views on Atherosclerosis and Coronary Disease," *New England Journal of Medicine* 292 (January 9, 1975): 105–7; T. R. Dawber, "Annual Discourse—Unproved Hypothesis," *New England Journal of Medicine* 299 (August 31, 1978): 452–58, and his 1980 book, *The Framingham Study: The Epidemiology of Atherosclerotic Disease* (Cambridge, MA: Harvard University Press, 1980), 141.

26. Cathy Young, et al., "Effect on Body Composition and Other Parameters in Obese Young Men of Carbohydrate Level of Reduction Diet," *American Journal of Clinical Nutrition* 24 (1971): 290–96.

27. Claude Bernard, *An Introduction to the Study of Experimental Medicine*, trans. H. C. Green (New York: Dover Publications, 1957 [1865]), 38.

28. Meyer Friedman, *Pathogenesis of Coronary Artery Disease* (New York: McGraw-Hill, 1969), 77.

29. Paul Johnson, *Modern Times: A History of the World from the Twenties to the Nineties* (New York: HarperCollins, 1991), 2–3.

30. Ibid., 3.

31. Taubes, *Good Calories, Bad Calories*, 25. On Navajos, see I. H. Page, L. A. Lewis, and J. Gilbert, "Plasma Lipids and Proteins and Their Relationship to Coronary Disease Among Navajo Indians," *Circulation* 13 (May 1956): 675–79; on Irish, see M. F. Trulson, et al., "Comparisons of Siblings in Boston and Ireland," *Journal of American Dietetic Association* 45 (1964): 225–29; on Swiss Alpine farmers, see D. Gsell and J. Mayer, "Low Blood Cholesterol Associated with High Calorie, High Saturated Fat Intakes in a Swiss Alpine Village Population," *American Journal of Clinical Nutrition* 10 (June 1962): 471–79; and on Trappist monks, J. B. Groen, et al., "The Influence of Nutrition and Ways of Life on Blood Cholesterol and the Prevalence of Hypertension and Coronary Heart Disease Among Trappist and Benedictine Monks," *American Journal of Clinical Nutrition* 10 (June 1964): 456–70.

32. G. V. Mann, et al., "Cardiovascular Disease in the Masai," *Journal of Atherosclerosis Research* 4 (July–August 1964): 289–312; A. G. Shaper, "Cardiovascular Studies in the Samburu Tribe of Northern Kenya," *American Heart Journal* 63 (April 1962): 437–42.

33. W. B. Kannel, et al., "Serum Cholesterol, Lipoproteins, and the Risk of Coronary Heart Disease: The Framingham Study," *Annals of Internal Medicine* 74 (January 1971): 1–12.

34. W. B. Kannell and T. Gordon, *The Framingham Diet Study: Diet and Regulation of Serum Cholesterol*, Section 24 of *The Framingham Study: An Epidemiological Investigation of Cardiovascular Disease* (Bethesda, MD: U.S. Department of Health, Education, and Welfare, Public Health Service, and National Institutes of Health, 1968), 15.

35. On Puerto Rico, see M. R. Garcia-Palmieri, et al., "Relationship of Dietary Intake to Subsequent Coronary Heart Disease Incidence: The Puerto Rico Heart Health Program," *Journal of American Clinical Nutrition* 33 (1980): 1818–27; on Honolulu, K. Yano, et al., "Dietary Intake and the Risk of Coronary Heart Disease in Japanese Men Living in Hawaii," ibid., 31 (July 1978): 1270–79; on Chicago, O. M. Paul et al., "A Longitudinal Study of Coronary Heart Disease," *Circulation* 28 (July1963): 20–31; on Israel, H. A. Kahn et al., "Serum Cholesterol: Its Distribution and Association with Dietary and Other Variables in a Survey of 10,000 Men," *Israeli Journal of Medical Sciences* 5 (November–December 1969): 1117–27. And there were many other studies still, not cited here, but available in Taubes, *Good Calories, Bad Calories*, notes on 465.

36. R. B. Shekelle, et al., "Diet, Serum Cholesterol, and Death from Coronary Heart Disease: The Western Electric Study," *New England Journal of Medicine* 8 (January 1981): 65–70.

37. Ibid.

38. "Linking of Heart Disease to High-Cholesterol Diet Reinforced by New Data,"

Washington Post, Jan. 8, 1981; "Long-Term Study Links Cholesterol to Hazard of Early Coronary Death," *New York Times,* Jan. 8, 1981.

39. A. Koryani, "Prophylaxis and the Treatment of the Coronary Disease," *Theraputica Hungarica* 11 (1963): 17; and Research Committee, "Low-Fat Diet in Myocardial Infarction: A Controlled Trial," *Lancet* 286 (September 11, 1965): 501–4.

40. "Diet Linked to Cut in Heart Attacks," *New York Times,* May 17, 1962.

41. I. D. France, Jr. et al., "Test of Effect of Lipid Lowering by Diet on Cardiovascular Risk: The Minnesota Coronary Survey," *Arteriosclerosis* 9 (January–February 1989): 129–35; Taubes, *Good Calories, Bad Calories,* 38.

42. Review Panel of the National Heart Institute, *Mass Field Trials of the Diet-Heart Question: Their Significance, Feasibility, and Applicability—Report of the Diet-Heart Review Panel of the National Heart Institute,* American Heart Association, Monograph No. 28, 1969.

43. Jean Meyer, "By Bread Alone," *New York Times Book Review,* December 15, 1974, 19.

44. Larry Schweikart, *The Entrepreneurial Adventure: A History of Business in the United States* (Fort Worth, TX: Harcourt, 2000), 274.

45. "Food Pyramid History," http://iml.jou.ufl.edu/projects/Fall02/Greene/history.htm.

46. Select Committee on Nutrition and Human Needs of the United States Senate, *Dietary Goals for the United States* (Washington, DC: Government Printing Office, 1977). After publication, there was a firestorm of protest from researchers, scientists, doctors, and nutritionists who insisted that the science was far from settled, and that there was no consensus.

47. Taubes, *Good Calories, Bad Calories,* 46.

48. Ibid., 48.

49. George Mann, "Diet-Heart: End of an Era," *New England Journal of Medicine* 297 (September 22, 1977): 644–50.

50. David Kritchevsky, quoted in Taubes, *Good Calories, Bad Calories,* 52.

51. Multiple Risk Factor Intervention Trial [MRFIT] Research Group, "Multiple Risk Factor Intervention Trial: Risk Factor Changes and Mortality Results," *Journal of the American Medical Association* 248 (September 24, 1982): 1465–77; "Heart Attacks: A Test Collapses," *Wall Street Journal,* October 6, 1982.

52. "Cholesterol: And Now the Bad News," *Time,* March 1984.

53. C. Everett Koop, "Message from the Surgeon General," U.S. Department of Health and Human Services, 1988, and the *Surgeon General's Report on Nutrition and Health* (Washington, DC: U.S. Government Printing Office, 1988), iii–iv, 3–4l; National Research Council, Committee on Diet and Health, Food and Nutrition Board, Commission on Life Sciences, *Diet and Health: Implications for Reducing Chronic Disease Risk* (Washington, DC: National Academy Press, 1989), 13.

54. Taubes, *Good Calories, Bad Calories,* 49.

55. Ibid., 66.

56. "In 4-diet Study, All Lost Weight if they Watched Their Calories," *USA Today,* February 25, 2009. See the disclaimers in the article, "Comparison of Weight-Loss Diets with Different Compositions of Fat, Protein, and Carbohydrates," *New England Journal of Medicine* 360 (February 26, 2009): 859–73. Nor did this very small study (811 subjects) reduce carbohydrates enough, nor increase fat intake enough, to make significant judgments.

57. Ancel Keys, "Sucrose in the Diet and Coronary Heart Disease," *Atherosclerosis,* September–October 1971, 93–202; "Cholesterol: Debate Flares Over Wisdom of Widespread Reductions," *New York Times,* July 14, 1987.

58. Robert C. Atkins, *Dr. Atkins' New Diet Revolution* (New York: M. Evans & Co., 2002), 20–21.

59. Ibid., 22.

60. Frederick L. Benoit, R. L. Martin, and R. H. Watten, "Changes in Body Composition During Weight Reduction in Obesity: Balance Studies Comparing Effects of Fasting and a Ketogenic Diet," *Annals of Internal Medicine* 63 (October 1965): 604–12.

61. T. L. Halton et al., "Low-carbohydrate-diet Score and the Risk of Coronary Heart Disease in Women," *New England Journal of Medicine* 19 (February 9, 2006) 1991–2002.

62. Iris Shai et al., "Weight Loss with a Low-Carbohydrate, Mediterranean, or Low-Fat Diet," *New England Journal of Medicine* 359 (July 17, 2008): 229–41.

63. A. J. Nordmann et al., Effects of Low-carbohydrate vs Low-fat Diets on Weight Loss and Cardiovascular Risk Factors: A Meta-analysis of Randomized Controlled Trials," *Archives of Internal Medicine* 3 (February 13, 2006): 285–93. The argument about LDL (low-density lipoproteins), which is entirely different from whether a low-carb diet is superior for losing weight, has subsequently become a fallback position for the antifat crowd, but a better measure of the risk than the so-called LDL cholesterol was the size and density of LDL particles and the number of ApoB proteins (the component of very low-density lipoproteins and low-density lipoproteins)—and in that regard, a comparison of carbs and fats shows that carbs produce denser LDL while fats make the LDL large and fluffy, or, generally, fats are far less harmful particles.

64. G. D. Foster et al., "A Randomized Trial of a Low-carbohydrate Diet for Obesity," *New England Journal of Medicine* 21 (May 22, 2003): 2082–90.

65. J. Powles, "Commentary: Mediterranean Paradoxes Continue to Provoke," *International Journal of Epidemiology* 30 (October 2001): 1076–77.

66. M. Nestle, "The Ironic Politics of Obesity," *Science* 269 (February 7, 2003): 781.

67. C. W. Enns et al., *Trends in Food and Nutrient Intakes by Adults: NFCS 1977–78, CSFII 1989–91, and CSFII 1994–95, Family Economics and Nutrition Review* 10 (1997), quoted in Atkins, *Dr. Atkins' New Diet Revolution*, 25.

68. H. E. Garrett, E. C. Horning, B. G. Creech, and Michael De Bakey, "Serum Cholesterol Values in Patients Treated Surgically for Atherosclerosis," *Journal of the American Medical Association* 189 (August 31, 1964): 655–59; D. Rittenberg and R. Schoenheimer, "Deuterium as an Indicator in the Study of Intermediary Metabolism. XI. Further Studies on the Biological Uptake of Deuterium into Organic Substances with Special Reference to Fat and Cholesterol Formation," *Journal of Biological Chemistry* 121 (1937) 235–53.

69. Kelly Brownell and K. B. Horgan, *Food Fight: The Inside Story of the Food Industry, America's Obesity Crisis, and What We Can Do About It* (New York: McGraw-Hill, 2004), 8.

70. Taubes, *Good Calories, Bad Calories*, 234; Centers for Disease Control and Prevention, "Physical Activity Trends—United States, 1990–1998," *Morbidity and Mortality Weekly Reports* 50 (March 9, 2001): 166-69.

71. "Taking Exercise to Heart," *New York Times*, March 27, 1977; "Passion to Keep Fit: 100 Million Americans Exercising," *Washington Post*, August 31, 1980.

72. J. D. Wright et al., "Trends in Intake of Energy and Macronutrients—United States, 1971–2000," *Morbidity and Mortality Weekly Reports* 53 (February 6, 2004): 80–82.

73. John Higginson, "From Geographical Pathology to Environmental Carcinogenesis: A Historical Reminiscence," *Cancer Letters* 117 (1997) 133–142, and his "Rethinking the Environmental Causation of Human Cancer," *Food and Cosmetics Toxicology* 19 (October 1981): 539–48.

74.   J. O. Hill and J. C. Peters, "Environmental Contributions to the Obesity Epidemic," *Science* 299 (February 7, 2003) 1371–74.

75.   David Pimentel and Marcia Pimentel, "Sustainability of Meat-based and Plant-based Diets and the Environment," *American Journal of Clinical Nutrition* 78 (September 2003), supplement, 660S–663S.

76.   Nathan Fiala, "How Meat Contributes to Global Warming," *Scientific American*, February 4, 2009.

77.   "Fatties Cause Global Warming," *The Sun*, April 21, 2009, http://www.thesun.co.uk/sol/homepage/news/article2387203.ece.

78.   Fiala, "How Meat Contributes to Global Warming."

79.   Eric Schlosser, *Fast Food Nation: The Dark Side of the American Meal* (New York: Penguin, 2002).

80.   Adam W. Shepard, *Scratch Beginnings: Me, $25, and the Search for the American Dream* (New York: Collins, 2008).

81.   "Childhood Obesity Report Calls for Government Regulations to Limit Access to 'Unhealthy' Restaurant Chains," CNSNews.com, September 2, 2009, http://www.cnsnews.com/news/article/53374.

82.   Peter Gwynne, "The Cooling World," *Newsweek*, April 28, 1975.

83.   Richard Lindzen, "Global Warming: The Origin and Nature of the Alleged Scientific Consensus," *CATO Institute* 15 (Spring 1992), http://www.cato.org/pubs/regulation/regv15n2/reg15n2g.html.

84.   B. Bruce-Briggs, *The War Against the Automobile* (New York: Dutton, 1977); John Heitmann, *The Automobile and American Life* (Jefferson, NC: McFarland, 2009).

CHAPTER 5

1.   Interview with Felix Cavaliere, Rascals founder, March 10, 2009.

2.   Ray Manzarek, *Light My Fire: My Life with the Doors* (New York: Berkley Boulevard Books, 1999), 14.

3.   Barry Miles quoted in Peter Doggett, *There's a Riot Going On: Revolutionaries, Rock Stars, and the Rise and Fall of the '60s* (New York: Canongate, 2007), 174.

4.   This was a well-established business trend of controlling the entire production process. See Larry Schweikart and Lynne Pierson Doti, *American Entrepreneur* (New York: Amacom Books, 2009).

5.   Doggett, *There's a Riot Going On*, 70.

6.   Jonathan Gould, *Can't Buy Me Love: The Beatles, Britain, and America* (New York: Harmony Books, 2007), 61.

7.   John Heitmann, *The Automobile and American Life* (Jefferson, NC: McFarland, 2009).

8.   Ray Kroc and Robert Anderson, *Grinding It Out: The Making of McDonald's* (Chicago: Contemporary Books, 1977); Kemmons Wilson, *The Holiday Inn Story* (New York: The Newcomen Society, 1968); Bob Thomas, *Walt Disney: An American Original* (New York: Simon and Schuster, 1976); Randy Bright, *Disneyland: Inside Story* (New York: Abrams, 1987).

9.   Gould, *Can't Buy Me Love*, 147.

10.   Doggett, *There's a Riot Going On*, 77.

11.   Gould, *Can't Buy Me Love*, 221.

12.   The influence of the Beatles on the American music scene was, in an understatement, massive. West Coast rockers such as Doors keyboardist Ray Manzarek and East Coast

"white soul" singer/keyboardist Mark Stein of Vanilla Fudge identified the Beatles as one of the most important influences in their music (interviews with Mark Stein, various dates, 2008–9). Dave Mason, of Traffic, observed that "they were raw, brand new, everyone copied them" (interview, April 14, 2009). The impact was not universal: Doors guitarist Robby Krieger cited edgier British bands, such as the Rolling Stones and the Animals, as his primary influence; and David Paich of Toto leaned toward American jazz and blues artists (interview with Robby Krieger, July 1, 2009; interview with David Paich, June 25, 2009).

13.   Fred Goodman, *The Mansion on the Hill: Dylan, Young, Geffen, Springsteen, and the Head-on Collision of Rock and Commerce* (New York: Times Books, 1997), 9.

14.   Manzarek, *Light My Fire*, 94–95.

15.   Aldous Huxley, *The Doors of Perception and Heaven and Hell* (London: Chatto & Windus, 1960).

16.   Ibid., 36–37.

17.   Jann Wenner, *John Lennon Remembers* (New York: Popular Library, 1971), 140.

18.   Gould, *Can't Buy Me Love*, 324; Hunter Davies, *The Beatles: The Authorized Biography* (New York: McGraw-Hill, 1968), 289.

19.   George Harrison, *I Me Mine* (London: Phoenix, 1980), 94.

20.   Peter Knight, *Conspiracy Theories in American History* (Santa Barbara, CA: ABC-CLIO, 2003): 427. This book suggests that some inside the radical movement thought Lennon was a CIA "plant" precisely because of his lack of enthusiasm for revolution.

21.   Doggett, *There's a Riot Going On*, 97.

22.   Ibid., 180.

23.   Glenn C. Altschuler, *All Shook Up: How Rock 'N' Roll Changed America* (Oxford: Oxford University Press, 2003), 175.

24.   "Jimi's Private Parts," http://www.thesmokinggun.com/archive/080305ljimi1.html; Charles Cross, *Room Full of Mirrors* (New York: Hyperion, 2005), claims Hendrix faked being a homosexual to get a discharge, but Hendrix told reporters he was discharged because he broke his ankle. In all likelihood, it was a combination of Hendrix's attitude and injury that led to his discharge.

25.   Cross, *Room Full of Mirrors*, 66.

26.   Steven Roby, *Black Gold* (North Hollywood, CA: Billboard Books, 2002), 15.

27.   Cross, *Room Full of Mirrors*, 248.

28.   Doggett, *There's a Riot Going On*, 338.

29.   Peter Ames Carlin, *Catch a Wave: The Rise, Fall & Redemption of the Beach Boys' Brian Wilson* (New York: Rodale, 2006), 98.

30.   Interview with Peter Rivera (Peter Hoorelbeke), July 22, 2009.

31.   Ibid.

32.   Doggett, *There's a Riot Going On*, 5.

33.   Ibid., 10–11.

34.   Ibid., 146.

35.   Ibid., 169.

36.   Ibid., 184, 195.

37.   Ibid., 196–97, 209.

38.   Kenneth J. Bindas and Craig Houston, "'Takin' Care of Business': Rock Music, Vietnam and the Protest Myth," *Historian* 52 (November 1989): 1–23.

39.   Ibid., 1.

40.   Ibid., 3.

41.   David A. Noebel, *Rhythm, Riots, and Revolution* (Tulsa, OK: Christian Crusade

Publications, 1966); Jerome L. Rodnitzky, "The New Revivalism: American Protest Songs, 1945–1968," *South Atlantic Quarterly* 70 (Winter 1971): 13–21.

42. Emily Edwards and Michael Singletary, "Mass Media Images in Popular Music: An Examination of Media Images in Student Music Collections and Student Attitudes Toward Media Performance," *Popular Music and Society* 9 (1984): 17–26.

43. R. Serge Denisoff and Mark H. Levine, "Youth and Popular Music: A Test of the Taste Culture Hypothesis," *Youth Society* 4 (1972): 237–55.

44. For one attempt to straddle these issues, see James E. Perone, *Music of the Counterculture Era* (Westport, CT: Greenwood, 2004).

45. Doggett, *There's a Riot Going On*, 214.

46. Goodman, *Mansion on the Hill*, 65. Stephen Stills later claimed that he wrote "For What It's Worth" to make a statement about Vietnam ("I wanted to write something that had to do with the guys in the field in Vietnam"), a convenient post hoc explanation that made him more "cutting edge." At the time, the evidence suggests it was about a minor episode in Hollywood, and in 1966, very few Americans were attuned to the "guys in the field in Vietnam."

47. Goodman, *Mansion on the Hill*, 317.

48. Doggett, *There's a Riot Going On*, 394.

49. Ibid., 212.

50. David Dalton, "Finally, the Shocking Truth About Woodstock Can Be Told, or Kill It Before It Clones Itself," *The Gadfly*, August 1999, http://gadfly.org/1999-08/toc.asp, and conversations with David Dalton cited in Larry Schweikart and Michael Allen, *A Patriot's History of the United States from Columbus's Great Discovery to the War on Terror* (New York: Sentinel, 2006), 703–4.

51. Gould, *Can't Buy Me Love*, 566.

52. Dalton, "Finally, the Shocking Truth About Woodstock."

53. Ellen Sander, "It's the Sound," *L.A. Free Press*, September 5, 1969.

54. Abbie Hoffman, *Woodstock Nation* (New York: Vintage, 1969), 91; Doggett, *There's a Riot Going On*, 275.

55. Hoffman, *Woodstock Nation* , 4–5; Doggett, *There's a Riot Going On*, 270.

56. Doggett, *There's a Riot Going On*, 516.

57. Ibid., 512.

58. Ibid., 513.

59. Artemy Troitsky, "Rock in the USSR: The True Story of Rock in Russia," http://www.planetaquarium.com/eng/pub/doc_at1.html.

60. Timothy W. Ryback, *Rock Around the Bloc: A History of Rock Music in Eastern Europe and the Soviet Union* (New York: Oxford, 1990), 26.

61. Ibid., 42.

62. Ibid., 58.

63. All this material is from ibid., 50–58 and passim. See also Tony Mitchell, "Mixing Pop and Politics: Rock Music in Czechoslovakia before and after the Velvet Revolution," *Popular Music* 11, 187–203.

64. Ryback, *Rock Around the Bloc*, 63–64.

65. Doggett, *There's a Riot Going On*, 95.

66. Ibid.

67. Ryback, *Rock Around the Bloc*, 93.

68. Ibid., 95.

69. Ibid., 109.

70. Ibid., 4.

71. Ibid., 5.
72. Barry Miles, *Zappa* (New York: Grove Press, 2004), 292
73. Ibid.
74. Ryback, *Rock Around the Bloc*, 184.
75. Ibid., 141–48.
76. Ibid., 138.
77. Ibid., 139.
78. "East Berlin Loses the Rock War," *Le Monde*, June 21, 1988.
79. Ryback, *Rock Around the Bloc*, 152.
80. Troitsky, "Rock in the USSR."
81. "Boris Grebenshikov's Russian Rock," http://www.planetaquarium.com/eng/pub/doc_em1.html.
82. Ibid.
83. Troitsky, "Rock in the USSR."
84. Miles, *Zappa*, 294.
85. Christopher Andrew and Vasili Mitrokhin, *The Sword and the Shield: The Mitrokhin Archive and the Secret History of the KGB* (New York: Basic Books, 1999), 548.
86. Ibid., 548.
87. Doggett, *There's a Riot Going On*, 120.
88. Mark Mazower, *Dark Continent* (New York: Vintage, 2000) 181.
89. Jolanta Pekacz, "Did Rock Smash the Wall? The Role of Rock in Political Transition," *Popular Music*, 1994, 13, 41–49 (quotation on 46).
90. Doggett, *There's a Riot Going On*, 164.
91. Pekacz, "Did Rock Smash in the Wall?," 48.
92. Ryback, *Rock Around the Bloc, 5.*
93. Ibid.
94. Ibid., 233.
95. Frederick Rudolph and John R. Thelin, *The American College and University* (Athens: University of Georgia Press, 1990), 48.
96. Adams, Washington, and Jefferson quoted in Buckner F. Melton, ed., *The Quotable Founding Fathers* (New York: Fall River Press, 2004), 25.
97. "Jefferson's Taste in Music," http://www.monticello.org/jefferson/dayinlife/parlor/profile.html; Sandor Salgo, *Thomas Jefferson: Musician Violinist* (Chapel Hill: University of North Carolina Press, 2001); Judith S. Britt, *Nothing More Agreeable: Music in George Washington's Family* (Mount Vernon, VA: The Mount Vernon Ladies' Association of the Union, 1984).
98. Miles Hoffman, "If Lincoln Had an iPod," http://www.npr.org/templates/story/story.php?storyId=100675699.

CHAPTER 6

1. Ronald Reagan, *An American Life* (New York: Pocket Books, 1990), 409. Nevertheless, there is no entry for "Islam" in the entire index of Edmund Morris's biography of Reagan, *Dutch* (Edmund Morris, *Dutch: A Memoir of Ronald Reagan* [New York: Random House, 1999]).
2. Reagan, *An American Life*, 410.
3. Douglas Brinkley, ed., *The Reagan Diaries* (New York: HarperCollins, 2007), 14.
4. Ibid., 14.
5. Ibid., 37.

6. Reagan, *An American Life*, 415.

7. Ibid., 411.

8. Ibid., 416.

9. Brinkley, ed., *The Reagan Diaries*, 24.

10. Ibid.

11. Ibid., 25.

12. Larry Schweikart, *48 Liberal Lies About American History* (New York: Sentinel, 2008), 61–68.

13. Reagan, *An American Life*, 416.

14. *New York Times*, June 27, 1982.

15. "Interview: Caspar Weinberger," 2001, http://www.pbs.org/wgbh/pages/frontline/shows/target/interviews/weinberger.html.

16. Ibid.

17. Ibid.

18. Paul Johnson, *Modern Times: A History of the World from the Twenties to the Nineties* (New York: HarperCollins, 1991), 513.

19. Ibid., 517.

20. James Dobbins, Seth G. Jones, Keith Crane, Andrew Rathmell, Brett Steele, Richard Teltschik, and Anga Timilsina, "The U.N.'s Role in Nation-Building: From the Congo to Iraq," RAND Corporation, 2005, xvi, at http://www.rand.org/pubs/monographs/2005/RAND_MG304.pdf.

21. Brett D. Schaefer, "United Nations Peacekeeping: The U.S. Must Press for Reform," Heritage Foundation Backgrounder #2182, September 18, 2008, http://www.heritage.org/research/internationalorganizations/bg2182.cfm.

22. Roy Licklider, "Obstacles to Peace Settlements," in Chester A. Crocker, Fen Osler Hampson, and Pamela Aall, *Turbulent Peace: The Challenges of Managing International Conflict* (Washington, DC: United States Institute of Peace Press, 2001), 697–718; Paul R. Pillar, *Negotiating Peace: War Termination as a Bargaining Process* (Princeton, NJ: Princeton University Press, 1993); Stephen John Stedman, *Peacemaking in Civil War: International Mediation in Zimbabwe, 1974–1980* (Boulder, CO: Lynne Rienner, 1991), and his "The End of the Zimbabwean Civil War," in Roy Licklider, ed., *Stopping the Killing: How Civil Wars End* (New York: New York University Press, 1993), 125–63; Barbara F. Walter, "The Critical Barrier to Civil War Settlement," *International Organization* 51 335–64.

23. U.N. General Assembly and U.N. Security Council, Report of the Panel on United Nations Peace Operations, A/55/305–S/ 2000/809, August 21, 2000, p. 10, at http://www.un.org/peace/reports/peace_operations/docs/a_55_305.pdf (September 1, 2008). The report is often referred to as the "Brahimi Report," after the panel's chairman, former Algerian foreign minister Lakhdar Brahimi.

24. Roy Licklider, "How Civil Wars End: Questions and Methods," in Licklider, ed., *Stopping the Killing*, 3–19.

25. Ibid., 14.

26. Licklider, "Obstacles to Peace Settlements," 697–718; Pillar, *Negotiating Peace*; Stedman, *Peacemaking in Civil War* and "The End of the Zimbabwean Civil War"; Walter, "The Critical Barrier to Civil War Settlement."

27. Reagan, *An American Life*, 436.

28. Ibid., 431.

29. Bernard Lewis, *Semites and Anti-Semites: An Inquiry into Conflict and Prejudice* (New York: W. W. Norton & Co., 1999), 12.

30. Thomas Friedman, *From Beirut to Jerusalem* (London: HarperCollins Publishers, 1998).

31. Bernard Lewis, "The New Anti-Semitism," *The American Scholar* 75 (Winter 2006): 25–36, http://hnn.us/blogs/entries/21832.html.

32. "Who Is Involved?" 10/30/83, box 43, Executive Secretariat, NSC Country Files, Ronald Reagan Presidential Library (RL), Simi Valley, CA.

33. Morris, *Dutch,* 462–63.

34. Paul Lettow, *Ronald Reagan and His Quest to Abolish Nuclear Weapons* (New York: Random House, 2005), 108.

35. Ibid., 109.

36. Paul Kengor, *The Crusader: Ronald Reagan and the Fall of Communism* (New York: Regan, 2006), 176.

37. Reagan, *An American Life,* 440.

38. Brinkley, ed., *The Reagan Diaries,* 218.

39. Reagan, *An American Life,* 440.

40. Ibid., 441.

41. "Lebanese Working Group," September 1983, Richard S. Beale Files, Box 90403, NSC, RL.

42. Ibid.

43. Nonie Darwish, *Now They Call Me Infidel* (New York: Sentinel, 2006), 9.

44. Ibid., 9.

45. Lawrence Wright, *The Looming Tower: Al-Qaeda and the Road to 9/11* (New York: Knopf, 2006), 11–12.

46. Ibid., 23.

47. Ibid., 58.

48. Ibid.; Peter I. Bergen, *Holy War: Inside the Secret World of Osama Bin Ladin* (New York: Free Press, 2001), 88.

49. Jane Mayer and Doyle McManus, *Landslide: The Unmaking of the President, 1984–1988* (Boston: Houghton-Mifflin, 1989), 125.

50. Karen DeYoung, *Soldier: The Life of Colin Powell* (New York: Knopf, 2006); Caspar Weinberger, *Fighting for Peace: Seven Critical Years in the Pentagon* (New York: Warner Books, 1990).

51. John F. Lehman, *Command of the Seas: Building the 600-Ship Navy* (New York: Scribners, 1988), 308–12.

52. Ken Duberstein to Howard Baker, Edwin Meese, October 26, 1983, ND 183642, RL.

53. A select few used the term *terrorists* in memos to the president, such as Special Assistant Wadiah Haddad.

54. Lou Cannon, *President Reagan: The Role of a Lifetime* (New York: Public Affairs, 2000), 383.

55. Folder "Questions on Lebanon," pre-brief, "Lebanon Bombing October 23, 1983," box 41, Executive Secretariat, NSC: Country File RL.

56. Bernard Lewis, *The Middle East: A Brief History of the Last 2,000 Years* (New York: Touchstone, 1995), 166.

57. Eric Weiner, *The Geography of Bliss: One Grump's Search for the Happiest Places in the World* (New York: Twelve Books, 2008), 105.

58. Philip Brickman et al., "Lottery Winners and Accident Victims: Is Happiness Relative?" *Journal of Personality and Social Psychology* 36 (1987): 917–27.

59. Lewis, *The Middle East,* 270.

60. Mark Sangemon, *Understanding Terror Networks* (Philadelphia: University of Pennsylvania Press, 2004); Richard Minitier, *Disinformation: 22 Media Myths That Undermine the War on Terror* (Washington: Regnery, 2004), 126–27; "Terror Arrests: The List of Suspects," London *Telegraph*, July 7, 2007, http://www.telegraph.co.uk/news/uknews/1556345/Terror-arrests--the-list-of-suspects.html.

61. Victor Davis Hanson, *Carnage and Culture: Landmark Battles in the Rise to Western Power* (New York: Doubleday, 2001).

62. Lewis, *The Middle East*, 375.

63. Ibid., 385.

64. Sandra Mackey, *The Iranians: Persia, Islam and the Soul of a Nation* (New York: Dutton, 1996), 215, 264–65.

65. Amir Taheri, *The Spirit of Allah* (New York: Adler & Adler, 1985), 223.

66. Nikki Keddie, *Modern Iran: Roots and Results of Revolution* (New Haven: Yale University Press, 2003), 235.

67. Jimmy Carter, *Keeping Faith: Memoirs of a President* (New York: Bantam, 1982), 438.

68. David Harris, *The Crisis: The President, the Prophet, and the Shah: 1979, the Coming of Militant Islam* (Boston: Little, Brown, 2004), 401–2.

69. Ibid., 402.

70. Ibid.

71. Bernard Lewis, *The Crisis of Islam: Holy War and Unholy Terror* (New York: Modern Library, 2003), 162.

72. Larry Schweikart, *America's Victories: Why the U.S. Wins Wars and Will Win the War on Terror* (New York: Sentinel, 2007), 18.

73. John Laffin, *The Arab Mind Considered: A Need for Understanding* (New York: Taplinger Publishing Company, 1975), 23–24. See also David Leo Gutmann, "Shame, Honor and Terror in the Middle East," http://www.frontpagemagazine.com, October 24, 2003.

74. Darwish, *Now They Call Me Infidel*, 26.

75. NSPG 0072, "October 14, 1983 (Middle East), Box 2, Executive Secretariat, NSC: National Security Planning Group, RL. The same NSPG memo emphasized working with Arab "moderates."

76. Reagan, *An American Life*, 447.

77. Ibid.

78. Ibid., 452.

79. "French Troops Heard Blast at Marine Headquarters, Then . . ." The Associated Press, October 30, 1983.

80. Reagan, *An American Life*, 453.

81. "Interview, Caspar Weinberger."

82. Ibid.

83. Ibid.

84. Cannon, *President Reagan*, 383.

85. Ibid.

86. Robert C. McFarlane, "From Beirut to 9/11," *New York Times*, October 23, 2008.

87. Robin Wright, *Sacred Rage: The Wrath of Militant Islam* (New York: Touchstone, 2004), 54.

88. Cable, 2025, printed December 14, 1983, folder "Lebanon, Marine Explosion, October 23-November 3, 1983," (4), Box 41, Executive Secretariat, NSC: Country File, RL.

89. Cable from U.S. embassy in Beirut referenced in "Lebanon, Marine Explosion Octo-

ber 23–November 3, 1983," (4), Box 41, Executive Secretariat, NSC: Country File, RL.

90. "The Terrorist Threat to US Personnel in Beirut," January 12, 1984, cited in cable from U.S. embassy in Beirut to Middle East and major embassies, Box 43, Executive Secretariat, NSC, Country File, RL.

91. Cannon, *President Reagan*, 398.

92. "Lebanon Bombing, October 23–24, 1983," Box 41, Executive Secretariat, NSC: Cable Files, RL.

93. E-mail from Paul Kengor to Larry Schweikart, May 7, 2009.

94. "Congressman Bill Nichols, Armed Services Committee, Report on Beirut Security," December 21, 1983, ND016 186262, RL.

95. Weinberger, *Fighting for Peace*, 166.

96. One of the most impressive letters in the Reagan Library came from a Grenada vet, a staff sergeant named Ferdinand Rivera (n.d.): "I have never voted for a public official [but] you have B–[s] and yes I am voting this year . . . if you stay on" (ND016 184434, RL). It was written on cardboard, which apparently puzzled Reagan, until a second "cardboard letter" followed, from Sgt. Kevin McCarthy (October 21, 1983), in which Reagan replied, "You must be a friend of Sgt. Rivera—he sent me a letter on a piece of cardboard too" (ND016 188551, December 12, 1983, RL). Also noteworthy in the Reagan files are the remarkable number of letters from civilians offering to volunteer in Grenada and Lebanon to lend expertise, skills, and time.

97. These and other correspondence of support and opposition are in the ND016 files. See ND016-144980, 1175774, and 176040, various dates, all in RL.

98. ND016 175705-80, various dates, RL.

99. ND016 176298, October 24, 1983, RL.

100. ND016 18272, October 27, 1983, RL.

101. Reagan, *An American Life*, 463.

102. John Prados, *Presidents' Secret Wars: CIA and Pentagon Covert Operations from World War II to the Persian Gulf* (Chicago: Ivan R. Dee, 1996), 379.

103. George Crile, *Charlie Wilson's War* (New York: Grove Press, 2003).

104. Reagan, *An American Life*, 466.

105. Schweikart, *America's Victories*, ch. 7, passim.

106. Reginald C. Stuart, *The Half-Way Pacifist: Thomas Jefferson's View of War* (Toronto: University of Toronto, 1978); Joseph Whelan, *Jefferson's War: America's First War on Terror 1801–1805* (New York: Carroll & Graf, 2003).

107. McFarlane, "From Beirut to 9/11."

108. "Marine Explosion, October 23–November 3, 1983," Box 41, Executive Secretariat, NSC: Country File, RL.

109. Bin Laden quoted in Mark Silverberg, "Paper Tiger," http://www.jfednepa.org/mark%20silverberg/papertiger.html.

110. John Miller, "Greetings, America. My Name is Osama bin Laden," *Esquire*, February 1999, 96–103. See also John J. Miller, Michael Stone, and Chris Mitchell, *The Cell: Inside the 9/11 Plot, and Why the FBI and CIA Failed to Stop It* (New York: Hyperion Books, 2003).

CHAPTER 7

1. See John Ziegler's film *Media Malpractice: How Obama Got Elected*, 2009, http://howobamagotelected.com/.

2. James L. Moses, "Journalistic Impartiality on the Eve of Revolution: The *Boston Evening Post*, 1770–1775," *Journalism History* 20 (Autumn–Winter 1994): 125–30. See also Bernard Bailyn and John Hench, eds., *The Press and the American Revolution* (Boston: Northeastern University Press, 1981).

3. Thomas C. Leonard, *The Power of the Press The Birth of Political Reporting* (New York: Oxford University Press, 1996).

4. Donald Lewis Shaw, "At the Crossroads: Change and Continuity in American Press News, 1820–1860," *Journalism History* 8 (Summer 1981): 38–50 (quotation on 48).

5. Gerald Baldasty, *The Commercialization of News in the Nineteenth Century* (Madison: University of Wisconsin Press, 1992), 47. See also Frederic Hudson, *Journalism in the United States from 1690 to 1872* (New York: Harper and Bros., 1873), 432–33.

6. *New York Herald*, May 6, 1835.

7. L. Edward Carter, "The Revolution in Journalism During the Civil War," *Lincoln Herald* 73 (Winter 1971): 229–24 (quotation on 230). See also J. C. Andrews, *The North Reports the Civil War* (Pittsburgh: University of Pittsburgh Press, 1955), 6–34; Edwin Emery and Henry Ladd Smith, *The Press and America* (New York: Prentice-Hall, 1954); and Havilah Babcock, "The Press and the Civil War," *Journalism Quarterly* 6 (1929): 1–5.

8. Carter, "The Revolution in Journalism," 231; Jeffrey A. Smith, *War and Press Freedom* (New York: Oxford University Press, 199), 103.

9. Smith, *War and Press Freedom*, 104–5. See also David T. Z. Mindich, "Edwin M. Stanton, the Inverted Pyramid, and Information Control," *Journalism Monographs* 140 (August 1999).

10. Dan Schiller, *Objectivity and the News: The Public and the Rise of Commercial Journalism* (Philadelphia: University of Pennsylvania Press, 1981), 4.

11. James Carey, "The Dark Continent of American Journalism," in Evea Stryker Munson and Catherine A. Warren, eds., *James Carey: A Critical Reader* (Minneapolis: University of Minnesota Press, 1997), 144–90 (quotation on 161).

12. See Jonathan Fenby, *The International News Services* (New York: Schocken Books, 1986), 25.

13. Sheldon R. Gawiser and G. Evans Witt, *A Journalist's Guide to Public Opinion Polls* (Westport, CT: Praeger, 1994), 13.

14. Ford Risley, "The Confederate Press Association: Cooperative News Reporting of the War," *Civil War History* 47 (September 2001): 222–39.

15. Thrasher quoted in Risley, "Confederate Press Association," 231.

16. Quoted in Risley, "Confederate Press Association," 231.

17. Robert W. Jones, *Journalism in the United States* (New York: Dutton, 1947), 322.

18. Mitchell Stephens, *History of News: from the Drum to the Satellite* (New York: Viking, 1988), 254.

19. David T. Z. Mindich, *Just the Facts* (New York: New York University Press, 1998), 67–68. Also see Donald L. Shaw, "At the Crossroads: Change and Continuity in American Press News, 1820–1860," *Journalism History* 8 (Summer 1981): 38–50, and "News Bias and the Telegraph: A Study of Historical Change," *Journalism Quarterly* 44 (Spring 1967): 3–31; and Michael Schudson, *Discovering the News* (New York: Basic Books, 1978).

20. Gobright quoted in Mindich, *Just the Facts*, 109.

21.   Harlan S. Stensaas, "Development of the Objectivity Ethic in U.S. Daily Newspapers," *Journal of Mass Media Ethics* 2 (Fall/Winter 1986–1987): 50–60; and Shaw, "At the Crossroads."

22.   "American and British Newspaper Press," *Southern Quarterly Review* 4 (July 1843): 235–38.

23.   William G. Bovee, "Horace Greeley and Social Responsibility," *Journalism Quarterly* 63 (Summer 1986): 251–59.

24.   W. S. Lilly, "The Ethics of Journalism," *The Forum* 4 (July 1889): 503–12; George Henry Payne, *History of Journalism in the United States* (New York: D. Appleton, 1925), 251–53. Also see standards in the *Minnesota Newspaper Association Confidential Bulletin*, no. 20 (May 17, 1988): 4–5, and those adopted by Will Irwin, published in *Collier's Magazine* (1911), reprinted in Clifford F. Weigle and David G. Clark, eds., *The American Newspaper by Will Irwin* (Ames: Iowa State University Press, 1969).

25.   Quoted in Bill Kovach and Tom Rosensteil, *Elements of Journalism* (New York: Crown, 2001), 53.

26.   Oswald Garrison Villard, "Press Tendencies and Dangers," in Willard G. Bleyer, *The Profession of Journalism* (Boston: Atlantic Monthly Press, 1918), 23.

27.   Richard Grant White, "The Pest of the Period: A Chapter in the Morals and Manners of Journalism," *The Galaxy* 9 (January 1870): 102–12 (quotation on 107), responding to Edwin Godkin, "Opinion-Moulding," *The Nation* 9 (August 12, 1869): 126–27.

28.   Thomas K. McCraw, *Prophets of Regulation* (Cambridge, MA: Belknap Press, 1984), 1–56.

29.   "Edwin Lawrence Godkin," *The Journalist*, July 11, 1891.

30.   John H. Summers, "What Happened to Sex Scandals? Politics and Peccadiloes, Jefferson to Kennedy," *Journal of American History* 87 (December 2000): 825-54.

31.   Casper S. Yost, *The Principles of Journalism* (New York: D. Appleton, 1924), 154, 110.

32.   Richard Grant White, "The Morals and Manners of Journalism," *The Galaxy* 8 (December 1869): 840–67 (quotation on 840).

33.   Ibid., quotation on 840.

34.   W. Irwin, *The American Newspaper, Part VII*, April 22, 1911, 21.

35.   Frederick L. Allen, "Newspapers and the Truth," *Atlantic Monthly*, January 1922, 44–54; quotation on the ASNE Web site, http://www.asne.org/index.cfm?ID=3460.

36.   Quoted in Bruce J. Evensen, "Journalism's Struggle over Ethics and Professionalism During America's Jazz Age," *Journalism History* 16 (Autumn–Winter 1989): 54–63, quotation on 55.

37.   Cited in ibid., 54.

38.   Cited in Jim Kuypers, *Press Bias and Politics: How the Media Frame Controversial Issues* (Westport, CT: Praeger, 2002), 201.

39.   "Code of Ethics," Society for Professional Journalists, http://spj.org/ethics/code/htm.

40.   "Associated Press, Code of Ethics," http://www.asne.org/ideas/codes/apme.htm.

41.   James L. Aucoin, "The Re-emergence of American Investigative Journalism, 1960–1975," *Journalism History* 21 (Spring 1995): 3–13.

42.   Robert D. Leigh, ed., *A Free and Responsible Press* (Chicago: University of Chicago Press, 1947), 23.

43.   White, "The Pest of the Period."

44.   As historian Robert Loewenberg observed, this resulted in a situation in which facts become interpretations (Robert Loewenberg, "'Value-Free' vs. 'Value-Laden' History:

A Distinction Without a Difference," *The Historian* 38 (May 1976): 439-54. CNN reporter Christianne Amanpour echoed Loewenberg's assessment: Objectivity meant "giving all sides a fair hearing, but not treating all sides equally. . . . So 'objectivity' must go hand in hand with morality" (Christiane Amanpour, "Television's Role in Foreign Policy," *Quill* 84 [April 1996]: 16–17).

45. Lou Guzzo to the author, January 27, 2001, via e-mail.
46. Ibid.
47. Ibid.
48. E-mail exchanges with Lou Guzzo, various dates, 2001.
49. Robert J. Donovan and Ray Scherer, *Unsilent Revolution* (Cambridge, England: Cambridge University Press, 1992), 266.
50. Gabriel Weimann, *The Influentials: People Who Influence People* (Albany: State University of New York Press, 1994), 91.
51. Joseph Keeley, *Left-Leaning Antenna: Political Bias in Television* (New Rochelle, NY: Arlington House, 1971), 28.
52. Theodore H. White, on William F. Buckley's *Firing Line*, quoted in ibid., 47.
53. Hugh Hewitt, "'Inbreeding' Among Royals, Pitbulls and Editors," July 12, 2006, http://www.townhall.com/Columnists/HughHewitt/2006/07/12/inbreeding_among_royals,_pitbulls,_and_editors.
54. Ibid.
55. Hugh Hewitt, "The Media's Ancien Regime: Columbia Journalism School Tries to Save the Old Order," January 30, 2006, http://www.weeklystandard.com/Content/Public/Articles/000/000/006/619njpsr.asp.
56. Barbie Zelizer, *Covering the Body* (Chicago: University of Chicago Press, 1992), 40.
57. Ibid., 35.
58. "President's Assassin Shot to Death," *New York Times*, November 25, 1963.
59. "The Marxist Marine," *Newsweek*, December 2, 1963.
60. An analysis of the failures of the media in the Kennedy assassination do *not* require one to believe in a conspiracy to conclude that both television and newspapers, perhaps because of their having been co-opted by "Camelot," or perhaps for other reasons, failed utterly to provide the public with *all* the relevant information. To have done so would have preempted dozens of conspiracy books and perhaps killed that cottage industry in its cradle. See Larry Schweikart and Jim Kuypers, "First, the Bad News," working title, ms. in authors' possession.
61. Keeley, *Left-Leaning Antenna*, 45.
62. David Frum, *How We Got Here* (New York: Basic Books, 2000), 36.
63. *Charlotte Observer*, June 26, 1977.
64. Chalmers Roberts, *The Washington Post: The First 100 Years*, (Boston: Houghton Mifflin Company, 1977).
65. Oscar Patterson III, "Television's Living Room War in Print: Vietnam in the News Magazines," *Journalism Quarterly* 61 (Spring 1984): 35–39, 136.
66. "Vietnam and Electronic Journalism," *Broadcasting*, May 19, 1975, 26.
67. Daniel Hallin, "The Media, the War in Vietnam, and Political Support: A Critique of the Thesis of an Oppositional Media," *Journal of Politics* 46 (February 1984): 2–24, table on 8.
68. Paul Johnson, *A History of the American People* (New York: HarperCollins, 1997), 895.
69. Ibid.
70. Ibid.

71. Ibid.
72. Gladys Engel Lang and Kurt Lang, "The Media and Watergate," in Doris A. Graber, ed., *Media Power in Politics* (Washington, DC: Congressional Quarterly Press, 1984), 202–9, quotation on 204.
73. Von Hoffman quoted in James Boylan, "Declarations of Independence," *Columbia Journalism Review*, Nov./Dec. 1986, pp. 29-45. The "frame" was ideological, not financial: Fred McChesney found no significant effects on the stock value of *The Washington Post* as a result of the investigation. See Fred S. McChesney, "Sensationalism, Newspaper Profits and the Marginal Value of Watergate," *Economic Inquiry* 25 (January 1987): 135–44.
74. Len Colodny and Robert Gettlin, *Silent Coup: The Removal of a President* (New York: St. Martin's, 1991). See also Schweikart, *48 Liberal Lies About American History* (New York: Sentinel, 2008), 134–38; *Maureen K. Dean and John Dean v. St. Martin's Press, Inc., Len Colodny, Robert Gettlin, G. Gordon Liddy, and Philip Mackin Bailey* (1996), http://www.nixonera.com/media/transcripts/liddy.pdf.
75. Richard Nixon, "Memo to President Bush: How to Use TV—and Keep From Being Abused by It," *TV Guide*, January 14, 1989, 26–30.
76. Ibid.
77. Seymour Martin Lipset and William Schneider, *The Confidence Gap* (New York: Free Press, 1983), 48–49.
78. Ibid., 55.
79. Stanley Rothman and Amy E. Black, "Media and Business Elites: Still in Conflict?" *Public Interest*, Spring 2001, 72–86, esp. 83–84.
80. John Leo, "Bad News," *New York Daily News*, April 15, 2000.
81. Ibid.
82. Jonathan Cohn, writing in the *American Prospect*, quoted in James Fallows, *Breaking the News: How the Media Undermine American Democracy* (New York: Vintage Books, 1997), 79.
83. Michael Kelly, "The Game," *New York Times Magazine*, October 1993, 65.
84. Joel Kotkin and David Friedman, "Clueless: Why the Elite Media Don't Understand America," *The American Enterprise*, November 11, 1999, 29.
85. Ibid.
86. Stephen Hess, *The Washington Reporters* (Washington, DC: Brookings Institution, 1981), 87.
87. Excerpts from David Weaver et al., "The American Journalist in the 21st Century," available online at www.poynter.org.
88. Shosteck's results are reported in Robert McFarland, "Conservatives Can Beat Liberal Media Bias," CNSNews.com, May 25, 2000.
89. K. Daniel Glover, "The NRA and the Press: A Case Study in Media Bias," Intellectual Capital.com, September 2, 1999.
90. Will Lester, "Web Attracts Younger News Audience," *Washington Post* online edition, June 11, 2000.
91. Matt Drudge, "Cable Quake: FOX News Beats CNN in Ratings; First Time During Breaking Event," www.drudgereport.com, June 27, 2000.
92. Paula Bernstein, "CNN Ratings Slip; FOX News Up 22% in 3Q!" Reuters, October 3, 2000.
93. Tom Bierbaum, "FOX News Trounces the Cable Competition on Inauguration Saturday," January 23, 2001, www.inside.com.

94.   "Study: Viewers Disgusted with Local TV News," www.DrudgeReport.com, April 20, 2000, citing a forthcoming *Los Angeles Daily News* article.

95.   Bernard Goldberg, *A Slobbering Love Affair: The True (and Pathetic) Story of the Torrid Romance Between Barack Obama and the Mainstream Media* (Washington, DC: Regnery, 2009), 12.

96.   Ibid., 66.

97.   Ron Robinson, Young America's Foundation, 2009, copy in author's possession.

98.   Robinson, comments in Speech at Young America's Foundation, 2009.

99.   Goldberg, *A Slobbering Love Affair*, 7.

100.   Ibid., 30.

101.   Ibid., 140.

102.   Ibid., 30.

103.   "Juan Williams Decries 'High Tide' of Media 'Kowtowing' to Obama," http://newsbusters.org/blogs/brent-baker/2009/06/20/juan-williams-decries-high-tide-media-kowtowing-obama; Goldberg, *A Slobbering Love Affair*, 153.

104.   "Love or Lust, Obama and the Fawning Press Need to Get a Room," http://www.sfgate.com/cgi-bin/blogs/bronstein/detail?blogid=47&entry_id=41380.

105.   "Obama's First 100 Days: How the President Fared in the Press vs. Clinton and Bush," Pew Research Center, April 28, 2009, http://www.journalism.org/analysis_report/obamas_first_100_days.

106.   Robert J. Samuelson, "The Obama Infatuation," *Washington Post*, June 1, 2009.

107.   "Media Boost Obama, Bash His Policies," Center for Media and Public Affairs, April 27, 2009, http://www.cmpa.com/media_room_4_27_09.htm.

108.   Goldberg, *A Slobbering Love Affair*, 5.

109.   Ibid., 9.

110.   Ibid., 152.

111.   "The Radical Roots of Barack Obama," *Rolling Stone*, February 22, 2007.

112.   Goldberg, *A Slobbering Love Affair*, 55.

Conclusion

1.   Mark R. Levin, *Men in Black: How the Supreme Court Is Destroying America* (Washington, DC: Regnery, 2005); Andrew Napolitano, *Constitutional Chaos: What Happens When the Government Breaks Its Own Laws* (Nashville, TN: Thomas Nelson, 2006), and his *The Constitution in Exile: How the Federal Government Has Seized Power by Rewriting the Supreme Law of the Land* (Nashville, TN: Thomas Nelson, 2007); and Stephen P. Powers and Stanley Rothman, *The Least Dangerous Branch?: Consequences of Judicial Activism* (Santa Barbara, CA: Praeger, 2002).

INDEX